NOT ALWAYS DIPLOMATIC

'Susan Boyd was not a stereotypical Australian diplomat of the late 20th century. Born into a British military family, this single (but not celibate) woman with a ribald sense of humour found herself more than once defending Australia's interests in a major political crisis. Her engaging memoir should be read by anyone interested in Australian diplomacy, and anyone interested in a woman's experience of what was, and to a lesser degree remains, a predominantly male profession.'

Peter Edwards, Australian diplomatic historian

'A thoroughly engaging read. Sue's book took me for a walk down memory lane, remembering the tumultuous events of 2000 in Fiji and the fall-out thereafter. Sue has a rare understanding of the Pacific Islands and its peoples. An enjoyable read. Part of it made me laugh out loud. From a gender perspective, it offers intuitions into the difficulties faced by women attempting to pierce the glass ceiling. Sue faced those difficulties with good humour and common sense, partly explaining why she has had such a successful career.'

Imrana Jalal, The World Bank

'Love it! It's just like talking to you! Just like the conversations I've had with the author – full of generous insight and wise counsel and above all, hugely entertaining. Sue is a highly accomplished corporate coach and this book is peppered with great advice on making a great career. Only Sue Boyd can get away with describing herself as a cat presenting the reader with a dead rat. Definitely not always diplomatic.'

Diane Smith-Gander, Non-Executive Director.

NOT ALWAYS DIPLOMATIC

An Australian Woman's Journey through international affairs

SUE BOYD

UWA PUBLISHING

First published in 2020 by
UWA Publishing
Crawley, Western Australia 6009
www.uwap.uwa.edu.au

UWAP is an imprint of UWA Publishing,
a division of The University of Western Australia.

THE UNIVERSITY OF
WESTERN
AUSTRALIA

ISBN: 978-1-76080-149-6

NATIONAL LIBRARY OF AUSTRALIA
A catalogue record for this book is available from the National Library of Australia

Cover by Alissa Dinallo
Typeset by Lasertype
Printed by McPherson's Printing Group

uwapublishing

For Lynda-Jane and Gerald

Contents

Whitlam's injunction

The Portuguese Carnation Revolution took place on 25 April 1974, Anzac Day in Australia and the day before I returned from Portugal to duty in the Department of Foreign Affairs in Canberra. Prime Minister Gough Whitlam called for someone to brief him and said he wanted 'someone who really knew'. So they sent me across the rose garden to the Old Parliament House, in my high heels and short skirt, long hair piled up, into the prime minister's office. I was twenty-eight.

'Well, Susan', he boomed. 'What's going on in Portugal? What does it mean for Australia? And what should we do about it?'

What it meant for Australia was the ensuing Timor crisis: civil war, evacuation of the Portuguese governor, muddled political aspirations, quest for and eventual independence, refugee flows, occupation by Indonesia, Australian journalists killed, sharing sub-sea oil and gas and a seabed boundary dispute.

The prime minister's three questions form the basis of the work of every Australian embassy and guided me through my 34-year career in international relations.

Foreword

The Hon. Kim Beazley AC

Not Always Diplomatic but effective whether or not, might be added to the long title for the book but Sue would be too modest to do it. This is a story of her experiences, perspectives, thoughts, feelings, grievances, judgements, ideals, hopes and fashion sense. However as befits a lifetime spent in the service of our foreign affairs department, it is a story of acute study of the desires, characters, fears, affections, hopes, objectives of others many of whom at either a modest or substantial level were capable of impacting on directions that were important to the Australian national interest. Sue is very funny but never frivolous. This is a book which is both a joy to read and one from which much can be learned.

Sue's story can be read at several different levels. At one level it is about a woman raised in the late phase of the British Empire in a family enmeshed in the business end of that Empire. A military family on constant deployment. Empire and Cold War. Schooled at a very early age in the value of multiple languages and cultural understanding. Then an almost accidental migration to Australia. Where despite misgivings she flung herself wholeheartedly into the opportunities and affairs of her new country. A pioneer for women in our foreign affairs department. With her female colleagues a change maker for her gender in that critical institution. Our first female head of mission in an Islamic country, Bangladesh. From time to time a trouble shooter in difficult situations. A target herself in an awkward time as high commissioner in Fiji during a coup. As such in an important South Pacific nation whose political forces always had Australia in focus. In focus for us in the knowledge that the country she represented was aghast at military coups and deeply committed to democracy. As such it is a rollicking good yarn. Concluding with a life well spent in her adopted State. A better fist made of retirement than many who have served us so well in the diplomatic corp.

At another level, Sue's book can be read as a view from the engine room of the making of Australian foreign policy. This is so important now. The world we now inhabit has seen many of the verities of the post-World War II international order severely challenged. How we do foreign policy, how we do broader national security policy, is increasingly challenged. National survival now critically depends on our adjustments and the skill of those entrusted with all elements of our national security, the Department of Foreign Affairs and Trade (DFAT) very much at the heart of it. Sue's service predated these developments but the skills and experiences she outlines remain important to those who must pursue these tasks. In some ways this book is a manual.

I spent six years in the department and came to respect my colleagues deeply. One thing is, they write superbly and concisely. Sue's skills in that regard were well developed before she entered the service, a product of her education and brief flirtation with journalism. Her reporting skills for the department are clear from her accounts here. But particularly in her early years, to get those views noticed was not easy in a masculine environment. By the time I served that had changed. When I think of the many senior women with whom I served it is hard to picture. There are many in debt for the pioneering work she and her few colleagues did. The nation, not simply women, are in their debt.

It was my experience that at least 90 per cent of the issues we worked on had little public exposure and none with the detail and mechanics of how we handle crisis events. Those who say all we need to know is in the public arena in various forms of media, could not be more wrong. About how we handle those events there is a backstory. That backstory is embedded in the department's records. Those who would understand it, or more particularly professionally understand, will find this book valuable.

Two events struck me. One was the early phases of our responses to Indonesian intervention in East Timor. As a very junior official Sue's experience in Portugal was important to an understanding of the likely consequences of its revolution for us and for policy toward Indonesia. That is the neighbour most important for us in South East Asia and deeply bound up in the Timor outcome. How heady it must have been for her when Gough Whitlam roared to her, 'Well Susan, what's going on in Portugal? What does it mean for Australia? And what should we do about it?' What a challenge for an officer deployed for her first posting to a seemingly peripheral country in Australian concerns. Prime Minister's relationships with junior officers (and Foreign Ministers as well) more usually extend to bag carrying on occasional visits to post.

The other was the Speight coup in Fiji where members of parliament, many who looked to Australia and were our friends, were held hostage. The crisis lasted 56 days with the coup masters deeply suspicious of Australian intentions and policy. Lives, including Susan's, were very much under threat. As hostages were released they came straight to Sue's mission. I was moved by Sue's description of her meeting with the oldest parliamentarian who told her 'he had managed to keep a simple daily journal, but Speight had found it and ripped it to pieces. I [Sue] found myself choking back tears of sympathy for this old man and all the others being held so long... Every morning I woke thinking who will we need to influence today?!' We may not think it but Fiji and the South Pacific is vital to us.

Sue's time in Fiji was not simply about the coup. She also had to handle the Howard government's 'Pacific solution' to the problems arising from boat entry to Australia. Here is a lesson many in DFAT have to learn. How do you handle a situation where you profoundly disagree with policy but have to implement it? Resignation is always an option but that is not why you joined the department. Rather you recognise you represent a democratically elected government. Cabinet makes the decisions and you do the best you can implementing them.

There is much more in this book. Sue has found herself in so many interesting situations. East Germany in the late Cold War. Her accounts enhanced by subsequent access to her Stasi file (East Germany's all intrusive secret service). Vietnam (as Ambassador) at a time when it was reaching out for relationships with the West. The U.N. engaged heavily with its arms control function. All laced with superb accounts of the relationships she built as she reached out to local movers and shakers. But also, her many relationships with ordinary citizens who provided a flavour of real life in the countries in whom she represented us. This is rich fare. Sue can be hilariously self-deprecating. But she is also deeply focussed on her primary task. Making sure she gave our policy makers the best understanding she could.

I knew Sue well when we were direct colleagues at the University of Western Australia. I have lost a number of elections in my time but only one in the public domain. That is for a position or constituency with which I was directly engaged. It was for President of the Guild of Undergraduates, when Sue became the first woman to hold the post. I was, after that, her Vice President and can attest she did the job really well.

As her life proceeded I would intersect with her from time to time when she came home. I never held the Foreign Affairs portfolio but my colleague, Gareth Evans thought the world of her and she him. I am glad she has a prodigious memory. I am glad she writes superbly. I learned a lot from this book and if you read it, you will too.

The Honourable Kim Beazley ac,
Governor of Western Australia

Introduction

Discrimination

I felt little discrimination growing up, at home or in my many schools in many countries. My parents soon got over the disappointment that their first born was not a boy and treated me throughout my childhood as if I had been. There was little I was not allowed to try, irrespective of my gender.

I remember the sense of injustice, however, when my father refused to let me take up rowing when I was fourteen or fifteen. He said it was not a suitable sport for girls, as it developed unsightly muscles. I felt very left out, as all my school friends, girls as well as boys were joining the club, which operated on the banks of the River Stour in Suffolk. But I accepted his judgement, as I knew deep down that he believed he had my true welfare at heart. And children need to know that there are some boundaries. In the village where we lived, I didn't really want to hang out with the adolescent boys and was secretly pleased when my father discussed with me why doing so was not a good idea. I could hide behind his veto, which was my protection.

But I remember no barriers through the rest of my schooling. Indeed, independence was encouraged, and early in my teens I was sent off to travel alone to visit relatives in London and Ireland, and to spend the summer holidays learning French with a family in France. And when I left school, aged eighteen, I was encouraged to go to Africa for a year as a volunteer teacher in a mission school.

Throughout my four years at the University of Western Australia the only two instances of discrimination I remember feeling were in my first year, when Professor Rex Prider refused to take women students on weekend geology field trips and, in my final year, when I was guild president, the elected head of the student body, and the head of the men's residential college St George's proposed a compromise to resolve a problem the college faced. The college formal St George's Day dinner was always a men-only affair, but they also always invited the guild president. This year the president was a woman. How to resolve this impasse? I was foolish enough to agree to the solution they offered. They would invite me, as guild president, but I would decline the invitation and send my (male) vice-president. A neat diplomatic solution but not one the sisterhood would have sanctioned.

It was 1970 when I entered the paid, very traditional, male workplace of the public service – the Department of External Affairs – that more examples of discrimination showed themselves. It began the day the class of 1970 were formally inducted, when I and the only other female discovered that we two women in the class of twenty-three recruits were to be paid 10 per cent less than our male colleagues – for exactly the same work. We had to wait and work another two years before we were paid the same as the men. The unequal treatment continued with the advice given to us on the rate of superannuation deduction we should choose. 'You girls will get married and leave, and take your contributions with you. There is no point in contributing at the optional higher rate'. So we were notionally worse off when we *did* retire – and I outlasted most of the men.

A potential career stumbling block appeared when I was made Foreign Affairs liaison officer to the High Court for the Asia Pacific Chief Justices Conference in 1980. Chief Justice Sir Garfield Barwick told me that my job was to help the visiting judges' wives with their hairdressing appointments. I dealt with that one. A more serious case was when the department decided not to send me to East Timor in 1975 on a short-term mission at the beginning of the Timor crisis, even though I was the best suited for the job. Why? Because if they sent me, it would be thought that the government was not taking the situation seriously, as they were only sending a woman. I protested firmly against this decision, and soon afterwards they did send me north, to open an office in Darwin to support Australia's involvement in the evolving crisis. I was housed on the Larrakia air force base, next to the office of the air force commander. Things went smoothly for a couple of days, until the commander returned from leave and proceeded to belittle, bully and harass me as he sought to undermine me and my mission. There were lewd comments, attempts to look down the front of my dress and disparaging observations about the stupidity of posting a girl to do a man's job. Others at the base, as well as the navy chief in Darwin and the army staff I worked with, supported me and gave me the strength to ignore this barrage and continue to do well the job I had been sent to do. I did not complain to anyone about this treatment, just swallowed it and got on with the work. Things would be different today.

The three-man selection committee which interviewed me in 1969 for entry to the Department of External Affairs observed that I was 'attractive and well groomed, but nonetheless intelligent and articulate'. I wonder how they described the male recruits.

This was the workplace I entered in 1970. In the ensuing years, I learned how to navigate the sexist minefield of low expectations, resistance, hostility and sometimes well-intentioned but harmful consequences of policy decisions, culture and prejudice to forge a successful, rewarding and enjoyable career for myself, advancing Australia's interests internationally. And I learned how to enable better conditions for others, men as well as women, married and single.

This book is about being a woman, finding a way through life and a traditionally male profession – diplomacy – and helping to form and apply Australian foreign policy for thirty-four years. Many women have told me they regard me as a role model in a field where there were few women to follow. I have helped, mentored and coached many other women, and also men. It has been a fulfilling life, in which I have felt able to provide some service.

This book is not an academic analysis of Australian foreign policy. It is rather the view from the trenches from a career officer serving Australia's interests internationally.

This is my story. I hope it is a useful and entertaining read.

1

Conceived in Quetta, born in Calcutta (Kolkata), brought up internationally, 1946–51

What formed me? Family history, spanning India, Europe, Middle East.

Father Victor Robert Hugo Boyd, was Irish and superstitious. He persuaded Dr Mitra in the Calcutta Nursing Home in India to induce my birth early, on 31 March, so I would not be born on April Fools' Day. Father was full of sayings like 'Play with salt, play with sorrow', 'Don't open an umbrella indoors', 'Never gift a bag or wallet without a coin in it' and 'Blunt the danger from a gifted knife, which could "cut" the friendship, by responding with a coin'. Coming from a British military family, he was posted in India during World War II as an artillery officer in the British Army. My parents were sure their first baby would be a boy and were bitterly disappointed when this girl popped out, a healthy 8-pound (2.9 kg) baby. All the baby clothes they had ready were blue.

As I grew up, I learned about the family history and was the one entrusted with family documents, by both father and his elder brother, Uncle Derek Boyd. Maybe it was because I was the eldest. But also, maybe they judged that, of my generation, I was the most capable of safe guarding and passing on the stories.

Father hero-worshipped his own father, Major General Sir Gerald Farrell Boyd (1877–1930) who was a British war hero. He was the general who led the 46th Midland Division in breaking the Hindenburg Line on the Canal de Saint-Quentin, in France, in 1918, the decisive action in ending World War I. He is described as the 'ranker general' in the biography Derek Boyd wrote about his father.[1] In 1895 the young Gerald Farrell Boyd had enlisted as a private soldier, a 'ranker', in the Devonshire Regiment, and fought in the Boer War as well as World War I and had risen rapidly through the ranks to become a senior officer. Much decorated, (KCB, CMG, DSO, DCM) he uniquely held both a medal awarded only to 'other ranks' and one given only to very senior officers. The French Government also granted him the Légion d'honneur.

His brother, Sir Harry Boyd, rose through the British Civil Service and became ceremonial secretary in the Home Office, the peak of a career including service in Shanghai and Beijing. Part of Harry's duties was to be present at all royal births, to certify that the new child truly belonged to the royal family.

Paternal Grandmother Grace Sophia Burdett (born 21 December 1885) came from the Irish gentry – a Protestant Anglo-Irish family that moved to Ireland from England in 1623 as part of the first Irish settler plantation. This was a scheme whereby the English King granted land in the colonised country of Ireland to English and Scottish settlers. The Burdetts lived in grand houses in Banagher and controlled extensive land holdings in King's County (now County Offaly), on the River Shannon. Their lands crossed over into County Galway. Grace and Grandfather Gerald Boyd married on 9 January 1913, while he was posted with the Leinster Regiment at Birr in Ireland – close to her home in Banagher.

The *Irish Times* carried details of the wedding on the front page in 1913, including a list of the presents they received and the chief guests. I am keeping some of these treasured gifts in trust for future generations. During childhood visits to my grandmother's house I was fascinated by one gift, the self-recording barograph, which makes a daily record of fluctuating air pressure. I loved the weekly ritual of changing the sheets of graph paper, making sure the recording needle had the right ink supply and winding the apparatus up to go for a full week. But I also love the small, silver evening handbag inlaid with tortoiseshell, containing a polished bone dance card and silver propelling pencil, with which grandmother could record the dances booked to successive partners at formal balls. And the gold-and-pearl-topped smelling-salts bottle. We have a hand-coloured photograph of her in her coming-out ball dress of Irish lace, carrying a coral pink ostrich-feather fan with a pearl embroidered silk handle. My grandmother's beautiful and valuable jewellery has been shared around the women of the family.

Our father, Victor Robert Hugo Boyd was the couple's second son, born at Dublin Castle on 23 July 1919, while Grandfather Gerald was serving there as officer commanding the British troops in Ireland. It was a tumultuous and historic time for Britain and for Ireland, as Irish nationalism grew and became violent – a long period of events leading to the partition of the country and independence for the south. The family were next posted to Quetta, in Balochistan, India, in 1923, where Gerald Boyd was appointed commandant of the military staff college. When my father was in his pram in Quetta, someone apparently commented, 'That baby looks just like a bulldog', and the nickname 'Bull' stuck.

Their tour of duty in India finished in 1927 and the family returned to London, where Grandfather Gerald became military secretary at the War Office. Their son 'Bull' Boyd was eight and was sent to boarding school, like his elder brother, Derek.

Grandfather Gerald died young, suddenly, of meningitis, in 1930, while at the War Office. Our father was ten. Grandmother Gracie went back to Ireland, to her family. In due course she met and married Fred Wood, an Irish widower, who had made his fortune as a tea planter in Ceylon (now Sri Lanka). There was a daughter, Pam, from his first marriage, and they all lived in Cloghan Castle, near Banagher. The boys spent their school holidays there, becoming proficient horsemen, riding point-to-point horseraces and show jumping. They also learned to use a shotgun in game-shooting and to manage and train gundogs. Father played tennis well and was in the school rugby first XV.

Pam got on well with her new stepbrothers and later became a glamorous favourite aunt of mine.

An army widow's pension was not generous, even for the widow of a famous British general, and Grandmother Gracie was not wealthy. She already had her eldest son Derek in public (that is, private) boarding school, at Winchester College in England. General Laurence Carr and his wife, Elizabeth (Elsie), were the Boyd's best friends and became their younger son's godparents. The Carrs had no children of their own and were very fond of the boy, whom they called by his third name, Hugo. They generously offered to make his mother an allowance to cover all the living and education costs and invited him to spend time with them in the school holidays. Laurence Carr arranged a scholarship for him to attend Wellington College in England which also served as a feeder school for the British Army. In due course, he introduced him to his own London Club, useful for a young gentleman entering society. The family papers include the very tactful letter from Uncle Laurence proposing to look after these expenses, and the deed of gift providing the regular allowance. In the letter he indicated that he could well afford this arrangement.

Upon my baptism Uncle Laurence and Aunt Elsie also became my godparents. When widowed, Aunt Elsie lived until her death with her sister's family at Crathes Castle near Aberdeen, in Scotland. I loved her dearly and visited her there several times. I felt very grand at the family dinners in the castle, with silver and candles. I never had the right formal evening clothes but was decked out appropriately by her nieces. Aunt Elsie had an old, green pet parrot, which wandered freely and often perched on her shoulder. It would attack any male who came close to her. This was a shock for my brother when we went to visit her together.

Our part of the Boyd family has a crest showing the three Prince of Wales feathers and the Latin motto 'Retro sed ultro'. This has been translated as 'backwards yet forwards' or 'backwards, but of my own accord'. The crest must have been granted by the king to one of our forebears, as a reward for particular bravery or military skill in battle. The oral family history has it that we are descended from the Boyds of Kilmarnock, part of the great Stewart clan of Scotland, which fought for Bonnie Prince Charlie in the wars against the English.

Retro sed Ultro has been a useful motto throughout my career. The way forward sometimes requires a step sideways or backwards first.

A gold signet ring is worn by all the Boyd men in our family and their wives. When I turned twenty-one, I asked my father for one of these rings. He refused: they were worn only by male members of the family, and I should wait until I was married and then wear the signet of my husband! I was furious: this was my family too, and what if I never married? He would not be shifted. But as my own little act of rebellion, I used money left to me when Aunt Elsie died and had a ring made myself.

Father was posted to India during World War II, as a young officer in the Royal Artillery. He and his regiment, complete with heavy anti-aircraft guns, were on a ship bound for Singapore in early 1942 when Singapore fell to the Japanese, and the ship was diverted to Bombay (Mumbai) in India, instead. With responsibilities for anti-aircraft warfare against Japan, Captain Boyd and his unit travelled by train across the country to Bengal, to defend the airfields of Chittagong and Dum Dum, in Calcutta.

In Calcutta he met Albert Cooper, a British manufacturer and racehorse owner. When after a few months, Captain Boyd was sent on sick leave to Darjeeling, in the foothills of the Himalayas, he met Cooper's daughter, Peggy, who was working there as a hairdresser. This was my mother. Peggy was nineteen, our father, twenty-five. They were deeply in love. Bull Boyd wrote letters to his mother in Ireland telling her of their plans and complaining bitterly that Peggy's father was insisting on a six-month engagement. 'Doesn't the man know we are in a war?!! They married in 1944 in Calcutta Anglican cathedral.

Maternal Grandmother (Granny) Phyllis Dagmar Rolfe Norris, was one of thirteen children whose own grandfather had in the mid-1800s taken four horse-drawn hansom cabs from England to Bangalore (Bangaluru) where he established a thriving business. Indian horse-drawn passenger carriages already existed, but the smart, enclosed hansom cab, with upholstered seats and privacy for the passengers, was a major step forward. There is still a Norris Road in Bangalore, where the hansom cab business was founded. Granny worked as a successful dress designer and milliner in Bangalore. She was also a talented contralto singer and travelled around India with a small concert-performing group, the Sparklets.[2]

Granny married Albert (Bert) Thomas Cooper, who was with the British Army in India, in Bangalore. He was born in 1881 in Warley Salop, Worcestershire, in the United Kingdom. They met when she was talking over the school fence in Bangalore with his two sons by his first marriage, Bertie and Archie. His first wife had died in India. Albert Cooper had seen the opportunities for business in India and, with his army demobilisation pay and in partnership with his friend MacFarlane (first name unknown to us), established paint factories in Bombay and Calcutta. MacFarlane Paints was a lucrative business, especially during WWII given the insatiable demand for camouflage paint and the war having blocked access to supplies from England. The humid climate in India meant houses and public buildings needed frequent repainting. Albert Cooper moved to Calcutta with his new wife, Phyllis, to establish and run the factory there. MacFarlane took responsibility for the Bombay operation.

Their daughter Peggy was born in Bangalore in 1924 and brought up in Calcutta (see picture insert figure 3). She was formally baptised in the Anglican Church with the names of her two grandmothers, Frances and Mary. But Phyllis had always wanted a daughter named Peggy, so that's what she was called.

Mother went to La Martiniere Catholic school in Calcutta, where her aunt Pat (Norris) Miller taught.

The Coopers were relatively well off. Their son David went to St Paul's boarding school in Darjeeling, which also educated Indian boys. Maharajas were in the family friendship group. Albert Cooper owned two racehorses, Phylter and Sylter, and was a stalwart member of the Calcutta Jockey Club. Mother said she loved going with her father to the racetrack in the cool of the very early mornings, as the horses were being trained and exercised.

When Peggy finished school in Calcutta, her whole family went to England on holiday, and she was then to attend finishing school in Brussels, where her father's sister lived. But this was in 1939, and the prospect of war in Europe was looming. The family scurried back to India on the last ship to sail before war broke out. There was to be no elegant European finishing school for Peggy! She chose instead to train in Calcutta as a hairdresser and beautician. We still have her documents of apprenticeship to Madame Korner at the Calcutta Beauty salon. There was a branch of the salon at the Gymkhana club in Darjeeling, and, having completed her apprenticeship, Peggy went to work there. Most of Calcutta's elite moved to Darjeeling for the hottest months, and the club was the centre of a lively scene. There was a busy social life, with tea-dances, cinema, swimming, tennis, horseriding and rollerskating. And it was while she was there that father arrived in Darjeeling on medical leave and met and fell in love with Peggy Cooper. For her part, she did not take immediately to 'Bull' Boyd – his name in itself put her off. But he persevered, and their wedding took place on 11 January 1944.

They spent their early married years in various army camps in India, and then in Quetta, where 'Bull' taught gunnery and studied at the staff college at which he had spent his early childhood years, when his father was commandant. Urdu was among the subjects taught.

I was probably conceived while they were in Quetta. (Which is now in Pakistan). They apparently used contraceptives which were individually wrapped in foil and kept in the icebox. There was great embarrassment on one occasion when the bearer thought they were sweets and took them to the table at a dinner party. Clearly one of these did not work!

Recording interviews with my parents for the family history some years ago, I asked, 'Mummy, did you sleep with Daddy before you were married?'

After some prodding, she admitted she did, on the train, in their private carriage, as they were both travelling to Darjeeling before they were married. 'But you see, darling, we just didn't do that in those days. For one thing I was terrified of getting pregnant. But I think Daddy knew what he was doing. I think he used a *condom*'. She mouthed the last word, looking at the tape recorder.

'Mummy', I said. 'You didn't *know* Daddy was using a condom?'

'Well, darling, I was very ignorant in those days and had no idea what was going on down there. For all I knew, he might have been using a banana skin!'

When I asked my father the same question a little later, he responded, 'I can't remember where we first slept together – somewhere in Calcutta or Darjeeling, I suppose!' It was clearly not of the same significance to him.

Before her engagement, Peggy had befriended an Australian air force pilot, Keith Dumas, who was based in Calcutta. They arranged to meet at the cinema one evening, but he did not turn up. He had been sent off on a sortie and never came back. And she could find out no more: official war secrecy. Years later, visiting the Australian War Memorial in Canberra together, we found his name inscribed among the war dead. When I was posted as Australian high commissioner to Bangladesh, in 1987, I visited the Commonwealth War Graves cemetery at Chittagong. There lie Australian airmen who, during the Burma campaign, were shot down and nursed at the military hospital, where many died. As I contemplated the graves of the young Australians, I mourned that carefree young man who had danced with the beautiful young woman in Calcutta during the war.

In 1946, six months after my birth , the army posted my father back to England, and our family of three boarded a troopship for the journey. In India, I had had an Indian Ayah (nursemaid) from birth. Now, suddenly, my parents had unassisted charge of a six month old and discovered that it was a full-time task. I did not sleep happily through the night, as they had believed. I needed regular feeding, burping, cleaning and entertaining. I was used to having every need anticipated and met. And my lullabies had been in Bengali. It was not exactly a romantic cruise. When they reached port in the United Kingdom, they learned that Grandfather Albert Cooper had died of cancer in Calcutta while they had been travelling. He had been seriously ill when they left, so his death was no surprise, but this made it no less sad as they arrived in austere postwar England.

After a short period of leave, which was spent with Boyd relatives, my father was posted to Germany, as part of the occupation forces. This was immediately after the war, and there were no married quarters available. So Mum and I stayed for a year with his mother in Ireland. Gracie Boyd, again a widow, then living in Clonoragh, a comfortable house with a big garden, in the village of Ballytore, County Kildare. Learning to talk, I called her 'Ulla'. The name stuck. We were next door to a dairy farm and collected a billy can of fresh milk each morning. Until then there had only been tinned or powdered milk in the diet. Ulla was by that time an experienced country woman, a skilled cook, a competent housekeeper, a knitter, handy with a needle, a knowledgeable gardener and adroit at storing and using produce. She made cheese, cream and butter and preserved all the seasonal fruits and vegetables. A jug of milk was left to sour on the kitchen mantelpiece each day and used the following morning to make fresh soda bread. Grandmother 'Ulla' handled children well. Mother, coming from a house with several servants in India, had no experience of cooking and knew nothing of any of this – but she could not have had a better tutor!

So, in 1947, when the family was reunited in Kiel, in Germany, Mum was quite ready to run a house, manage the domestic staff, look after me and cook passable meals. In 1948, twins were born in the British military hospital at Rinteln. They were desperate for a boy, so there was some anxiety when the first baby born was a girl, Lynda-Jane. There was huge joy and relief when, ten minutes later, Gerald Alexander Laurence popped out. They had their son and heir.

I loved and was very proud of the twin babies, but as they grew up I came to resent the sometimes preferential treatment given to Gerald just because he was the boy, even though I remained the adored eldest child. He was an indulged, noisy, naughty, disruptive baby and toddler. And when I learned later that he was to inherit all the family silver, I smarted under this injustice. When I was older I eventually came to terms with the situation – it was the property of our parents and they could dispose of it as their culture and upbringing determined.

The British postwar policy objective of rebuilding and normalising Germany as quickly as possible included promoting full employment. So we had two nannies: one for me and one for the twins. We also had a cook, a gardener, a housekeeper and the boilerman, who tended the coal-fired central heating and cleaned snow from the footpaths in winter. Army wives were expected to undertake voluntary work, and there was an active social life as well. So, we children grew up spending more time with the German-speaking staff. Thus, I grew up bilingual. My father had learned French and German at school and some Urdu and Hindi in India. He was a firm believer in the value of languages, so this was encouraged.

My father's hobby was breeding and training German short-haired pointer gundogs and helping re-establish the populations of game birds which had lived on the surrounding moors and heathlands before the war. Most of the original birds had, of course, been eaten by the German wartime population. Replacement chicks were imported from England to build the stock of wild birds. He worked closely with the local foresters, speaking German with them, and I played with their children and enjoyed sleepovers at their houses, sharing the children's feather beds. I remember one German mother becoming very cross with me and her little daughter as a tickling match in bed resulted in a ripped cover and feathers all over the room! I would have been about four.

The German-language skills were useful at home. Mother told of my serving as an interpreter at age three when painters arrived at the house unexpectedly. And when the twin babies came home from the hospital – I was two and a half – I was so proud of them I would go out on the street and invite German strangers to come in to admire the babies and then offer cigarettes from the silver cigarette box. Nanny told our mother, who put a stop to this.

I was, however, quite surprised when my parents brought two little humans home from the hospital. Whenever she had been away for pre-natal appointments, Mummy had always brought me a special little cake, formed like a frog, with green icing. That's what I thought you brought home from the hospital!

I adored my father and spent a lot of time with him when I was little, learning how to train the dogs and trailing around helping him as he did all the practical jobs. He was a member of the British Army's equestrian team – and had a way with horses he had learned growing up in Ireland. There are photos of me on a horse with Daddy when I was very small. He was pleased that I learned practical skills from him and flourished in school – I learned to read very early. My mother said I was a determined little person who would not accept warnings, always pushing the boundaries and needing to learn from experience, and I was very independent. In Kiel we lived in the former Danish Consulate, on the Kiel Canal.

When I was five, the army moved us to another German town, Bad Oeynhausen.

I started school there in a little British Army primary school near our house in Roon Strasse. It was a great house for children to play in. One childish adventure included the twins' raiding the neighbour's coal cellar, loading briquettes onto a little toy cart and hauling them back to our cellar. We received a lecture about stealing.

But my naughtiness was more serious. Once, I was in bed recovering from measles and was bored. During the afternoon I felt cold, so I crept into our parents' room and took the forbidden matches from their bedside table drawer and set fire to a pile of comics heaped up against my bedroom wall. The leaping flames also ignited the curtains and the chest of drawers. The updraught made the bedroom door slam shut. The doorknob on the inside was broken. I was trapped! Nanny was downstairs and ignored my yells, as all morning I had been calling her up to 'pick up my pencil' and other menial jobs. It was a real case of 'crying wolf'! Luckily, people in the house across the road saw the flames and rushed over, pushed Nanny aside, ran up the stairs, flung the door open and grabbed me, taking me downstairs wrapped in a blanket; then they fought the fire. The fire brigade came, and I remember feeling very cross that they wouldn't let me go and look at the fire engine! Our mother was walking home with another army wife and saw the fire engine speed past. 'Your place or mine?' they joked! Father kept a copy of the report to the army on the damage and circumstances. I dared not strike a match for years.

In 1952, when I was six, the army moved us from Germany to Holywood, County Down, in Northern Ireland. We lived just outside the Palace barracks where Father was based. I attended the little multiple-class, single-teacher primary school in the barracks, headed by Mr R. T. Evans. I adored him. Already a good reader, I could help the younger students with their books and lapped up greedily all the learning opportunities provided. Even at that early age, however, maths was not my favourite subject. I told Mr Evans one morning that I was not in the mood for arithmetic that day. He replied firmly, 'We do not teach moods in this school. We teach arithmetic'. Doing homework one evening, I asked Mummy how many farthings there were in a penny. She told me eight (there were actually four), and I was very cross when all my sums turned out to be wrong! I continued to exchange letters with

Mr Evans for long afterwards, until one day I received a sad note from his widow, telling me he had died. She said I had been his favourite student.

Years later, when I revisited mother's mistake about farthings, she defended herself. 'Well, how should I know about farthings? I was brought up in India. If you'd asked me about rupees and paise I would have known the answer!' And my older self is now ashamed at how I misunderstood and under-appreciated our mother. She was separated from her own family, grieving for her father and struggling with three small children in a culture with which she was not familiar. Being Raj British in India was one thing. Being Raj British in England and Ireland was another. What she was very good at was loving and protecting us, looking after us, being home when we came back from school, cooking good meals and baking cakes and biscuits and dressing us well. Our father could be very strict and gruff and controlling and there were times when she had to intervene and take our part and console us. All in all, I found our home a safe base from which to launch risky adventures. I was learning how to manage our father.

For the twins it was more difficult. Father had been sent to boarding school when he was eight, had nannies and governesses and saw relatively little of his own parents. He had no experience in a modern family himself. As the favoured child, clever, and competent, I was loved and nurtured. But for my brother it was a different story. He was the son and heir and expected to shine, but he fell short of our father's unrealistically high and inappropriate expectations. Father had little real understanding of his son and little skill in showing his love. His manner was invariably gruff. Sister Lynda tells me that she was in perpetual fear of him. At his public school, Hurn Court in Dorset, England, Gerald did well in practical subjects – technical drawing, carpentry and practical farming. He made lasting friendships easily. He was a good sportsman and a competent sailor. But he was not strong in the traditional academic subjects, and, term after term, his school reports were heavy with criticism. This disappointed and enraged our father, who had little respect for the skills Gerald did have. He imposed punishments like taking away my brother's bicycle for the holidays. He would shout at us over any misdemeanour. I remember Mummy once berating him, saying, 'Stop treating the children like your soldiers!'

Gerald was always being compared with me, which did little for our sibling relations. We fought a great deal, and this only stopped when he grew big enough to win every physical fight; then the combat took the form of taunts and teasing designed to provoke my ire. This continued into our adulthood.

Sister Lynda adored her twin brother. She was like our mother in being loving and playing the peacemaker. She was self-sacrificing, accepting the blame and punishment for the naughtiness Gerald committed but was too terrified to own up to. He was very naughty. Lynda was always most genuinely the nicest and most loving of the three of us. She occupied the neutral, central ground of the middle child. She was neither the eldest nor the boy. So, she was pretty much left to her own devices, was a quiet achiever at school and made very solid lifelong friends. She was creative and was due to enter art school when she finished secondary school, in Clevedon, in Somerset in the United Kingdom, but it was at that point, in 1966, that the family decided to emigrate to Australia.

Mummy had never really liked living in England. Her brother, David, had emigrated from the United Kingdom to Adelaide in 1964 and Granny had gone to live with him and his family. Their letters were glowing. And they judged that employment opportunities for Daddy and for us children were better in Australia than in Harold Wilson's United Kingdom. Wilson was the Labour Party Prime Minister of the United Kingdom, elected in 1964. His government quickly enacted a range of social reforms which found little favour among more conservative elements.

I had always been enthralled by the stories of my parents' life in India and wondered why they found settling in England so difficult. The chance to make several visits to Calcutta came with my posting as Australian high commissioner to Bangladesh (formerly part of Bengal) from 1986 to 1989. The city was a short flight from Dhaka, Bangadesh's capital, and I first revisited my birthplace in 1987. I called at the jockey club, explained the family connections and asked to look around. The club secretary told me politely that this was a men's club, and so I could not be received. However, he relented and became suddenly much more cooperative when I told him I was the Australian high commissioner.

I also visited mother's old school and the apartment building which had been her family home. The school was in good condition and continued to operate successfully. The apartment building was, however, quite run down, and each apartment housed several families. The street was dirty and crowded. I took many photographs of Calcutta and sent them back to Perth. She was very depressed at the run-down state of the place. In our mother's youth it had been a beautifully manicured and well-maintained city, the former grand capital of British India. She refused my invitation to revisit the place with me.

Being brought up in a family like this helped me to adjust to different countries and schools, to put down roots quickly and to pull them up again when it was time to move on. I learned about different cultures, values and religions. I knew that different was not necessarily inferior. I grew up in houses with domestic staff, so when I was serving abroad, and I employed and managed people helping in my various homes, it was not a new experience for me. Many Australians are unhappy with this aspect of their service abroad and find it hard to coexist with strangers living and working in their midst. In the High Commission in Bangladesh we had one wife, on her husband's first posting, who was terrified of her local domestic staff and refused to let them touch her baby: she thought their brown skin meant they were dirty. Other newly posted staff did not understand that being employed by a foreign diplomat and earning a good salary for their work was an honourable profession and conferred considerable social status on the domestic staff among their contemporaries. It was not exploitation, and the staff did not expect to become their best friends. I also grew up knowing that my job in life, like that of my father and grandparents, was to be of service to others, a leader, and to be confident of my place in society.

Both our parents have now died, and I have no-one in front of whom, like a cat, I can lay my dead birds or mice. They were proud of me and my life. I hope that they would have been pleased with this book.

2

Schools and Africa, 1951–65

International schooling and volunteer teaching in Africa

Art has been important to me in all my postings. I have included reference to an artwork in some chapters of this book. References to the images are included where relevant.

A local village potter near Masuku Mission in Zambia fired several clay pipes and a black bowl in the campfire (see artwork insert page 1). I thought they were beautiful and packed them carefully in a basket I carried while hitchhiking and travelling by boat, bus and train around Central Africa on my way back to the United Kingdom in 1965, at the end of my volunteer teaching year, aged eighteen. They have been with me ever since.

Thirteen schools in five countries educated me as we moved around the world with the British Army. Fortunately, all were on the same British model and curriculum, and we were taught in English. I have strong memories of only a few of the dozens of competent teachers who contributed to my education in Germany, Ireland, England, Egypt and Cyprus, Germany again and then back in England.

I was removed from only one school, the British Army high school in Limassol, Cyprus. My family was living in Nicosia, where there was no army secondary school, so at age eleven I was boarded on the army base at Limassol with a nice family who had a daughter of the same age. Away from home for the first time, I tested the boundaries of my new freedom and became very naughty: didn't do homework, was cheeky and rebellious with the teachers and to my host 'mother', went walkabout by myself and led my hosts' daughter, Joanna, astray. It was the midnight feast adventure which was the final undoing. While her parents were away at a dinner party one night, I led Joanna into the pantry to raid for biscuits and cake for our feast. There, we met a large rat, which scared us enough for me to telephone the parents at their dinner party. Their first question was, of course, 'What were you doing in the pantry?'

My parents took me back to Nicosia, where the army agreed to pay the fees at the private British Council international school. This was excellent: my classmates were Greek, Turkish, Cypriot, French and Armenian as well as British. And the city of Nicosia was much more interesting than the Limassol army barracks. As a family we walked around the walls of the city in the early evening and ate kebabs in the Turkish quarter. When I went with our mother to her dressmaker's I learned that it was not polite to leave until the coffee cup was cold. I learned some Greek and coached my mother in a Greek oath she should shout if the male drivers gave her a hard time when she drove in the local traffic. Luckily, my mother checked out the oath with our housemaid, who was horrified.

The family had moved to Cyprus from Egypt, as part of the British Army's defence of the colony and British determination to contain the pro-independence movement EOKA, which was escalating its terrorist campaign. We children were trained in avoiding bomb and other attacks and in how to take shelter, and we had army soldiers as guards on our school bus and at school. They were nice, fresh-faced, young national servicemen, who amused themselves and us by peeling our playtime oranges with their bayonets.

Despite the dangers, Cyprus was a lovely place for us to live. The family drove over the Kyrenia Mountains to the beach at several weekends, and to the salt flats at Larnaca to see the massed hordes of flamingos. We spent a summer holiday in the mountains at Troodos. At home, we played in our sandpit and in the street with the children of our Greek and Turkish neighbours.

Other weekends we spent at the army saddle club at Athalassa, learning to ride the army horses. Our father told us that, even though modern artillery weapons were already towed by military vehicles, when we were there in 1957 the formal army instructions still called for horses to be supplied to do the job, and the gun crews still listed men to hold the horses' heads. Soldiers who handled livestock in their civilian lives looked after these horses and taught us to care for them and their tack, and how to ride.

One of the grooms once sat me on his lap while he explained the details of a horse's bridle. I was conscious of some strange movement against my bottom and as I reached out to grasp the bridle I was groped. I felt instinctively that this was not a good thing and ran away. That evening, I told my mother what had happened. She was outraged. 'I'll come with you tomorrow and I want you to point him out. I'll horsewhip him! I'll horsewhip him!' I wasn't sure I wanted my mother to horsewhip anyone, so I was quite pleased that the offender was nowhere to be seen the following day.

Father liked to ride with us, but he pushed us beyond our limits of current competence. He had done the same in Egypt, when we sailed on the Great Bitter Lake at Fayed, on the Suez Canal. We had been posted in Egypt there until the Suez crisis erupted in 1956, when the British forces and their families were hurriedly relocated to Cyprus. I was sailing with my parents when I dropped a precious Red Sea sponge off the boat. My father shouted at me and ordered me to jump off and get it back, despite my protests that I could not yet swim. This was not an acceptable excuse, and I was forced to jump off the boat into the water – and found that I could, indeed, swim. This was typical of my father's way of instructing his children, though he could also be painstakingly patient, as when teaching us how to train dogs and use a shotgun.

At the end of our posting in Cyprus, in 1957, my father was once again sent by the army to Germany, this time to Münster. He was very happy to be in a German-speaking environment once more and able to resume his sporting interests. I was by now in high school. The British Families Education Service had three boarding schools around Germany to cater for kids like us. I went to Windsor School, in the town of Hamm. This was located near the Moehne Reservoir, the site of the audacious skip bombing of the Moehne Dam carried out by the Royal Air Force Dambusters in World War II. The school, which was coeducational, was housed in a former German Army barracks and was well equipped, with a swimming pool, sportsground and chapel. The boys' and girls' houses were in parallel accommodation blocks separated by a garden. I realised that I had become short-sighted when I could no longer see clearly from inside the girls' block the activities going on in the boys' dormitories and I asked Matron to organise an eye test. I had noticed no problems with reading the classroom blackboard.

I flourished in boarding school, with the time available for sports and extracurricular subjects such as pottery, drama, archery and Girl Guides. I could swim well, having learned in the warm waters of Egypt and Cyprus, and was elected house swimming captain. I received a useful life lesson when I drew up the team for the interhouse swimming carnival and put myself down for every event: breaststroke, freestyle, butterfly, backstroke, diving – the lot. I only included other girls for the relay teams. Our house mistress explained patiently that a team contained other members besides the captain. I might well be the best swimmer in the house for each of those events, as I claimed, but I was unlikely to perform to the winning standard in all of them on the same afternoon. So I revised the team list. Our team did well.

Like many German towns, Hamm had a good concert hall, and our music master took us out of school on special evenings to classical concerts. These were a revelation to me and opened up a whole new world of music. I loved the vigorous applause delivered by the German audiences, with stamping on the wooden floorboards and banging on the wooden pews in appreciation. Much more satisfying than the polite British hand-clapping! I sang in the school chapel choir, and we learned and performed works like Handel's *Messiah* and psalms and hymns, but the classical concerts provided my first encounters with orchestral music. We'd heard nothing like this in our home – we did not even possess a record player. I was hooked for life.

The family moved back to the United Kingdom in 1959, and my father was assigned to the War Office, in London. He came home to us at weekends. Our Grandmother Gracie, Ulla, had died while we were away in Egypt and left her house to us. We settled there when we returned. She had moved from Ireland to a seventeenth-century thatched cottage in Stoke by Clare in Suffolk, to be near her sister Aunt Maudie Firth, who lived in the next village, Wixoe. Stoke by Clare was typical of that part of the country: a main street lined with thatched or slate-tiled cottages painted either white or Suffolk pink. The Red Lion pub was opposite us, and the Norman Anglican church was down the road. We used the two small general stores, Bean's and Ling's, a garage and a post office, the last of which was an annex built onto the house of Mr Skeets, the postmaster. Mr Skeets also worked part-time in our garden. The railway station was next to the small primary school, which the twins attended. Mrs Bruty, who helped our mother in the house, cycled the 2 miles (3.2 kilometres) to and from her council house. Her house had recently been fitted with electric lights, but she refused to turn them on, just as she refused to use our vacuum cleaner. 'Modern fandangled things!' We never knew or used their Christian names. The River Stour was a short way down a hilly lane next to the cottage. We walked the German short-haired pointer, Sonia, there each day, and my brother and I went home with bruises and bloody scrapes one day when the billy cart Gerald had made crashed on its test run downhill, with us aboard.

31

The school I attended was Sudbury Girls' High School, a thirty-minute school bus ride away, coming home by train if there were after-school activities. I sat the General Certificate of Education 'O' level exams in 1962 and shocked everyone by failing four of my eight subjects: maths, Latin, history and German. It had been a busy year, playing in the school hockey, swimming and tennis teams and attending ballroom-dancing classes with pupils from the boys' grammar school. I was a school prefect and had founded a school music society. Willing teachers had taken us to the famous Christmas carol service at King's College, Cambridge, and to churches with notable organs around the county. A classmate and I had represented the school in Anglia TV's interschool quiz program, winning a television set and books for the library. I just hadn't studied very well. It was a wake-up call: I could no longer cruise along.

Father retired from the army early. The British Army had moved to nuclear weapons, and modern war strategy required fewer actual soldiers, so there were attractive packages for officers, like my father, who had become redundant. He found a job with the publishing house George Newnes which produced *Chambers's Encyclopaedia*. They promoted him to run the business in the West of England, so in 1962 we left our pretty village and thatched cottage home and moved to Somerset.

The family bought an old stone farmhouse, 'Moorgates', near the pub in Kenn, a village near Clevedon, some distance away from Bristol. I had an hour-and-a-half's journey each day to school. First, there was a 2-mile (3.22 kilometre) cycle along lanes over Kenn Moor to the main road to meet the bus to the Bristol City terminal. In winter, there was rain, sleet and snow to contend with. I took a local bus to Bristol and then a city bus to school. The travel time was useful for the heavy study load.

Colston's Girls School, in Bristol, one of the best girls' schools in the region, had accepted me on the basis of the glowing recommendation from my headmistress in Suffolk, written before my disastrous exam results came out. Miss Amy Dunn, my new headmistress, was stern at my opening interview. She was an Oxford graduate, and the school had high academic standards. She made it clear that she was shocked and angry at my 'O' level failures and said that the school would certainly not have accepted me with that record. But all was not lost. Both she and my previous headmistress believed I still 'had it in me', and she established a clear academic plan for my rescue. I would work extra hard in the two years remaining of my schooling, proceeding with the study of the three 'A' level subjects I had chosen: English, French and German. I would do extra German study to bring me up to the expected level. In addition, with extra support from teachers, I would study for and resit the 'O' level exams in Latin and maths. This was a heavy load, but I liked Colston's and knuckled down to the work. There were new friends, the hockey, swimming and tennis teams, and the school play. In my final year, 1964, I was made a prefect, a member of the student leadership team. It was a relief when I passed all three of my subjects at the General Certificate of Education 'A' levels, as well as the 'O' level subjects I resat.

The school had partner relationships with two boys' schools: Bristol Grammar School and Bristol Cathedral School. We had some mixed classes, worked with the boys on school plays and enjoyed mixed ballroom- and Scottish-dancing classes. I formed a special friendship with a boy from each school, both of which lasted for years afterwards. Roger and Paul were my first boyfriends, and I loved and admired them for their knowledge, sense of humour, different points of view and great company. I drank my first glasses of cider with them in Bristol pubs. (They took their school ties off before going into pubs after school.) I met their parents and they met mine. The hormones were racing, and there was a lot of yearning and kissing and fumbling but nothing serious. Once there was a bit of rolling in the hayfield with Roger, but procedures were halted by both my attack of hayfever and interference from the family dog, which was with us and was protective against what she interpreted as an attack on me. Roger had a great gift with the English language and was a poet, and this was all very romantic.

In 1964, when we finished school, Roger and I deferred university study and each had a year with the British volunteer organisation Voluntary Service Overseas (VSO): Roger in Coimbatore, India, and I in Northern Rhodesia (now Zambia). Roger sent me beautifully crafted letters while we were away and brought me back a fine woollen shawl, which I still use. He went on to Oxford University, and I paid him a gorgeously romantic visit, including punting on the river.

My other boyfriend, Paul, joined the Royal Air Force and invited me to his graduation ceremony and ball at Cranwell RAF College in 1965. It was my first ball, and I chose a beautiful green brocade fabric and sewed my formal gown for the event. My mother allowed me to wear a priceless emerald and diamond brooch which had belonged to Grandmother 'Ulla'. I had my ears pierced so I could wear the matching earrings. That dress served me well through many university balls. Paul was later posted to Hong Kong as a helicopter pilot; he was too tall to eject safely from a jet fighter, which he really wanted to fly. He visited me later, when I was twenty-one, and we went on a camping trip together in the stunning southwest of Western Australia. He wanted to develop our relationship, but I could not move on past a good friendship. I was at university and set on a good career. The prospect of being an air force wife did not appeal. I had seen at home what that looked like.

September 1964 saw me as a VSO volunteer teacher at Masuku Mission Upper Primary Girls' School, in the southern province of Northern Rhodesia. We were not far from the Zambezi River, and an hour's walk through the forest brought us to the top of a ridge from which we could see Lake Kariba and its dam. The dam was an important project, constructed in 1959 on the Zambezi River, to produce the world's largest artificial lake and reservoir, lying along the border with Zambia and Zimbabwe. It supports an important hydro-electricity scheme.

The nearest town to our school, Choma, was on the north–south railway line and had two banks, a grocery store, a butcher, a post office, a small hospital, schools, churches and a railway station. It was 75 kilometres of dirt road and two river ford crossings away from Masuku Mission. The mission's driver, Noah, made the trip each Saturday in the mission's sole vehicle, a jeep, to collect mail, food, and school and hospital supplies. The teaching and nursing staff at the mission each took turns to accompany him on this bumpy trip, once or twice a term. In the rainy season the road was sometimes impassable, and on several occasions Noah had to wait at the fords for several hours until the water level over the road dropped.

I had a small, furnished two-bedroom brick house to myself, with an internal bathroom and a wide front veranda. The first night I slept alone, I was quite nervous. I awoke during the night to the sound of rustling paper. Was someone in my house? I lay in bed rigid and sweating with fear, afraid to move and make a noise. I listened intently as the paper rustling continued and gradually realised the sounds were coming through the window, from outside the house. Overcoming my fear, I tiptoed across and peered outside, through the curtains. In the bright moonlight I saw a herd of cattle browsing through the grass and dried fallen leaves. I never felt nervous there again.

There was no electricity at Masuku. Tilley paraffin pressure lamps produced light and there were kerosene fridges. Running water and modern toilets in the houses were available only when the pump was working to lift water from the well to the single central water tank. There was a deep-drop pit toilet at the top of the hill behind my house, with the best view over the forest of Masuku fruit trees after which the mission was named. I bathed while standing in a large plastic basin placed in the bathtub, and afterwards, in the dry season, I watered the small flower beds around my house with the bath water.

A farmer from a neighbouring village kept us supplied with eggs and fresh fruit and vegetables, including the first avocados

I had ever encountered. Whenever he came, the missionaries bought his complete offering and shared it among the staff. He also provided vegetables for the students' meals.

I paid one of the schoolgirls to clean my house and to wash and then use the iron filled with charcoal from the fire on the four cotton dresses I owned. The school took small fees from the parents of the students, and we often accepted eggs, chickens or firewood in lieu of money. I was paid the same small salary as the African teachers.

There were two Methodist Missionaries at Masuku. Sister Connie Howard was the experienced matron in charge of the small hospital. The headmistress of the school was Eileen Hoyle, a gentle English north-country woman. She appointed me class teacher for Standard 8, the senior class in the school. There were thirty students, from the Tonga tribe, whose territory straddled the border with Zimbabwe. The girls ranged in age from about eight to thirteen, depending on when they had started primary school. We taught in English, but the daily and Sunday church services were in the local language, Chitonga. The missionaries encouraged me to learn the language and to conduct the morning service sufficiently well. Early missionaries had produced a Chitonga-language Bible and hymnal. The girls were talented singers, with natural harmony. The final evening prayer and hymn, sung in a circle outside the dormitory – lit by Tilley lamps placed on the ground, providing a cocoon of soft light – created an emotionally peaceful way to end each day.

VSO had given the group of volunteers some pre-departure training in England in teaching and community development. I remember the mantra: 'Start with what the community says it needs'. I was asked to teach almost every subject to the class, including science, maths, English, African history and geography, and physical education. In addition, one of the three African teachers taught domestic science, and an African nurse from the small mission hospital taught hygiene and first aid. The Northern Rhodesian Education Department provided a curriculum guide, and

I just had to keep a couple of lessons ahead of the girls. Amazingly, this was mostly successful. But science was a particular challenge. We had almost no laboratory equipment so had to improvise with bottles and a small spirit lamp. For an experiment designed to show that air expands when heated, we used the lamp to heat an empty bottle inverted into a bucket of water. Soon, bubbles came out of the bottle's mouth. 'What do you see, girls?' I asked.

'The water in the bucket is boiling, Miss Boyd'.

'Aha! And what do you know about boiling water?'

'It is hot'.

'So, put your hands into the water to see if it is hot'.

'Oh no, Miss Boyd, we will be burned'.

'Well, let's see what happens when *I* put my hand into the water. See? My hand is not burned'.

'Ah, but you are the teacher. You have magic!'

A difficult topic was aerodynamics. These children had never seen a plane but had observed birds. How did they fly? The curriculum dictated that we should teach this by constructing and flying paper kites. We had a lot of fun. But the external end-of-term exam contained a multiple-choice question: 'What keeps kites up in the air? A. The string. B. Magic. C. Air pressure'. They all ticked 'magic'!

I enjoyed our physical education lessons. The girls loved to run and jump, and we constructed a hurdle course with piles of sand and boxes. The class suggested we accompany the movements with drum music, which they were good at. But the missionaries vetoed this suggestion: drums would lead to dancing, which was sensual and might lead to overexcitement and trouble!

I learned a little about the local culture. I volunteered to sew the screens for the new maternity ward at the hospital using a donated bolt of red fabric. But no woman was willing to have her baby in the new ward. It seemed that red was an unlucky colour and signalled death.

I liked teaching and was deeply committed to all the young women in my class. They were keen students, avid to learn and reluctant to have the lamps taken away at the end of the evening's homework period. I got on with and respected the two missionary women. The three African teachers and the two African nurses at the hospital, who were close to me in age, offered friendship and taught me a great deal. The schoolgirls all knew that education was the key to development, and they studied hard and were deeply appreciative of the opportunities offered. Fifteen of my thirty girls succeeded in passing into the local high school at the end of the year; there were only thirty-five places on offer for the whole district. I was proud of them. This was the largest number of entrants Masuku had ever achieved. Those who did not get into secondary school went into nursing or teachers' college or found other jobs.

I taught adult literacy classes at night in the lower primary school in a nearby village. The class consisted of a group of women in colourful dresses and head-wraps, each with a baby in a sling, and a couple of men. I rode my bicycle alone with my Tilley lamp through the bush to the school, with absolutely no fear. The two women missionaries and I were the only white people in the area and seemed to be respected by all the villagers. We were teaching their children and looking after their sick people and pregnant women, and we took the seriously ill to the Choma hospital in our sole vehicle. Many came to worship in the mission church when the minister visited on circuit once a month.

Once, a survey team came through the mission, planning the course of a new road to Kariba Dam. The Batonga people called them 'Ba Mappas'. The team contained a couple of good-looking, fit, young white men. We had few outside visitors and I invited them to my house for a cup of tea. The missionaries were quite nervous at this and suggested I leave all the doors and curtains wide open during such visits. They were also cautious when I went to visit a fellow volunteer who was working at a Catholic mission not far away. I was warned that the Catholic priests drank alcohol, played cards and danced. I thought all this was a nice change! But I nonetheless admired, respected, liked and learned a lot from those wise, dedicated women, and I enjoyed my year in their company. We kept up a regular correspondence afterwards.

While I was at Masuku the Standard Chartered Bank teller in Choma, whom I had met while doing my banking, thought I might be interested in a wider social event and invited me to his sister's twenty-first birthday in Kitwe, on Rhodesia's copper belt, and he drove us there and back. Kitwe is a day's drive from Choma and this would have been the longest road trip I had made in Rhodesia. I savoured the changing scenery en route. Once at the party, I was shocked at the extravagant expenditure on food and drink. The money would have paid school fees for 100 students at our school. His mother saw the simple cotton dresses I had packed and kindly decked me out from her own wardrobe in a more suitable white lace party dress, evening stole and gold sandals and handbag, plus a necklace. When I returned to Masuku, I found the kind woman had secreted all these clothes in my suitcase, and a few more besides. That turned out to be a very useful party dress for several years.

In the first moments of 1965, Northern Rhodesia became the new independent state of Zambia. While the whole school sang the new national anthem at midnight, the newly formed Girl Guides company, using the correct knots we had learned, proudly raised the new Zambian flag to the top of the flagpole erected in the school playground, made from a tree chopped down in the forest. It was an utterly peaceful transition throughout the country, with Kenneth Kaunda as the country's new president. The Africanisation of the country's civil administration upon independence, and the withdrawal of British colonial public servants, created many new employment opportunities for educated local men and women, and our girls eventually moved into those jobs.

I left England with £20 in my purse and returned a year later, in September 1965, with the same amount, having travelled by bus and ship and having hitchhiked through Zambia, Uganda and Tanganyika before catching a charter flight at Entebbe, which took all the English volunteers home from East and Central Africa at the end of their assignments.

In September 1980 I revisited Lusaka, the capital of Zambia, as adviser to the Australian parliamentary delegation to the Commonwealth Parliamentary Association conference. I was overwhelmed to find that one of my Masuku girls was deputy clerk of the Zambian parliament. She rounded up a few of the other Masuku old girls, who had all moved into national leadership roles. One was head of the national teacher training college; one was matron of the Lusaka hospital. I was told that only one had 'gone back to the village'. Many of the women had not married: they told me that men were not interested in educated women.

But one of my favourites at the school, Siziwe, had married a much older man, to whom her family had 'sold' her. The Batonga people were cattle owners, and in their system, women had a bride price of several head of cattle and other goods. While I was at Masuku, a young man from a neighbouring village had proposed marriage to me. In a letter he told me he wanted me to 'wave the blue flage [sic] to keep away my loneliness'. I asked what bride price I was worth. He said that I was not very strong and therefore would not be able to work very well in the gardens, but I was educated. So I was probably worth two head of cattle. Other, more hefty, volunteer Englishwomen were worth more.

Looking back, I can see that I was a product of my English class structure. We were confident that we were born to rule, and inherent in that was a duty of service. All my school reports described me as a natural leader. In going to Africa, I thought I was an incredibly privileged, well-educated eighteen-year-old, and I had a duty to 'give back'. On arrival, I saw myself as inherently superior to all these 'poor' black African children and staff at the school and hospital at Masuku Mission. I'd had a better formal education and what I thought was a wider experience and a better standard of living than they'd had. I was a little, racist, white supremacist.

During the Masuku school holidays I was working in Lusaka, the capital, at the Young Women's Christian Association when that self-perception changed radically. I met a black woman who was better educated than me, with wider experience, who had an inherent dignity and was a high achiever. Inonge Wina was president of the association, was university educated and, upon independence, became a member of the first Zambian delegation to the United Nations. She went on to become vice-president of Zambia. This was a woman I admired and could look up to, and she was smarter than me! It was a life-changing moment. I went back to Masuku and the rest of my life with a different attitude.

I grew up in that year at Masuku. It was an intensely happy time, and I learned a lot about myself and my abilities. My capacity for making new friends, for leadership and for independent action, my ability to innovate and my curiosity and willingness to learn all contributed to a successful and happy year.

The missionaries had a battery radio telephone, used only for emergencies. I wrote to my family every week and received aerogram letters back. I did not speak to my family in my whole year away. Telephone links were difficult and expensive. We didn't even think about making personal calls. In one of the last letters from my mother, towards the end of my stay, she wrote that my parents had decided that the family, including our maternal grandmother, who lived with us, were going to leave England and migrate to Western Australia. I was shocked and furious. I had a place waiting for me at The University of London. My mother wrote that I could attend the University of Western Australia, in Perth. I was not reassured. What was a degree from there going to be worth? Who had ever heard of the university?

When I got back to England I told my parents that I would stay behind in London, and the rest of the family could leave! But the family refused to go without me, and I was persuaded that I could study and my father, brother and sister would find better work in Western Australia than they could find in Britain. WA was a state which was 'on the move', both ripe for investment and avid for a capable workforce. And they were right.

3

Ten-pound Poms and The University of Western Australia, 1966–69

Family migration to Western Australia and my time at The University of Western Australia

The artists Guy and Helen Grey-Smith were the parents of Sue Grey-Smith, one of my earliest friends at St Catherine's College at the University of Western Australia. Sue took me often to the family home in Darlington in Western Australia, where I got to know and admire Guy, Helen and their son, Mark, then a budding sculptor. In 1974, on a visit home to Perth, I telephoned Guy and told him I now had some money and would like to buy one of his paintings. He said Mark was up at the house. There was a stack of his paintings in the shed and I could make my choice.

I chose an untitled painting (see artwork insert figure 2) and a serigraph called *Rock Fishermen*. Mark had no idea of the prices but assured me they would be reasonable. A few years later I received a letter from Guy saying the taxman was on his back and could I please pay? I asked how much he wanted and sent off a cheque. I can't recall and did not record how much I paid for either work. But they have accompanied me around the world and have been a great and constant joy.

On 14 February 1966 the whole Boyd family was up at dawn, catching a first glimpse of Western Australia over the ship's rail.

We arrived in Fremantle on the SS *Canberra* on Decimal Currency Day. We were assisted migrants – ten-pound Poms. The twins, who were only seventeen, travelled free. The family left Southampton, in the United Kingdom, during a snowstorm and arrived in Western Australia three weeks later in temperatures over 40°C. But we adjusted and settled in quickly: this was just another posting. But we were surprised to find some subtle cultural changes. My father had found a job in the General Agency Company, which had sponsored our migration and provided us with temporary rented housing in the Perth residential suburb of Floreat Park. The agency's representative Ozzie Oswald and his wife, Joan, met us off the ship, took us to our new home, befriended us and helped us settle in.

The day we arrived was truly sweltering, with no afternoon sea breeze. At around 4.00 pm in the hot afternoon, we were all sleeping in our new beds, following the very early start to the day. A nice Brit from the Good Neighbourhood Council knocked on our door, introduced himself and offered to return later that evening and take us to the beach. This was at a time before widespread air-conditioning, and it seemed that the whole population of Perth was on Floreat Beach that hot, windless night! There were beach cricket, volleyball and barbecues, whole families cooling off on the sand and in the water. We thought we were good swimmers and rushed into the sea, only to be dumped by the huge waves. What a welcome!

Before leaving England my godmother gave us an introduction to two sisters who lived in the West Australian town of Guildford, close to Perth. Madge and Helena King had lived with my god-mother's family in England when they had visited when they were young. We phoned them soon after arrival and a few days later they invited us to afternoon tea, where we met the Blair family. John Blair had been a British civil servant in Africa and was now a classics teacher. His wife, Mary, had been born in southern India, like my mother. Their son, David, was a second-year student at the University of Western Australia, and his sister, Anne, was about to start her studies there with me, as was their cousin Sue Grey-Smith. It was a good match for us all. They were our first friends in Australia and we remained close over the years. David became a professor and prominent physicist at the University of Western Australia, and his research team became famous in 2017 when they were part of the international consortium which first recorded a gravity wave.

A week after we arrived, David invited my brother, Gerald, and me for a sail on the Swan River. We were in the sailing boat and well underway from the university club at Crawley, when a sudden gust of wind propelled Gerald across the boat on the trapeze. His feet hit my back and pushed me into the water. The boat capsized, and the automatic self-righting airbags that David had designed and installed in the boat didn't work. Luckily, we were not hurt and were all good swimmers. David and I stayed with the capsized boat, in the middle of the river, while Gerald swam to the nearest land, knocked on a stranger's door and used their phone to call the water police. David and I were rescued ignominiously, and the boat was towed back to the Crawley shore.

Gerald had finished his schooling in England and was due to travel that very afternoon to Esperance, to start work with our Irish cousin John Trench, a pioneer farmer. Esperance is 714 kilometres from Perth, on the Southern Ocean. The land had recently been opened up to farming, following the discovery of the fertiliser superphosphate which compensates the soil for natural lack of vital trace elements. Gerald just made it to the bus for the ten-hour journey and his farming job.

The family settled in to Perth quickly. Lynda had also finished her schooling in England and found a job with a photo laboratory, the beginning of her successful career in sales and marketing. Father began work in real estate and took the family car to the city each morning. It was hard for our mother at first. She was left alone at home in the rented house during a heatwave. She had no new local friends and frequently walked in the heat to the local shopping centre to visit the hairdresser, just to talk to someone.

After a few weeks, my father bought our first Australian home, in South Perth, close to shops and on a bus route, giving Mum plenty to keep her busy. My grandmother, who arrived from her son's in Adelaide to live with us, also bought Mum a small car. She gradually made friends with other British migrant families who had more recently arrived and had bought houses through my father.

I started almost immediately at the University of Western Australia, moving into St Catherine's College, then the women's college, and quickly fitted in with all the other students. Many were all new together, so it was easy to integrate and make friends. I studied for a bachelor of arts, and included a unit of geology as a broadening study in my first year. Geology was a course in which I could study with men; my arts units were heavily feminised. A new friend from St Cat's was Shona Robinson, whose family had moved to Perth from Canberra. We joined the judo and jujitsu club together, wanting to try a new sport and thinking it was useful to learn self-defence. We were the only two women members. My first boyfriend at university was an extremely handsome judoka. We spent much time at the beach together that summer, and he also taught me to drive. His family were refugees from the Ukraine, and his parents made sure we young people understood the situation of postwar East European migrants and their hatred of communism. They were extremely nervous about socialist student activism.

I became Miss Judo, the judo club's entrant in the Miss University Quest, for 1966. This was the university students' annual fundraiser for the World University Service, and most students were involved. I did not win, though we raised a fair amount of money by raffling off a dinner with me at a prominent, smart restaurant. Helen Wildy was Miss St Catherine's College, and we jointly took over management of the quest in 1967, a first significant organisational experience at the university. After we graduated, the Miss Uni Quest was seen as a non-politically correct activity and duly abandoned. I also heard that the

World University Service was discredited as being a CIA front organisation. But at the time it was a lot of fun, and it helped new and older students to mix and meet each other.

Another annual fundraising event for the World University Service was the Winnie-the-Pooh Reading, which took place on the stage of our very formal Winthrop Hall. A range of eminent professors read the parts of characters from the Pooh stories. It was very amusing to hear, for example, the professor of philosophy reading out, 'I am a bear of very little brain, and long words bother me'.[3] Our rather overweight professor of mathematics read the part of Piglet. His lines were mostly confined to 'Yes, Pooh', 'No, Pooh' and 'Anything you say, Pooh' in a very high voice.

There was plenty of social life at the university, with many opportunities to make new friends, both male and female, and I had some interesting and attractive boyfriends and lots of personal exploration on warm night-time beaches and in parked cars.

In 1967, Professor Gordon Reid was appointed by the university to introduce a new area of study: politics. I was really interested in this subject and made it my joint major, along with English drama. Gordon Reid and Bob Hetherington, the new Senior Lecturer, were energetic and inspiring teachers who brought the topics alive, drawing on their own practical experiences in Australian domestic politics. Professor Reid was a former usher of the black rod in the federal House of Representatives and knew parliamentary processes and the ins and outs of party activities firsthand. Both he and Bob had engaging stories to share as they introduced us to the history of democracy, comparative government systems and examples of governments in the United States, Russia, Britain and other European countries. The subject matter was relevant and engaging. Scott Macwilliam was also an inspiring tutor in politics at St Catherine's College, reinforcing study material and providing clarification where necessary, and he left us wanting to find out more. I worked hard at the subject. Scott was a close friend of Peter Edwards, my boyfriend at the time, and I did not want Peter to think I was a dummy. Peter was the 1967 guild president, then became the Rhodes scholar and left us for Oxford. He had a stellar career as a historian, including being the Australian official historian of the Vietnam War.

For me, active political engagement seemed to follow naturally. In 1967, I was elected to the council of the student governing body, the Guild of Undergraduates, though it was hardly an election. The number of men and women on the guild council reflected the ratio in the total student body. There were eight places for men and four for women, and exactly four women were nominated. There was a lot to get involved with in the university, including in the residential colleges. I joined a number of clubs and societies, was Education Vice President in the Guild of Graduates and organised a number of campaigns and events. There were seminars and conferences and I took part in amateur dramatics. In 1968, I was persuaded to run for election for guild president for 1969. This would be the first woman guild president and possibly the first woman to head any Australian university student governing body. It would be a tough battle to shift the student body out of its conservative apathy, and a major achievement. Many thought it an impossible challenge. But I sensed that this was a time of change and that there was a wave of activism I could ride.

There were two other candidates, the Rhodes scholar designate Tim Blain and the Labor Club president Kim Beazley (who later became Governor of Western Australia), so it was a tough election battle. I campaigned hard, speaking at all the colleges and making short presentations before lectures. Voting was compulsory for full-time students but not for part-time students, who mostly attended the evening lectures. For two years I had worked for two days a week at the afternoon newspaper the *Daily News* and to compensate attended many evening lectures, so I spoke before them, asking the part-time students to exercise their vote and support me. In all my election pitches my strong track record and experience were emphasised, which would make me an outstanding president, irrespective of my gender. And I promised to install soft lavatory paper in all the toilets. My election speeches ended with the words, 'I'm not asking you to vote for me because I am a woman. But I am asking you not to vote against me because I am a woman'.

The other two candidates both had factors working against them. Tim Blain had already been named as the Rhodes scholar for 1969 and would be leaving for Oxford halfway through his term as guild president. So it was easy to undermine him. And Kim Beazley had strong Australian Labor Party affiliations, he was president of the university branch of the Labor Party, and his father was a shadow minister in the federal parliament. At that time, students were not comfortable in supporting a candidate with strong political party connections, and many came from families with longstanding conservative affiliations.

I won the election and became the first woman guild president. This followed a long line of former presidents who had gone on to be prominent in Australian public life, including judges, senior officials and ministers of state and federal parliaments. They included Australian prime minister Bob Hawke.

The two failed candidates were close friends, and I asked Kim Beazley to be my vice-president. He took his turn as guild president in 1970 and also went on to win a Rhodes scholarship to Oxford and have a stellar career in federal politics. He then became the very successful Australian ambassador in Washington during Barack Obama's presidency and in 2018 became Governor of Western Australia. I jokingly say that I launched him on his political career; he genially plays along with this.

Following his studies at Oxford, Tim Blain joined the Australian foreign service, served in the Australian Embassy in Washington, DC, and then moved to the United Nations Secretariat in New York. He was exceptionally witty, musically gifted and a great debater. He was a star at the annual University Camp for Kids events, where student leaders took disadvantaged children for a week's residential holiday at the Point Peron campsite on the beach south of Perth. One child I particularly remember was the only member of his family who was not blind.

He was unusually mature for his young age and was used to being everybody's helper. The student leaders played games with the kids, put on concerts, rode on antique fire engines, provided good food and generally gave them a great time – and had a lot of fun. University Camp for Kids is the oldest not-for-profit charitable organisation in Western Australia, so there was a well-established tradition. It was still going strong in 2019 when I wrote this book.

It was an eventful period to be in student politics. There was growing controversy about US and Australian involvement in the Vietnam War, and student riots in Paris and in cities and university campuses in the United States and in Australia. University administrations were anxious about a rise in campus activism and students' demands for change. At the University of Western Australia, the guild ran a Vietnam Information Week and a protest march through the streets of Perth.

It also held a Sex Education Week after the tragic death of a former St Catherine's student resident following an illegal backyard abortion. Another student was killed at night while crossing the busy Stirling Highway, which separates the university from its colleges and halls of residence, so we campaigned for a tunnel under the highway as a safe pedestrian passageway for student residents in the colleges. We were impatient at the delays in approving and constructing the tunnel so thought up a number of stunts to pressure the five authorities with jurisdiction over the project to come to a speedy decision and move things along. St George's students won media attention by turning up on the median strip of the highway in front of their college dressed in dinner jackets and starting to dig the tunnel themselves with spades. And I led 1,000 students in a sit-in on the university side of the highway to block traffic. It was a well-run sit-in, with one traffic lane kept clear for emergency vehicles and an ample rotation of students to replace those directed by the police to move. The student newspaper, *Pelican*, irreverently dubbed the pedestrian underpass 'Boyd's passage'. The media pressure helped to move the plans forward through the multiple stakeholders, and it was a valuable experience in how to successfully negotiate a major project.

There were other issues which occupied us, too. The university accepted the students' petition to include the guild president in the university's governing council – the senate – and I was the first president to be so included. I was also the last guild president to be a full-time student, during my year of study for a postgraduate diploma in education. The university was growing, demands on the president left little time for study, and I was grateful for the understanding and support of the education faculty, which helped me get through. We persuaded the senate to allow subsequent presidents to suspend their studies for a year and to receive a modest stipend. At times of stress throughout my post-university life I have had the recurring nightmare that I have failed my university exams and face the question of what I am going to do for a living.

Jean Rogerson was a prominent businesswoman in Perth and the only woman on the senate. She took me to lunch and gave me some guidance on success. 'Read all the senate papers thoroughly', she advised. 'The men never do'. And she said she had trained her male colleagues not to tell dubious jokes in her presence. She'd be glad if I did not do otherwise! Jean was an independently wealthy woman and made significant bequests to the university and St Catherine's College.

We students wanted to change the world. As well as agitating for an end to the Vietnam War, we worried about the state of public education and campaigned for better schools and for Aboriginal land rights.

In 1969, the guild's Aboriginal affairs officer was Kim Akerman, who went on to a distinguished career in anthropology and museum administration. Kim led a student occupation of the iconic State War Memorial shortly before Anzac Day, to draw public attention to a blatant violation of an Aboriginal sacred site which had taken place near Leonora, in country Western Australia. Kim and I went further, by obtaining a mining right entitling us in general to prospect for sand, limestone, gravel and sandstone.

This legally entitled us to either peg out our claim area or define it by digging ditches. So we pegged our claim area around the War Memorial, and a group of local Noongar people danced nearby to celebrate their entitlement to the land. As we had anticipated, this attracted media attention and the ire of the police and the powerful Returned Services League, whose members protested over the violation of *their* sacred site. Of course, we didn't actually dig up the site to look for minerals, but as a result of our action the Aboriginal sacred site near Leonora came under protection.

When the guild produced a special edition of *Pelican*, the student newspaper, devoted to censorship, the state police seized most of the print run and charged us with producing a pornographic publication. The editor had included as part of a book review some extracts of the banned novel by D. H. Lawrence, *Lady Chatterley's Lover*, and Philip Roth's *Portnoy's Complaint*. In the same issue *Pelican* also reproduced allegedly offensive theatre posters and greeting cards which had been seized from local newsagencies. Both Alastair MacKinlay, the *Pelican* editor, and I, as guild president and publisher of the newpaper, were prosecuted, went to court and were found guilty, despite a brilliant defence by our lawyer, Ian Temby (see picture insert figure 11). We appealed, and as a consequence of our case the censorship law was soon after changed.

Student politics helped develop political awareness and knowledge of the institutions of government. Since the guild ran student facilities, including the refectory and other services, which were sizable businesses and employed staff, I also learned about business administration and funds management. At the licensing court I won a liquor licence for the new Guild Tavern on campus, despite strong opposition from breweries and nearby pubs.

Interstate meetings of the National Union of Australian University Students (NUAUS) also provided the chance to visit the other Australian capital cities for the first time and to build knowledge of Australia and of international affairs. There were active and spirited debates on a variety of current political issues, including Israel and the position of the Palestinians, the Vietnam War, nuclear disarmament, the Soviet invasion of Czechoslovakia, South Africa and apartheid, and a range of political prisoners. The NUAUS meetings also provided an excellent Australia-wide network of outstanding student friends, many of whom became state and federal leaders in their fields. John Bannon, president of the Adelaide University Student Representative Council, became premier of South Australia. Jim Spigelman, from the University of Sydney, became chief justice of the Supreme Court of New South Wales. Andrea Hull, also from Sydney University, became a leader in arts education and administration, including heading the Western Australian Department of the Arts and the Victorian College of the Arts, in Melbourne. Alan Cameron, from Sydney University, became a senior lawyer and headed the Australian Securities and Investments Commission. Greig Pickhaver, from Flinders University in South Australia, became the leading satirical commenter known as H. G. Nelson. And there were many more.

I thrived in the activist energy of the university environment and, as I became more aware of party-political matters, realised that my father's family in Britain and Ireland had always been staunch conservatives. They were shocked when the Conservative Party lost power in the United Kingdom in 1964 and believed the advent of Harold Wilson and the British Labour Party caused changes in British society which were unacceptable, driving people like us to emigrate and seek a better life.

When we arrived in Australia, the conservative parties had retained power in both the federal and the WA state governments for over twenty years. However, the university branch of the Australian Labor Party was strong, and many of my university friends were members. The mothers of two of my university friends were active Labor Party supporters, feminists and early women's libbers. The mother of my friend Jeremy Dawkins had been particularly influential. Muriel Dawkins had long been a Labor Party activist. It was a surprising new thought that mothers could have independent political views: my own mother automatically voted the same way as her husband. In 1967 I was asked to be a Labor Party scrutineer for the re-count of the senate vote for Dame Dorothy Tangney and became aware of the workings of electoral officers. In 1943 Dame Dorothy was the first woman elected to the Australian Senate. She served Western Australian continuously thereafter but was defeated by only a few votes in the 1967 Senate election. A re-count of the vote was called. It did not change the outcome.

In 1969, while I was still in Perth, there was a federal election and the work of the Women's Electoral Lobby was impressive, so I handed out how-to-vote cards for them at an election polling place in one Perth suburb. A couple of nuns asked what it was all about. They seemed influenced by the explanation that we had surveyed all the candidates on issues which were important to women and families and had compiled a list of the candidates which were recommended as a result. As the nuns walked away with their how-to-vote cards, the person who had been handing out Labor cards and had been listening to my explanation, laughingly said, 'Didn't tell them you were for abortion, did you?' I was, in fact, very much for legal abortion and had been ever since my university friend had died from the complications of a backyard abortion, which touched us all deeply.

Despite many friendships with ardent Labor party supporters and my own political inclinations, I never joined any political party, judging it best to work impartially as a public servant without any particular party membership. This served me well in my career, working closely with and serving successive foreign ministers from both the major political parties.

After leaving university I was very touched when the Guild of Undergraduates named a room after me in the new Guild Building. In later years, when interviewing a Foreign Affairs candidate, Sally Mansfield, she asked, 'Are you the Sue Boyd of the Sue Boyd

Room? I thought you were dead!' And an academic visiting from Hong Kong asked me how, as a public servant, I had amassed enough wealth to endow a room at the university. That was the norm in Hong Kong.

From 1967 I had enjoyed free university education supported by a Commonwealth Scholarship. This was provided by the government and covered all tuition costs, and included some allowances for books. It did not, however, fully cover accommodation costs at St Catherine's and I was grateful for the salary paid by the *Daily News*, the local afternoon newspaper, which employed student cadets for the long summer vacation each year as well as in term time. As I mentioned before, I worked there part-time throughout three of my four years at university and this income covered my fees in college. The work was also a great way for a 'new chum – fresh off the boat' – a newly arrived migrant – to learn about the state, as we covered human-interest stories, the courts, politics and sport. The more established and seasoned journalists and photographers enjoyed setting me up and playing on my naivety. The paper's photographer and I were once on a late-night airport assignment greeting new migrants and without any leads looking for interesting stories. The photographer tricked me by directing me to a passenger whom he described as 'an English earl who was giving it all up to come to Australia and work as a brickie'. I took the bait, approached the unwitting, innocent migrant and was left looking silly! On another occasion, I was doing vox pop interviews on St Georges Terrace, the main business street in the city, and a man told me he was 'Joe Blow, of Gage Roads, Fremantle' (the Australian slang for 'Everyman' – and Gage Roads was the offshore ocean area where ships waited before entering Fremantle harbour). Our editor, Len Owens, had a good laugh when I submitted that story.

It was all great experience, interviewing politicians, families of Vietnam War victims, community heroes, winemakers and the duxes of local public schools, and covering sporting events, fashion, fires and magistrates courts. We received excellent

English-language coaching from the cadet counsellor at the newspaper, Jim Dunbar. A job was waiting there after graduation, as well as with the Australian Broadcasting Commission's television service, for whom I had done a couple of stories. I was also now a qualified teacher. But it was time for me to find a bigger pond to splash around in. And that led to Canberra in 1970 and a life in the Australian foreign service.

4

To Canberra: the start of a career in diplomacy, 1970

Joining the Department of External Affairs and training for the foreign service

When young people ask about a career path into international relations, I tell them it doesn't matter what subject you choose to study. You must really love it, so you will study hard and do well. International affairs organisations, both government and non-government, including the Australian Department of Foreign Affairs and Trade (DFAT), choose staff with a wide variety of university degrees. But the starting point is high university marks. To be successful you must also have broader interests and experience outside your formal study. You need cross-cultural awareness. When you have a good portfolio of competencies, experiences and educational achievements, you are ready to grab opportunities when they appear.

I don't believe in life plans. Things change, sometimes rapidly, and jobs you never expected suddenly become possibilities. New technology drives radical changes.

Take my own experience. At the University of Western Australia in 1969, I was enrolled for a diploma of education – studying to be a teacher. I did not have a lifelong yearning to be a diplomat. There were precursors along the way, to be sure. I had lived an international life and spoke several languages. A favourite cousin,

Pam Firth, had led an international personal and professional life, which I wanted to emulate. The family understood that she had been a British intelligence agent during World War II. I admired her enormously and had taken short holidays with her in her glamorous London apartment early in my teens. She had been married to Vladimir Peniakoff, a dashing White Russian. He was ethnically Russian but born in the area between Russia and Poland, and belonged to those who had resisted the Soviet Red Army in the Russian Civil War (1918–21). He was known as Popski, renowned for the formation and operation of Popski's Private Army, which fought with the British forces in the Middle East during World War II.[4] I never knew Popski, who had died of a brain tumour. In the 1960s Pam married a wealthy American newspaperman, Tom (T. S.) Matthews, who was a founding editor of *Time* magazine. They bought back and refurbished the former Firth family home, Cavendish Hall, in Suffolk, not far from our home in Stoke by Clare. Pam and Tom lived at Cavendish Hall for many years, providing warm hospitality and stimulating conversation to many visiting friends and family members from all over the globe. Pam provided ongoing and intelligent encouragement.

Uncle Derek Boyd, my father's brother, was the first in our family to attend university. He and his wife, Ann, had no children, and he took a particular interest in me, encouraging study, giving books as birthday and Christmas gifts, discussing the Middle East, where he had served, and supporting me to think about university study.

An influential meeting during my second year at university was with Alan Edwards, an Australian diplomat home on leave from the Vietnam War. Alan was posted in the Australian Embassy in Saigon (later called Ho Chi Minh City), and he spoke in graphic and exciting terms about the Tet Offensive, a significant assault by the Viet Cong against the South Vietnamese capital city, which he had witnessed. He described his work in Saigon and relationships with the various political leaders and with the Americans. This all sounded interesting and a great job – for someone else.

I had studied politics and international relations and could write and analyse. But I had arrived in Australia only four years earlier, was a British citizen, did not think of myself yet as an Australian and did not dream that I might be eligible to join the Australian foreign service.

Then, in my final year at university, I bumped into a university friend, Tim Kendrew, who told me excitedly that he had been provisionally accepted as an Australian diplomatic trainee. He was no more Australian than I was. Like me, his father was a British Army officer – we had played together as children in Cyprus – and he had been in Australia with his parents for a relatively short time. His father was the governor of Western Australia. Well, I thought, if they'll take Tim, they should surely take me.

At the university careers office they said that applications closed the following day. 'If you send a telegram to External Affairs today and follow up in the next couple of days with a full application and supporting documents and references, that will be accepted', they told me. I rushed off. I had a good application and strong referees, including the university vice-chancellor, Sir Stanley Prescott. It turned out that a British passport was no hindrance. At that time British immigrant citizens had the same status as Australians: they could vote and be employed in government services.

The Department of External Affairs liked my application, and I travelled to a shortlist interview in Canberra. The interview panel consisted of three senior male officers from the department. The group of shortlisted candidates came from all around Australia, and took part in small-group discussions of current international relations questions. We were observed, and notes were taken of our individual level of knowledge, our presentation and persuasion skills, and how we interacted within the group. Later, all the candidates were invited to a reception in the Canberra house and garden of Mick Shann, a senior foreign affairs personality. We suspected that the examiners were looking at our social interaction skills and how we handled our plates, drinks and cutlery. We all seemed to pass this test, except one of our number who drank far too much, threw up in the shrubbery and tried to move in on Shann's daughter. He did not make it to the next stage of the selection process. The group of trainees from the previous year's selection also held a party for us, and there we met a very bright cohort of (all) men, most of whom became valued colleagues in the department and at overseas posts. Almost all rose to very senior ranks in the Australian Government service.

I got in, and I joined External Affairs in early 1970, four years after first setting foot in Australia. It seemed more appropriate, as I was serving the country, to do so as an Australian citizen. Becoming one then was a simple procedure. So I became a dual national. Through accidents of birth, it turned out I was also eligible for Irish and Indian passports, which I did not pursue. Over the years, the Department of External Affairs morphed into the Department of Foreign Affairs and then merged with the Department of Trade to become DFAT – the Department of Foreign Affairs and Trade.

Two other graduates from the University of Western Australia joined External Affairs at that time: David Irvine and Peter Cross. The twenty-three of us in the class of 1970 trained together in Canberra for a year and then went to our various postings throughout the world. A special bond unites us still, and there are reunions now and then, even though many have since moved to other jobs or have retired. Just one other woman was recruited initially in 1970: Jennifer Turnbull, from Melbourne. This was a 100 per cent increase on the previous year, when they had admitted only one woman (who soon left). A third woman, Wendy Field, joined us later, transferring from the general public service intake. The foreign service was very male. Senior officers, who were mostly supported by very able and selfless wives, did not at all welcome the idea of women colleagues. They expected we would marry and then have to resign, thus wasting all that expensive investment in our training. Until 1966 women who married were forced to resign from the public service. There was no provision for maternity leave, so women who had babies, and needed time off, were also obliged to resign. The men assumed women were inherently weaker, and so would need more medical leave. They also believed there were limited posts in which we could be deployed successfully, as they maintained that we would not be locally accepted, and would thus be ineffective, in Asia or the Middle East. And they thought that our recruitment would displace more suitably qualified males. In short, we would be a net drain on the system.

In 1963, A. R. Taysom, an officer of the Trade Commissioner service sent the director an internal minute which included a note from Nick Parkinson, then secretary (ie the public servant head) of External Affairs, on the recruitment of women:

> (They) have to be trained for 18 months before going to their first post. The average marries within five years.
>
> It is a very expensive process, but External Affairs lack courage to slam the door because of parliamentary opinion, pressure groups and so on.[5]

By 1970, however, the federal government was committed to improving gender balance and had directed the public service to recruit more women. Later legislation mandated equal opportunities throughout the public service, applying especially to women, Aboriginal and Torres Strait Islander people, people with disabilities and citizens from non-English-speaking backgrounds. The department gradually moved to include people from all of these groups successfully.

But in our time, a reluctant Department of External Affairs, sighing deeply, half-heartedly recruited a token small number of women. But we few females were a feisty lot and were not prepared to accept a second-class status. Throughout our careers, however, we always felt we were being judged not as officers of the department but as women officers, and we felt some pressure that the reputation and future of all professional women sat heavily upon our shoulders. We were mindful of and appreciated the saying 'To get half as far as a man, a woman has to be twice as good. And luckily that's not difficult'.

On induction, the first question asked was 'When are you going to retire?' This was a surprise, but it was a superannuation choice we were being asked to make. We women were strongly urged to nominate sixty-five as our age of retirement, rather than sixty. Our fortnightly superannuation deduction would be less, and as we would surely retire early, on marriage, we would get all the money back anyway. This was the first piece of discriminatory advice we received; it was offered with the best of intentions but was based on false assumptions. It meant that our superannuation entitlements when we did retire – and I outlasted most of my male peers – would be considerably less than the figure for males. (There were opportunities later in our careers to correct this anomaly).

It was a shock to discover that we were initially paid 10 per cent less than the men. In 1969 the federal government had decreed equal pay, but it was to be introduced gradually: phased in over the following two years.

The marriage bar and the absence of maternity leave meant there were very few women diplomats in External Affairs and really no role models for us. Penny Wensley, recruited two years before, was already on posting in Paris, at the start of her own stellar career, so we only met her later. We appreciated the splendid Tonia Shand, who had to resign twice – on marriage and on maternity – and restart at the bottom each time, while her male colleagues passed her and shot up the promotion ladder.

The idea of mentors was not common then, but one senior male officer, Robin Ashwin, strongly supported the idea of women in the department and went out of his way to help and advise us. He told me in detail how he had advocated for me in a promotion process and explained how the system worked. Our small group of women, including those recruited in the years following us, gradually formed an informal support network, and in due course, when in Canberra, we joined with other women from the wider public service at a regular networking dinner appropriately entitled 'The Seraglio', where we exchanged information and advice and provided support for each other. Among these were several women who had failed to get in to Foreign Affairs and were jealously and stridently critical of us and the department.

Before our various overseas assignments, the class of 1970 shared six months of the year-long training course with a group of junior foreign ministry officials from countries of the region. Some countries, such as Fiji and Papua New Guinea and some in Africa, were on the cusp of independence and needed to build foreign ministries from scratch. We all lived together in two Commonwealth hostels in Canberra – the Kurrajong and Brassey House – and got to know each other a little. We Australians took our host roles seriously and were expected by the department to remain in the hostels and support the overseas trainees for the duration of our joint training courses.

This period of living and training together provided us with a lasting and invaluable network of friends from other foreign services, and we served together with some of them at overseas posts during our careers. Our international friends came from Nepal, India, Pakistan, Malaysia, Laos, Cambodia, Papua New Guinea, Nigeria, Ghana, the Philippines, Singapore, Indonesia and Fiji. We began our careers with a ready-made professional international network.

My first on-the-job training assignment in Canberra was in the Protocol Section. The printing proofs of the diplomatic list arrived, and it was my job to proofread them. The diplomatic list gives the contact details of all the foreign embassies and high commissions in each capital city, and the names, addresses and positions of staff members and their partners. (For historical and legal reasons, countries which are members of the Common-wealth of Nations exchange high commissioners as the heads of their respective diplomatic missions, while non-Commonwealth countries exchange ambassadors. The two roles involve the same work.) Once proofreading was completed, the list was published as a little booklet, multiple copies of which were sent to each diplomatic mission in Canberra. We soon received a request from the US Embassy for an extra dozen copies – their staff list included a 'Counsellor for Pubic Affairs'. Whoops! Luckily, they thought it was funny.

Besides work placements in the department, the Australian trainees and the international colleagues were sent in 1970 on a ten-day familiarisation visit to Papua and New Guinea. At that stage it was not a united, independent country, and Australia was still responsible for its two separate territories and their international representation. We visited Port Moresby, Goroka, Lae and Rabaul and were well briefed on both Papua and New Guinea and their multiple cultures, histories and challenges. Western Australian judge Gresley Clarkson was then on circuit in Rabaul, the capital of New Britain, the largest island in the Bismarck Archipelago, on the northern coast of New Guinea. He invited us for drinks at his splendid residence, looking over the harbour and out to islands, and he took us on a cruise the next day in his official boat.

During our training year, we also made field visits as a group within Australia, to learn more about our own country before representing it abroad. The most challenging visit for us feminists was to Broken Hill in New South Wales, Australia's most significant mining town at the time. The mining unions ran the town through the Barrier Industrial Council. Employment of married women was not allowed. The policy was 'one breadwinner per family', and that breadwinner had to be male, although some exceptions were made for single women and widows. Mining superstition dictated that no women were allowed underground in the mines. So, while our male colleagues were taken on mine visits and briefings, we two women were taken shopping. It didn't stop there. Our male colleagues were given complimentary membership of one of the town's social and drinking clubs for the duration of our visit. The clubs admitted men only, though women were allowed in a sole designated 'ladies lounge' if escorted by a man. Membership was not offered to us women. All of this was quite eye-opening and infuriating for me, as I had encountered little prejudice or discrimination in my four years at university. Each of the Australian capital cities had men-only clubs, and some also had clubs in which membership was limited to women. But it was in the men's clubs that key business networks were established and maintained and business relationships of trust between business and political leaders were pursued. Exclusion from these opportunities was a serious barrier to women's capacity to compete on an equal footing with men in the workplace. I developed a personal policy of not accepting speaking invitations at events held in men-only clubs. If they wanted me as a guest speaker, they could choose a venue which operated on an equal opportunity basis.

DFAT paid a club membership fee for the head of each of its regional offices in Australia's capital cities. During a later posting in Sydney, I carefully chose a club that did not discriminate against women and used it for much of my official entertainment. When entertaining male guests in the club, I was clearly established as the host, and there was no embarrassing confusion about who was paying the bill. I objected formally to the department about my male counterparts in other capital cities who chose membership of men-only clubs. I thought it improper to use public funds for such memberships. But when I discussed this with the relevant departmental deputy secretary, my complaint was dismissed as 'a second order issue'. The boys were clearly not going to tell other boys they could not join such clubs, when these were the most prestigious business venues in town.

In the early 1980s, equal opportunities legislation came into force. Ten years after I had joined, DFAT, under Secretary Stuart Harris, started to look seriously at why there were so few women in its senior positions – and at why the department also scored badly against the other equal employment opportunity targets – Aboriginal and Torres Strait Islanders, those from non-English-speaking backgrounds and those with disabilities. Fellow

Western Australian Cisca Spencer was appointed as the first equal employment opportunity director in the department in 1983, and she undertook research to compare the career patterns of men and women in DFAT. She also studied the department's recruiting and deployment patterns to identify the internal blocks to promotion and retention of women. Cisca's internal study identified a number of factors both cultural and systemic, which needed to be addressed. Recruitment of well-qualified women was not difficult, but from that point the lack of equal opportunity policies seriously affected their promotion and retention. Patterns of overseas postings were also an issue. The few women officers who had been sent on overseas postings had gone to 'easy' posts, such as Paris, New York and London, and had performed exceptionally well. Those posts, however, were not in Australia's major policy focus. In addition, 'hardship' posts were of two years' duration, as compared with three years for the others. Thus, when it came to promotions, women were less competitive. In a ten year period, the men had a record of experience in five posts, whereas women, with the 'easy' posts under their belt could boast of only three. In addition, posts with difficult living conditions, comprised most countries of importance to Australia and aligned to its policy focus. The work in these posts was challenging but important to Australia, and good performance was noted and rewarded. Excluding women from the posts made them less competitive in the promotion processes and was therefore discriminatory.

There was also no formal, transparent promotion process at that time. A selection panel, all male, somehow made decisions on promotions, drawing on hearsay and material in our personnel and in our X files. These were informal files, outside the official filing system, in which miscellaneous material pertaining to each of us was held. In the late 1980s, the X file system was deemed illegal, and our personal X files were destroyed. Those of us who wanted to read our files beforehand could do so. They were shocking.

My X file revealed that one senior officer had made a judgement that affected a promotion decision, and he had never met me. I had been given no opportunity to refute his misleading information. The file also contained the report of the selection panel which had recruited me to the department, which claimed that I was, 'well groomed and attractive, but nonetheless intelligent and articulate'. The man in charge of our initial training year had written that I was extremely persistent in getting my own way and was not much liked by my male colleagues. Supervisors wrote comments about us that we did not see, and there was no process to judge their fairness or otherwise. Following Cisca's work a new, formal promotions process was established: it had to be transparent, and selection panels had to include at least one woman. The second stipulation actually became onerous to the few women in the department, as they spent more time on selection panels than doing their normal jobs. So, a few qualified women outsiders were invited to join some of the selection panels, bringing useful external perspectives.

Cisca's report also addressed discrimination connected with marriage, family concerns and maternity leave as well as the challenges of 'tandem couples' – marriages between two officers. It was eventually agreed that partners could work together in one of Australia's larger missions, provided one was not reporting directly to the other. There were also cases when husband and wife took postings in neighbouring embassies. In due course, a non-working accompanying spouse was entitled to leave without pay for the duration of an officer's posting. And after a few more years, same-sex couples were accepted with the same posting conditions. When we joined, it was illegal within the public service for officers to be homosexual. To be so was seen as a security risk. That changed. Family allowances were introduced to provide for frequent family reunions when children were in boarding schools in Australia or overseas. And better provision was made for children at overseas posts. This largely came about through effective lobbying by foreign service wives, who had formed their own organisation. Foreign Affairs also negotiated treaties with some countries to provide reciprocal rights for accompanying spouses to take outside employment while on posting overseas. It was at last recognised that women who chose a path which included marriage and children were equally valuable members of the foreign service and should be supported.

The performance of the wife in supporting the (male) diplomat posted abroad used to be evaluated by the department, and it affected the husband's performance appraisal. This ceased. Another positive development was that partners who provided catering services to support official diplomatic activities became entitled to be paid for their service.

In the early 1980s, when DFAT first decided to send a female diplomat to the staff of an embassy in an Islamic country, the head of mission was reluctant to accept her, arguing she could not be effective. Stuart Harris, the then secretary, however, persisted, and the posting proceeded successfully. By 1986, there was no resistance when I was sent as high commissioner to Bangladesh – the first Australian woman head of mission in an Islamic country. And when the first wheelchair-bound personal assistant was posted overseas, the embassy ensured that structural alterations were carried out to accommodate her needs.

Given the absence of role models, I had to find my own path to success in the organisation. I had successfully led teams and achieved a lot in student politics, and I went into DFAT in the same spirit. I was hardworking, creative, open, friendly and prepared to take risks and make mistakes – and learn from them. Part of my strategy for thriving and advancing was to fit into the prevailing culture and be as blokey as the blokes – to play them at their own game at the same time as advancing mine. I had a repertoire of dirty and daring jokes, and I used them as shock and awe tactics. I was good at languages, could imitate accents amusingly and was a good raconteur. I could talk about sport.

Like many women, I spent a bit of energy in ensuring the men around me felt comfortable. But I was firm in standing up to male colleagues when required. One particularly odious senior colleague to whom I presented a piece of work with which he could find no fault invaded my personal space egregiously, looked me over from very close range and said, 'You're really quite an attractive woman, if you just lost a little weight'. I responded by telling him I was sure he also had a big dick, but I was not interested. He retreated. I know that would not be an appropriate method today – I might equally be had up for harassment. Interestingly, in a later overseas post, a female staff member successfully lodged a formal sexual harassment charge against this particular male.

In 1990, my job entailed briefing the foreign minister Gareth Evans each day just before Question Time in parliament. He was always agitated and edgy during our briefing sessions, before going in to bat: combative, demanding and bullying. He was reported to have thrown an ashtray once in frustration, but I did not witness this. I liked and admired him and enjoyed being involved in the daily cut and thrust of national politics, but I had to stand up to him. On my first day working with him, he berated me and the department on a grammatical error in a briefing. 'Haven't you read the fucking style manual? It should be "first", not "firstly".'

I asked whether he was as concerned about the use of 'presently' in place of 'currently'.

'No', he said. 'Is that one of your concerns?'

I said it was.

'Well, I don't care about your concerns. I'm the fucking minister, not you!'

I calmly replied, 'For the moment, Gareth'. (An election was due).

There was an electric silence in room, and I thought, 'Oh shit, now I've blown it'.

But then he roared with laughter. 'Well said!'

Everyone else in the room laughed, too. And I was launched.

I worked out that the most useful approach in working effectively with him was to play one of two roles: either the governess or the whore. As the governess, I could firmly bully him back, calmly encourage him to settle down and focus on the material he had to absorb before going into the house. And when I told him a dirty joke, he was shocked enough to stop and regroup. A photograph was taken of us at a staff party in which it looked as if he was sitting on my lap (see picture insert figure 16). Gareth signed it with the comment 'For Susie. Not normally a girl to be sat upon…'.

Led by Paul Keating, language around Parliament House in Canberra was graphic, creative and unrestrained. 'Oh, why don't you stick your head up your bum so we can carry you out like a suitcase?' was one colourful suggestion.

Gareth Evans and I got on well together. I admired him greatly. I could deal with the unusual but entertaining language and the stresses and strains in the daily workplace, and I appreciated the strong foreign policy lead he gave the department. He led us; he was not led by us. I served with twelve foreign ministers, seven ministers for trade and one minister for Development Cooperation and Pacific Island Affairs. In my opinion, Gareth was the best minister during my whole career.

In 1991, Gareth invited me to dinner with him at Parliament House on the evening before I moved on to my next position, as regional director of DFAT in Sydney. He was late arriving, coming from a Labor caucus meeting. He was extremely irritated with another senator, who had apparently called out across caucus, 'The trouble with you, Gareth, is that you're so far up Bob's bum that all we can see are the soles of your fucking feet'. (Bob was Prime Minister Bob Hawke.)

The hardworking, effective, creative, blokey yet feminine strategy worked, then, for me. And I was well accepted by my peers, particularly the fellows in the classes of 1969 and 1970, who became good friends. They were intelligent men who were very helpful to me professionally at crucial times. Most rose to very senior positions.

When moving to the regional office job in Sydney, in 1991, I found that the office culture was more proper and very different. I greatly appreciated it when the equal employment opportunity officer warned me quietly that my language and jokes were not appreciated by the staff and that I was leaving myself open to a charge of harassment. So I adjusted.

In 1994 when the recommendation to post me as ambassador to Vietnam came up, the secretary, Mike Costello, was not impressed. He said that my sense of humour was not suited to a posting in Asia. He was married to a feminist and had also come to appreciate the value of diversity, with women in the organisation as women, with women's qualities, and I did not fit this model. I had told, in his presence, an unfortunate joke of which he was the butt, and this had been a potentially career-limiting move. Luckily for me, I had friends in court who persuaded him that he had misjudged me and that I would be a very good ambassador in Hanoi. I had, after all, survived and performed well as the first woman posted as high commissioner in Bangladesh and had been successful in negotiations with people of all nationalities and cultures at the United Nations. The secretary agreed to my appointment to Hanoi, but he was straight-shooting enough to call me in and tell me face-to-face of his reservations. He invited me to tell him he was wrong, which I did. But it was a useful and timely lesson: things had changed in the public service, and I needed to adjust my style.

The episode also reminded me of the importance of understanding the role of humour and the way it works. Most jokes work either by putting someone else down or through shock or surprise. I was reminded of the necessity to anticipate the impact before using a joke. Cross-cultural humour is a minefield, but a well-developed sense of humour is essential in travelling through the vagaries of human life.

The situation of women in DFAT, and in government generally, continued to improve. In 1986, when I was high commissioner in Bangladesh, there were only three other Australian women heads of mission: Rosaleen McGovern, in Singapore; Penny Wensley, in Hong Kong; and Diane Johnstone, in Nepal. By the time I became high commissioner in Fiji, thirteen years later, in 1999, there were so many Australian women heads of mission that the number was not such an issue – although there were still more men than women, the gap had narrowed significantly. I am proud of the role I was able to play in changing things.

In 2016, Frances Adamson became head of DFAT, the first woman so appointed. Her qualifications and skills had been recognised and rewarded over a long and successful career, which included an ambassadorship to China. She had four children, and her career included four periods of maternity leave. This would have been unthinkable in 1970. She also served under Australia's first woman foreign minister, Julie Bishop.

This has made a different department from the one I served in my early career.

5

Portugal and East Timor, 1971–76

First posting Portugal, the determined colonial power, revolution and East Timor's quest for independence

In 1971, following my initial Foreign Affairs training in Canberra, I was excited about actually working as a diplomat and being in a new country, especially one as beautiful and historic as Portugal. Postings were decided arbitrarily by the staffing section of External Affairs, taking into account the needs of the overseas posts. They might or might not take into account preferences or language ability. There was no opportunity to say where you wanted to go. We all took a language aptitude test on entry. Staffing said that they wanted to grow the pool of officers with Chinese and Japanese skills, and offered me the chance to spend two years studying one of these difficult languages, after which I could expect a posting to China or Japan. I was not attracted by this offer. Having just spent four years studying at university I was itching to get on with actual work.

I learned of my posting through gossip. My future ambassador, Kevin Kelly, had said at a Canberra cocktail party how pleased he was that Sue Boyd was to be his third secretary at the newly created Embassy to Portugal in Lisbon. No-one had asked me! I was surprised to hear this but not unhappy. The idea of getting out of Canberra, going to my first post and learning the language there was attractive. Before leaving Canberra, we each had an interview with the head of the Department of External Affairs, Sir Keith Waller. He said I would enjoy the country. 'Interesting history, wonderful architecture, great wine and food, nice people'. When I asked about the work, he said something like, 'Don't you worry your pretty little head about that'. He explained that Australia had been forced to open the new embassy in the Portuguese capital of Lisbon to process the large migration flow to Australia: the Portuguese Government would not allow Australia to process migrants through regular visits by staff from the large immigration section in the embassy in Paris. Waller said that the immigration officials at the new post in Lisbon did the migration work, and not much else was expected from the embassy. So I could go and enjoy myself.

I was third secretary at the embassy – the bottom rung of the diplomatic ladder. I was the only political officer, from the career diplomatic stream: the other staff came from the consular and administrative stream of the department or came from other specialist departments. They had the titles of First or Second Secretary (Consular and Administrative) or (Consular). More senior staff, could be called Counsellor. I ranked higher than all the other staff in Lisbon, who were, in turn, all more experienced than me. I would be chargé d'affaires – the acting head of mission – in the absence of the ambassador: what the Americans call the 'deputy ambassador'. So I knew I had to be sensitive and develop positive and respectful relations with the rest of the embassy staff. They were all welcoming, though the head of the Immigration Section was prickly about his separate standing: he did not belong to the Department of Foreign Affairs and had reporting lines to his own department in Canberra. The three other staff from Foreign Affairs made me very welcome; they were the senior administrative officer and consul, Second Secretary Bruce Scott; the administrative attaché, Vic Rebikoff; and the ambassador's secretary and communicator, Brenda Kelly. Helen Abreu was our expert, loyal, professional, helpful, locally engaged Portuguese translator and interpreter.

Kevin Kelly was an experienced old-school ambassador, and he taught me a lot about the craft of diplomacy. He was in naval intelligence during World War II and had a continuing interest in history, literature and languages. He spoke Spanish, learned during his previous posting as ambassador in Argentina, and tried hard to build a competence in Portuguese, which has similarities but important differences. He also chose to learn Gaelic during his posting – just for the interest of it. The day after my arrival, he and his wife, Margaret, took me to Fátima, the place of pilgrimage since the Virgin Mary was believed to have appeared to three young children there in 1917 and to have shared important prophetic information with them. As the embassy received a large number of Catholic pilgrims from Australia, I needed to know how to look after them, he said.

Kelly's family were devout Roman Catholics. He had two teenage daughters at the post, Anne and Barbara, of whom he was very protective, and he was a bit challenged about how to handle an independent young woman third secretary in her early twenties – not much older than his daughters. His wife was a sensible, capable, experienced woman and kept a motherly eye on all of us. She invited me to tea soon after I arrived and warned me that her husband could be a bit eccentric but said that he had always dealt with his staff very fairly and generously. When I became ill with hepatitis six months into the posting, she personally supervised my home nursing and organised a roster of the other wives to visit and cook meals for me.

A Portuguese maid, Senhora Augusta, came each morning to look after me in my rented penthouse apartment in Benfica. Portuguese custom is to identify all women by their given names – they do not generally adopt their husband's family names on marriage. The small apartment was luxuriously furnished in an overdone Portuguese baroque style – oodles of gold velvet, marble, gilding and oil paintings in heavy gold frames. There was a fold-down bed next to the kitchen and a small bathroom designed for a live-in maid. She also worked for the landlady and so kept a proprietorial eye on the place. She did all the cleaning, laundry and shopping. And I could practise my Portuguese with her. A large rooftop terrace ran around the apartment and looked out over a lovely seventeenth-century palace and garden. My street was a leafy cul-de-sac; it led off the main street and a tramline which linked Benfica with downtown Lisbon. Travel to work was by tram and underground. Benfica was the location of the main soccer stadium, which was just down the road, and it was hard to get home on nights of big matches due to the traffic and crowds on public transport.

The hepatitis was a blessing in disguise. It came just as I completed a six-month intensive Portuguese-language course in Lisbon, working at the embassy in the mornings and studying at the language school in the afternoons. The illness confined me to bed for a period, and I could read the daily Portuguese newspapers and watch Portuguese television. And then the doctor recommended a three-week convalescence at the small fishing village of Sines, south of Lisbon. No-one there spoke English, and I was befriended by a fishing family with a daughter around my own age, so this was all excellent for practising and continuing to learn the language. (Sines has since been developed as a major port; some of the initial underwater surveying was carried out during my posting by an Australian dive company.)

Before leaving Canberra in late 1970 my pre-posting interview with Secretary Waller had been a disappointing send-off for this little, overachieving, ambitious alpha female, suggesting there was little of real interest to Australia in Portugal. So when I got to the post I set about finding something that mattered, and I found Portugal's colonial policy.

Portugal was one of the last of the European states to grant independence to its colonies, in Angola, Guinea-Bissau and Mozambique in Africa; the Atlantic islands of the Azores; Macau, next to Hong Kong; and, of course, East Timor, close to Australia. Portugal was a small European state proud of its history. It founded the state of Brazil and had developed its economy, with the help of thousands of slaves mostly from its African colonies. Brazil had fought for its own independence from Portugal in 1824. Portugal's fascist dictator, António de Oliveira Salazar, had died in 1968, but the Prime Minister when I was in Lisbon, Marcelo Caetano, maintained an ultraconservative, repressive regime. It was supported by a notorious secret police and was popular with the large landowning class and the business community. The opposition Socialist Party was well organised with sensible leaders and was growing in membership. Portugal's wealth came from the colonies, producing diamonds, minerals, fish and agricultural products. The economy, especially its agriculture and the wine industry, were controlled by influential wealthy families employing large numbers of poor tenant farmers. This was particularly so in the south, in the Alentejo, where the Portuguese Communist Party was growing.

Resting on its historical laurels, Portugal was not about to reduce its global footprint voluntarily. The government held on doggedly to its African and other colonies. They were a source of national pride to the country, once a wealthy, proud and seagoing nation, which had made major maritime discoveries and significant scientific contributions to the art of navigation and mapping. Ferdinand Magellan was the first sailor to circumnavigate the world, in 1522, and Prince Henry the Navigator sponsored the voyages of discovery in the fifteenth century. It claimed that Christopher Columbus, who 'discovered' America in 1492, had a Portuguese wife. Portugal had the oldest bilateral treaty in existence, the Anglo-Portuguese Alliance, sealed in 1386 by the marriage of the daughter of the English John of Gaunt, Philippa of Lancaster, with the Portuguese King John I.

But the 1970s saw the international age of decolonisation. The colonial powers, including Britain, France and even Australia, were moving their colonies towards independence. This was a result partly of the activities of independence movements in the colonies and partly of trusteeship allocations of the former German colonies by the United Nations following the two world wars. The newly created nations greatly expanded the membership of the United Nations as they achieved independence.

I had been working in Northern Rhodesia when that British colony moved peaceably to become the independent state of Zambia, in 1964, and, as mentioned, in their training year the Australian diplomatic intake were sent to learn about Papua and New Guinea in preparation for the creation from those two colonies of the new independent state of Papua New Guinea.

The Portuguese Government had no intention of letting go of its colonies. Goa had already been forcibly absorbed by India, and the Chinese Government had signalled that it wished Macau to remain a colony until Hong Kong's status was settled. But there was growing civil and military discord in mainland Portugal, as well as armed independence movements in each of the country's African colonies, where the rebel movements were gaining momentum. These colonies were governed through the Portuguese armed forces, which increasingly saw their role there as futile and Portugal's colonial policy as resisting the global tide of decolonisation. Portugal's Senior General António de Spínola returned from his posting as Commander in Guinea-Bissau and had become a public critic of the government's policy. This senior military hero became the focus for the large number of disaffected military who had returned to the country following their overseas tours of duty. It was clear to us in Lisbon that change was afoot.

During the three years of my posting in Portugal I had made many contacts within the Portuguese armed forces, as well as friends among both wealthy families and members of the Socialist Party. Some of these were Australians who were married to Portuguese. I met younger army officers socially. It is the work of an embassy to get to know a wide range of significant, influential and knowledgeable political and social leaders. Our secretary, Brenda, was married to a Portuguese officer posted to Mozambique, and she related stories of military concern.

One of my early boyfriends in Portugal was a scion of the Braganza family, of the last king of Portugal. José took me for a weekend to the castle at Estremoz in the Alentejo which had been the family home since it was built by King Diniz in the thirteenth century. It had recently been converted to a splendid state-owned *pousada*. *Pousadas* were significant grand buildings which had been taken over by the state and turned into luxury hotels. As he guided me around the castle, the staff showed him great deference and called him Dom José (Prince José) – many of their families had worked there for generations. One of the old women told me about the miracle of Saint Queen Isabel, the wife of King Diniz, who died in 1366. The queen spent much of her time visiting and taking gifts to the poor of the area, against the wishes of her husband. One winter day, King Diniz caught her leaving the castle and demanded she reveal the supplies she was hiding under her cloak.

'But they are only roses', she protested.

He was disbelieving. 'Roses in December?' He made her open her cloak. And, lo and behold, she opened her cloak, and the goods had been transformed into roses.

'And this is true', the little old lady assured me, with quiet sincerity. 'This was the miracle of the roses'. She spoke as if this had happened the day before.

The ambassador was away, and I was chargé d'affaires, when the Portuguese Government informed us they were planning to send a trade mission to Australia. I told the head of the economic relations division of the Portuguese foreign ministry that, given Australia's position on decolonisation, it would be wiser for Portugal not to include people from the colonies in the mission. When formal notice of the delegation came, however, we were instructed by Canberra to refuse visas for the two nominated delegation members from Angola and Mozambique. On the following Saturday, when the embassy was closed for the weekend, I was summoned to the foreign ministry to receive an official protest about this decision, and they gave me notice that, as a consequence, Portugal was threatening to sever diplomatic relations with Australia.

This was serious stuff. I needed to quickly send an encrypted cable to Canberra. We were using very basic communication means for classified messages, which involved a slow and laborious process. (This, incidentally, encouraged brevity and concision by the originators of messages, unlike the longwinded messages which fly around the world today.) The resulting message, a series of four-number groups, was then manually typed into an ordinary telex machine. This was an old telecommunications device, using telephone lines, which produced a perforated paper tape. The tape was fed into the telex machine for transmission to Canberra via our telecommunications hub at the high commission in London.

Brenda, our communicator, was in hospital, and no-one else from our small embassy was in town and available to help. I had to encrypt and send the message myself. I had no idea how to do this, so I visited Brenda in her hospital bed and got blow-by-blow instructions on each step in the process. Armed with detailed notes, I returned to the office and some hours later managed to send off the message. I originally fed the paper tape in backwards by mistake, but a helpful communicator telephoned me from London and set me on the right track. Junior diplomatic officers have to be resourceful.

The stand-off between Australia and Portugal was eventually averted, and having made its protest Portugal quietly reduced the delegation. When he returned to Lisbon after his holiday and retook control of the embassy, Ambassador Kelly made known his satisfaction with the handling of the matter. When I returned to Canberra at the end of my Lisbon posting, Robin Ashwin, the senior member of the department who was supportive of women officers, congratulated me on the handling of the situation, which he said had been noted and approved in the department. This was rare and welcome feedback.

Before coming to Lisbon, Kevin Kelly had served in Argentina during its time of violent unrest, and he was obsessive about personal security. He had been worried about the apartment in Benfica, outside the usual diplomatic area, where he thought I might not be safe. Once while he was away, new office furniture arrived and we rearranged his office, so that it might work better. When he returned he was furious that we had placed his desk chair with its back to the window – a sniper might be able to pick him off from across the street. When Australia mandated compulsory car seatbelts, Kelly cabled back to Canberra saying he would refuse to enforce this law, as, with a seatbelt on, his driver would not be able to duck an assassin's bullet. Another day, at a time when we were all alert to the danger of possible parcel bombs, a heavy parcel arrived for him. He called me in. What did I think about this parcel? Could it be a bomb? I picked it up and said I thought it was a book. Well, he wasn't expecting any books. Didn't I think it was too heavy for its size? He picked it up and said he was going to test it. He went into our registry and hurled the book into our walk-in safe, quickly slamming the safe door shut. There was no explosion, so he shamefacedly retrieved the parcel, now somewhat battered, and, taking his penknife from his pocket, went to his office to slit open the packet. He told me, 'Stand back, Miss Boyd! No point in both of us getting killed'. It was indeed a rather large book, on Portuguese wines, sent to him following his recent visit to a winegrowing region. Bruce Scott, our very calm senior administrative officer, who was responsible for security and had not been consulted, was very cross with the ambassador.

Another rather large parcel did set off the metal detector through which all our mail was passed, and we called in the bomb-disposal squad. It turned out to be a parcel of migration applications, each one stapled carefully. The ambassador wrote indignantly to the migration office in Paris, which had posted the forms, chastening them for using metal staples at this time of heightened security.

Kelly once visited the northern town of Guimarães, the birthplace of Fernão de Magalhães commonly known to us as Ferdinand Magellan, and was telling us about it at a staff meeting shortly after his return. I quietly joked that Magellan was the first man to circumcise the world with a 60-foot clipper. The rest of the staff laughed, but as Kelly was a bit hard of hearing, he did not get the joke, and was discomfited. He called me in after the meeting and warned me about my inappropriate sense of humour, which he said would get me into trouble one day. I should have heeded this warning. It did get me into trouble later in my career.

But in the meantime, it was very funny when I attended a lunch given by the American Chamber of Commerce. They had as their speaker the famous and much-decorated American rear admiral Eugene Fluckey who was head of the NATO Allied Joint Force Command, headquartered in Lisbon. The chairman introduced him, but unfortunately he used word association as a way of remembering names, and so we were introduced publicly to Rear Admiral Clunty. (My father, incidentally, used the same method to remember names and was known to have introduced a Captain House instead of Curtin and a Lieutenant Chambers instead of Potts.)

For all his eccentricity, Kevin Kelly taught me a lot about the formalities of diplomatic discourse and relations between diplomatic missions and their host governments. For example, the official order of precedence between the various diplomatic missions in any capital city (the diplomatic corps) is determined strictly by the order in which the newly arriving ambassador formally presents their letter of appointment (credentials) to the head of state of the host government. So everyone knows their place. And this information is used to ensure people are seated properly at official lunches, dinners and other official events, like lining up at the airport to meet the pope or visiting heads of state on their arrival. The long established agreed processes prevent squabbles between countries on who is more important and who should sit or stand where.

A newly arrived ambassador, once credentials have been presented to the head of state, will call on all the other ambassadors (or high commissioners, in the case of a Commonwealth country). They will call strictly in order of precedence.

There are also formal routines for receiving an ambassador when they are calling at your country's embassy. So, 1972, our receptionist was rather surprised when the new Spanish ambassador suddenly appeared, without notice, in the embassy reception area and said he had come to call on our ambassador. I was hurriedly summoned and showed the new ambassador courteously into Kevin Kelly's office. I then quickly telephoned the Embassy of Austria. Were they expecting a call from the new Spanish Ambassador? Yes, they replied, they were waiting for him, and he was late. So we rescued the new ambassador from Kelly's office and sent him on his way to the Austrians. This confusion between Austria and Australia was quite common. When I was visiting the Alentejo, a small boy commented on my car number plate and asked where I came from.

'Australia'.

'You speak German there?'

'No, we speak English. You know, Skippy?'

Ah yes, he knew! 'Australia is that island south of Timor!' So it was to a small Portuguese.

Portugal had very formal protocol procedures. I arrived in Lisbon in time to accompany Ambassador Kelly when he presented his credentials, as the first Australian ambassador, to President Américo Tomás at the heavily baroque presidential palace. The reception room was modelled on the Versailles Hall of Mirrors. All our senior embassy staff accompanied Kelly. I was dressed in a smart raw-silk day dress and jacket, but the men needed to wear formal morning dress, which included black trousers and a frock coat with tails. The opera house was the only place you could hire such suits in Lisbon, and the clothing was designed for rather short Portuguese men. Our immigration officer, Mort Barwick, was an especially tall, lanky Australian, and the only black trousers which were anywhere near long enough for him were full of moth-holes. So we sent him out for this special occasion with the rather-too-short trousers suspended on string under his jacket. And we coloured his legs with black texta behind the various moth-holes, so no hairy pink flesh could be seen! He looked sufficiently smart, if you didn't look too closely.

The ambassador and I were included in the formal annual presidential new year reception for the corps. Each ambassador and deputy of the other embassies arrived in a single official car. In our case, Kelly decreed every year that I should take a second car, lest anyone presume I was his wife and look askance at him for having such a young partner. Margaret Kelly had warned me about his eccentricities, so I took it all in my stride and was very fond of him and grateful for the solid start to my Foreign Affairs career.

I travelled widely within Portugal and explored the historic towns and castles. I met academics, politicians and business leaders as well as military officers. There was a congenial friendship group among young diplomats on their first postings: American, British, French, Canadian and Italian counterparts as well as a number of young Portuguese. We had dinners in famous *fado* restaurants and went away together for weekends, around Portugal and into Spain. Once, we drove overnight to Pamplona, in Spain, to participate in the Running of the Bulls festival. One of my women friends was full of bravado and was outraged to be told women could not run with the bulls. But when we actually watched the run, safe on a balcony overlooking the street, we were very glad not to be down there, as we witnessed one young Spaniard being trampled by a bull below.

Another time, six of us made a special excursion to the Portuguese island of Madeira – famous for its wine and lace. We planned to split into two groups, drive to opposite sides of Madeira's main mountain, leave the cars at the foot and hike up, meeting at the top. We would then cook dinner and sleep overnight in the small lodge there and the next day swap car keys and each group hike down the opposite side. In beautiful sunny weather, my group escorted the other group to its side of the mountain, kissed them goodbye and said we looked forward to meeting at the top. We then drove to our side of the mountain, where we found that a thick, cold, wet fog had descended and that the guides we had hired were nowhere to be seen. But the beginning of the track was discernible, so after waiting a while we decided to plunge into the fog without our guides and start the walk. It was too late to recall the others and abort the adventure. There were no mobile phones then. We had no views and could see the track only for a few metres ahead. After about half an hour we heard the guides behind us in the fog, and they shouted that they would soon catch up with us. But they did not, so we toiled ever onwards and upwards, through the fog, on the wet track.

Late in the afternoon, we arrived at the summit to find the hut locked and no sign of the others. We settled down to wait, but as the sun started to set, the fog dropped and formed a plateau across which we could see another, higher peak, and then we heard the voices of our friends coming clearly across the fog table. On the other peak we could also see another, larger hut, with wood smoke curling tantalisingly from its chimney. We were at the top of the wrong peak. And it was rapidly getting dark and very cold. The guides shouted out that they would come and get us, so we broke into our hut for shelter, while we waited. The guides eventually arrived, after dark, complete with torches, and led us back down the mountain to the fork we had missed in the fog and up the right peak to join our friends. They had dinner ready, and we spread our wet clothes in front of the fire to dry and got stuck in to the spaghetti, eggs and wine. We had a good laugh about our misadventure. Next morning produced bright sunlight on both sides of the mountain, and we descended the opposite sides as planned. We all had glorious views all the way down. We were sore and jealous. This experience proved very bonding. Two members of the group, a Canadian and an Italian got married, I formed a lifelong friendship with Tain Tompkins, a very fine American (though he married someone else, Grace, who also became my friend), and we all remained in contact through the rest of our careers, visiting each other in our various posts around the world.

In early 1974, as the posting in Lisbon was coming to an end, the embassy judged that the political tide was turning in Portugal and significant political developments might be imminent. There were reports of unusual military meetings outside Lisbon, and none of the officers invited to my farewell party was able to come. I visited Mozambique and Angola on my way back to Australia, and in both countries spent time with Portuguese army friends, as well as local business leaders and foreign diplomats. All feared the changes in the air.

I took up duty in the West Europe Section of Foreign Affairs in Canberra on 26 April 1974, the day after the Carnation Revolution took place in Portugal. Led by the Senior General Spínola, who had been urging a change of colonial policy, the Portuguese armed forces had mutinied and overthrown the Caetano government. It was a peaceful coup, what became known as 'the carnation revolution'. The tanks and troops which entered the cobbled streets of Lisbon were welcomed by the population, many placing carnations in the barrels of the guns of the tanks and in the weapons carried by the soldiers. No-one was hurt. The change was welcomed by the ordinary people, who were ready for social and political change and by the socialist party and communist movement. The ruling class was however fearful of the change and of the emergence quickly of a communist-influenced government.

The revolution was extremely helpful to my career. I was the first officer from the embassy in Lisbon to return to Canberra after the coup, and I spoke fluent Portuguese. I have already related my summons by the Australian Prime Minister, Gough Whitlam. I was a junior second secretary in my twenties (having been promoted while I was at the post), back from my first posting, but I had returned to Australia via the Portuguese African colonies of Angola and Mozambique, where everyone I met was worried about what might be about to happen. I went off to Old Parliament House through the rose garden in my miniskirt and high heels. As I entered his office, the prime minister boomed, 'Well, Susan, what's going on in Portugal?' He seemed to be impressed with my briefing and was a great champion of me right through the rest of my career.

Incidentally, at that time it looked as if General Francisco Franco, the leader of Spain, might be about to die. The West Europe Section judged it prudent to have an official message ready to send to the Spanish Government for when the dictator passed away. I drafted something appropriate and sent it to the prime minister's office for approval. Whitlam sent it back with a comment handwritten in the margin: 'When and if the old bastard actually dies, we'll keep our condolences to ourselves!'

In the Department of Foreign Affairs' West Europe Section, my work focussed first on Portugal. The small number of staff had to monitor the reporting from all of our embassies in West Europe and keep abreast of any trends or developments which were important to Australia. Developments in Portugal and in the colonies were moving quite fast, as the new revolutionary government found its feet. There were concerns in Indonesia, about the prospect of a communist government in the neighbouring island of East Timor. The department organised itself to involve the rest of the relevant Australian agencies to consider developments and advise government on policy positions and actions it should take. It was my job to attend these meetings and keep the records. As the situation in Portugal developed, my time was increasingly taken up with East Timor, as the revolution in Lisbon spread to that Portuguese colony. Three political parties formed there: Apodeti (The Popular Democratic Organisation) which favoured integration into Indonesia; UDT (The Timorese Democratic Party), which supported continued union with Portugal; and Fretilin (The Revolutionary Front for an Independent East Timor), which wanted independence. The leaders of all three parties travelled in turn to Canberra to lobby the government to support their position. I escorted each delegation through their programs of meetings with Australian ministers and officials and interpreted for them when necessary. In the department there were strong debates about what Australia's policy should be towards East Timor. I personally favoured independence. I argued that the Portuguese Communist Party was really only an organised means for expressing Portuguese nationalism, that is, a quest for popular democratic representation and an end to feudalism. There was little evidence of fanaticism. But I was too young and inexperienced to understand how policy was made in Canberra and how to inject my ideas effectively. The pro-Indonesia group in the department was strong, and the task of running Australian policy and activity was shifting out of the Europe Branch and into the Asia Division. I remained involved in the policy processes, as representative of the West Europe Section. I read in the newspaper one morning in 1975 that the Australian Government was sending an official to inspect the situation on the ground in Dili, the capital of East Timor, and that the official was not me but the most junior administrative male officer who had been with us in the embassy in Lisbon. I was furious and remonstrated with the Asia Branch head, Lance Joseph. He agreed that I was the officer who should have been sent but said that if they had sent a woman, the public would say that the government was not treating the situation seriously! I was outraged and let him know what I thought about that.

Shortly afterwards, armed conflict erupted in Dili, the capital of East Timor. In August, Lance Joseph asked me to travel urgently to Darwin in the north of Australia to open a small temporary office to monitor events in East Timor, including public radio broadcasts in Dili and the arrivals in Darwin of refugees. After a few hours of briefings, I was on a plane. I was assigned a small office on the Darwin air force base and given temporary honorary membership of the air force mess. A few months before, Cyclone Tracy had destroyed much of Darwin, and most of the women and children had been evacuated. So a single young woman was made very welcome, and I was inundated with offers of dates. But there was no time for social activities, as the situation in East Timor deteriorated.

On 27 August 1975, the Portuguese governor, Mário Lemos Pires, and the army abandoned Dili, sailing to the island of Atauro. They had no communications equipment with them, so the Portuguese Government asked Australia for help, and a Royal

Australian Air Force plane and crew arrived in Darwin with equipment and sufficient cable to establish an aerial on the hill on Atauro, which had an airstrip. An Australian navy vessel also arrived in Darwin, on orders to stand-by in case of need in East Timor, and I joined the chief naval officer in Darwin in briefing the ship's captain and officers. A Dutch merchant navy ship, the MV *MacDili*, detoured to pick up refugees from Dili and take them to Darwin. Along with army intelligence officers, I went onboard the ship and interviewed civilian and military refugees to try to establish exactly what was going on in Dili. I was ignorant of the protocol which I should have followed as an Australian Government representative boarding the ship. It would have been courteous to call on the captain, and he let Canberra know that he was not pleased that I didn't. This was passed on, and I was instructed to contact the captain and apologise, tell him how grateful Australia was and try to make things up. It was very busy that day, and it was relatively late in the evening when I had the time to make the call. The ship was sailing early the next day. I went down to the dock on my own and walked along the quay to the ship's gangway, hailed the sailor on guard and asked to call on the captain. He was surprised at this lone young woman appearing out of the darkness at that late hour, but I eventually persuaded him who I was and the seriousness of my mission. He disappeared up the gangway and, some considerable time later, came back and ushered me aboard and into the captain's cabin. The captain was accompanied in the cabin by a mature woman in cocktail clothes, sipping a drink. Naively, I assumed this was his wife and commented how good it was that the shipping line allowed captains to travel with their family. The captain smiled, did not clarify the situation and listened gravely to my apology for failing to do him the courtesy of visiting that morning when the ship had docked. He offered me a drink, and we had a conversation about the situation in East Timor and the details of his passengers who had boarded in Dili. But it suddenly dawned on me that I had interrupted a delicate situation. This was *not* his wife, and I was de trop. So I thanked him for his work on behalf of the Australian Government, said my farewells and was escorted down the gangplank and back to the dock, where my self-drive Commonwealth car was waiting. I kicked myself for my naivety and the foolishness of going alone on this mission at a late evening hour.

The Portuguese Government in Lisbon despatched a peace mission to Darwin, led initially by the Portuguese consul general in Sydney, Dr José Eduardo Mello Gouveia. He had been close to former Australian prime minister Harold Holt and his wife, Zara. I had worked and socialised with him in Lisbon, where he had been head of the international economic department of the foreign ministry and had a charming apartment in the Lapa district of Lisbon, full of beautiful, antique, blue-and-white ceramics from his earlier posting in Jakarta. The other two members of the peace mission were Portuguese naval and army officers and I was to liaise with them.

The work was relentless. But during a rare lull one afternoon, I told the Australian air force commander that I was going to take a break at the hotel swimming pool and invited him to join me there for a beer. Leering down the front of my dress, he said that if he came, he wouldn't be getting the *outside* of his bathers wet. Charming.

That night I was asleep in my hotel bed when a telephone call from Canberra came in soon after midnight. Australia had intelligence that the Indonesians were planning to invade East Timor. I was instructed to pass this on to the Portuguese peace mission. Following Cyclone Tracy, my hotel was the only one in town with a night telephone service, so I sent a Commonwealth car to the hotel where the peace mission was staying, with a message for the consul general to contact me. Next thing, there was a phone call from reception at my hotel. The consul general was downstairs. Would he come up? No – he would prefer it if I came down.

I had dressed by this stage and went down to find Mello Gouveia in the Commonwealth car in his pyjamas, in front of the hotel. I gave him the news, and he asked if he could use the phone in my room to call Lisbon and the Portuguese Embassy in Jakarta. His pyjamas were of blue-striped cotton, with the pants held together by a tied cord. He hurried across the hotel foyer in his bare feet, holding the cord. In my room, he sat on my unmade bed – the telephone was on the bedside table – and made his calls. Soon afterwards the rest of the Portuguese peace mission arrived, the naval and army officers in full uniform, and stood formally in my hotel bedroom. It was a rather bizarre scene.

A couple of days later, the Portuguese minister for overseas territories, Dr António de Almeida Santos, arrived from Lisbon to take over leadership of the peace mission. Canberra sent Rawdon Dalrymple, just home from being Australian ambassador in Israel and a more appropriately senior officer, to replace me in Darwin and work with the Portuguese.

Soon after Dalrymple arrived, a phone call from DFAT alerted us that a Red Cross plane had been hijacked in Balibo, East Timor, by a group of refugees and was headed for Darwin. Prime Minister Whitlam ordered that the aircraft be landed at a remote corner of the Darwin base, away from media eyes, and that the hijackers be arrested and held in Darwin gaol.

The air force commander convened an emergency planning meeting at the base, including the Northern Territory police commissioner. Our instructions from Canberra were that the prime minister had directed Foreign Affairs to coordinate this operation, so Dalrymple moved to take over as chairman. The air force commander refused to cede: it was his base, and he would run the meeting. Dalrymple persisted, repeating that it was under the prime minister's orders. The commander said he didn't give a fuck about the prime minister; this was *his* base. And he physically pushed Dalrymple into the corridor. The police chief politely refused Dalrymple's invitation to join him in the corridor, and the planning meeting resumed. Time and fuel were running out as the plane circled overhead, awaiting clearance to land. I judged it more practical to remain in the planning meeting than to join Dalrymple in solidarity in the corridor outside.

The plane was cleared, and we moved quickly into vehicles to reach the corner of the airfield where the plane would land and disgorge its passengers. Uncomfortably, Dalrymple and I were forced to travel with the commander, as his vehicle had the appropriate equipment and clearance to operate on the airfield. Despite our precautions, the media were there in force. But the plane, its hijackers and other passengers were appropriately handled.

With Dalrymple taking over the temporary Foreign Affairs office in Darwin, I could finally get a good night's sleep and return to my regular job in Canberra. But the sense of being in the thick of it all, the long hours, the level of responsibility, the different tasks and duties crammed into this short assignment – and the knowledge that all this mattered – were exhilarating.

Years later, in 1998, I was posted to Hong Kong and also accredited as consul general in neighbouring Macau – still then formally a Portuguese colony. There, I found that the head of the Portuguese governor's office was a former army officer who had been in Timor on that governor's staff in 1975. He had accompanied the governor to Atauro. We naturally exchanged notes about our experiences at the time. He told me that the Portuguese had assumed that the Australian Government would have bugged the telecommunications equipment they supplied, so that Australian authorities could monitor the Portuguese radio traffic, and the Portuguese had deliberately planted messages in their communications on the assumption that Australia would read them. They were puzzled, however, that there had been no reaction from the Australian side. At the time, I was told that the Australian intelligence agencies had in fact proposed to fix the equipment, so we could read the Portuguese communications traffic, but this had been vetoed by Prime Minister Whitlam, who was not in principle a fan of the intelligence agencies at that time. So there were messages we had missed. I wonder if that would have made any difference.

In 1975, there were strong pressures on the Australian Government to support Fretilin and an independent East Timor.

Groups of former Australian servicemen who had been helped by Timorese during World War II to survive against the Japanese had an intense loyalty to the little island and argued strongly that to repay this debt Australia should support an independent East Timor. Jakarta wanted East Timor to become part of Indonesia as had happened in the case of West Papua. Under a UN supervised process in 1969, a vote of village councils had decided that West Papua should be incorporated into Indonesia. There was serious scepticism about the legitimacy of that process and the role played by the United Nations, and there was no appetite for a similar process involving East Timor now.

Unlike West Papua, East Timor had never been a Dutch colony, and so Indonesia could not mount a similar case for its incorporation. There were calls from some quarters for Australia to commit a peacekeeping force to maintain order in East Timor until a referendum could be held. The experience of Vietnam was, however, extremely fresh in the Australian Government's mind, and at this juncture it was reluctant to commit Australian troops to serve outside Australia's own borders.

The emergence of a communist-influenced government in Portugal following the 1974 revolution had alarmed the Indonesian Government, with the experiences of recent communist insurgencies in the region, including Malaysia. Fretilin had declared the independence of East Timor in August 1975, following the Portuguese withdrawal. The idea of an independent East Timor with a communist government right on the border was an alarming prospect to Indonesia. In this situation, it saw the integration of East Timor into Indonesia as the most desirable option. Whitlam, in an historic meeting with the Indonesian president Soeharto, abandoned any commitment to self-determination for East Timor and led Soeharto to believe that Australia understood and was sympathetic to Indonesia's preference for annexation of the territory. For Australia at that time, Indonesia's nervousness about a communist government in East Timor was persuasive. In December 1975, Indonesia invaded and took over East Timor.

The history of what unfolded in East Timor is well known. The killings of the four Australian journalists at Balibo, the invasion and occupation by Indonesia, the continued resistance by Fretilin fighters, the eventual decision of Indonesia to withdraw, the national referendum supported by the United Nations which led to independence, and the creation of the new state of The Democratic Republic of Timor-Leste are well documented elsewhere, as is the history of post-revolution Portugal. And I, moving from the Portuguese to the German language, now had a new focus and a new posting: to the German Democratic Republic, in East Germany.

6

East Germany with the Stasi, 1976–79

An abrupt change from my preoccupation with Portugal and East Timor was my second posting as first secretary and deputy head of mission at the Australian Embassy to the communist state of the German Democratic Republic (GDR), in East Berlin, from 1976 to 1979. Because of my childhood upbringing in Germany and school studies, I spoke German quite well, so it was a good fit. I had also attended a refresher course at the Goethe-Institut in Goettingen before joining the embassy.

Western countries had refused to recognise the Russian-created communist GDR. There were early signs of a thaw in the Cold War in the early 1970s, however, and talks began between the governments of the two German states. Australia's Whitlam government was one of the earliest to formally recognise the GDR, in 1973. The resident Australian Embassy opened in East Berlin in 1975, shortly after the establishment there of the Permanent Mission of the Federal Republic of Germany. Australia also maintained a consulate-general and military mission in West Berlin – a relic of its membership of the western alliance in World War II.

Ambassador Malcolm Morris OBE was the first resident ambassador, appointed in 1975. He had served as a British

Coldstream Guards officer in Germany during the war and was an excellent German speaker. Following the war, he was recruited into the fledgling Australian diplomatic service and had a strong career. He had been the first ambassador in Laos and in Austria, then ambassador to Vietnam and high commissioner in Pakistan.

I arrived as his deputy a year later. The embassy had just moved into its new purpose-built office, on Grabbeallee in Niedershoenhausen, a suburb a little out of the centre. It was near the newly built official Australian ambassador's residence and the older, established house in leafy Platanenstrasse, where I lived. My house had been built before the war by a Nazi sympathiser: a large swastika was built into the foundation brickwork. When I revisited Berlin in 2006, after reunification, my house had been converted into four apartments, and the swastika had been bricked over.

The embassy's task was to encourage trade and to monitor developments in the GDR and in the Eastern bloc generally, to provide our government with some understanding of the Soviet Union and the Cold War. We were also to help influence policy and opinion leaders to understand Australia. Morris and I formed a good team. He recognised my competence and allowed me great autonomy and independence of movement. He persuaded Canberra to relax the rule that, for security reasons, we should not travel alone but always be accompanied when travelling in the Eastern bloc. The system had to accommodate the novelty of a single woman first secretary without a convenient and protective accompanying spouse. I travelled widely within the GDR, as well as in the neighbouring communist Eastern bloc countries of Poland, Czechoslovakia, Hungary and Bulgaria. I also visited Moscow, and Kiev in the Ukraine. These countries were all behind the Iron Curtain and seldom visited by westerners, so it was a special privilege to travel there. Staff from Berlin often drove across Poland to visit the Australian Embassy in Warsaw, and I travelled a little within that country with my counterpart there, John Tilemann, who was also single.

I visited Budapest in company with Les Luck, first secretary at the Australian Embassy in Vienna, which had responsibility to cover Hungary. I accompanied him on the official calls he had to make and found those discussions illuminating when compared with similar discussions in Berlin. They were much more free and open than the East German officials I normally dealt with. We enjoyed the architecture, atmosphere and friendliness we encountered in the many restaurants and cafes. I had found my Hungarian and Romanian colleagues in Berlin the most open and approachable of all the Eastern bloc diplomats, and they helped me greatly in understanding what was going on and the uneasy relationship of these states with the Soviet Union.

Soon after my arrival in Berlin, I met graphic artist Gigi Ruth Mossner – a professional book illustrator and a free spirit – and I enjoyed times spent with her and her partner. (See art insert figure 4 for the cover of one of the illustrated books she gave me.) In summer 1978, I joined Gigi and her partner for a long weekend during their annual camping holiday at a beach on the Baltic. It was a nudist camp – what the Germans call FKK, or *Freikoerperkultur* ('free body culture'). Such beaches were more common in the GDR than what were called *Textilien Straende* ('fabric beaches'). Baltic beaches are often windy and on the chilly side. Every campsite was dug down and enclosed in a sand wall, to protect it from the wind. (I remembered these from a family holiday at the East Frisien island of Norderney when I was about five.) The weather being typical on the weekend of my visit, almost everyone was wearing a warm top but let the lower part of the body swing free, and images of men riding their bicycles and playing beach volleyball stick in the memory. Thor Magnus Bronder, my bachelor Norwegian diplomatic colleague, had earlier told me that in his opinion East German women looked better in the nude, while women in the west looked better covered up – a reflection, perhaps, of the relative unavailability of fashionable clothes in the communist state and the greater availability of fattening foods in the west.

In 1982, after my departure, the media reported that Gigi had had an affair with the West German political figure Klaus Boelling while he was head of the West German permanent mission in East Berlin.[6] She had accompanied him to Bonn when he was recalled to be the official West German Government spokesman. The affair had reportedly ended shortly thereafter. What exactly was Gigi's role in this affair? Intelligence and security agencies get very worried about intimate relations such as these. There is always the suspicion that official secrets are shared, as well as pillows. Was Gigi in fact targeting the West German permanent mission staff and spying on them, meaning the Australian Embassy was, in comparison, less of an interest? Or, due to my friendships and professional relationships with the diplomatic staff at the West German mission, was I a way for her to gain contact with them? She was, in any case, interesting and fun to be with.

She does not appear in the file kept on me by the East German intelligence organisation, the Stasi, which suggests she was not reporting back to them on her contact with me.

I spent a morning with Gigi back in Berlin in May 2019 in her bohemian apartment in Prenzlauer Berg, which was full of decorative treasures. She told me that the price she had had to pay for maintaining contact with her parents, who had moved to West Berlin, was her agreement to report for the Stasi. She said she thought the whole system was stupid; she had given them harmless titbits from time to time but had never told them anything about me.

I asked her about her affair with Boelling. She told me that she had heard that he was divorced and she had connived to meet him at a reception at the US embassy in East Berlin. There had been an immediate mutual attraction; he had visited her apartment, and the wild affair had begun. When, some time later, he had been recalled to Bonn, she had agreed to go with him. Gigi's exit from the GDR had not been easy: the authorities took away a house she had inherited as payment for her exit visa, and Boelling had needed to seek support for her exit from Erich Honecker, the head of the Communist Party. Gigi said that once in Bonn she realised she had made a great mistake. Bonn, she said, was boring – a small village with no cultural life and without the street life and vitality of Berlin. She ended the affair and came home to her narrow Bohemian apartment, three floors linked by a spiral staircase, where her son, Max, had continued to live. She settled back in and continued her professional art career.

I met many writers and artists in Berlin, many of whom were also published in the west, including Christa Wolf and Walter Kaufmann, the latter of whom was an Australian citizen. As a child during World War II, Kaufmann had fled Germany to Britain and had then been evacuated to Australia on HMT *Dunera*. He became a writer in Australia and as an adult had returned as a communist to East Germany. He continued to write and was published in both English and German. I wondered about the price such cultural figures might be paying for their artistic freedom and the good housing many of them enjoyed. Were they Stasi informers? After the fall of the Berlin Wall the Stasi archives became available, and the answer for many of the figures has been found to be 'yes'.

The Federal Republic of Germany (West Germany), along with most countries in the west, did not formally recognise the communist state of the GDR, so it could not have a normal embassy in Berlin. Diplomatic relations were conducted through the permanent missions in Bonn and Berlin. This is a common diplomatic device – the way to have useful and necessary exchanges short of formal diplomatic recognition.

I found contemporary East German painting on the whole dark and depressing. Music, rather than painting, was the art which engaged me most in Berlin. On the second evening after my arrival at the embassy, I went to a concert in the historic Staatsoper Unter den Linden, the home of the Berlin State Opera and the Staatskapelle Berlin. The arts were heavily subsidised by the communist state, and tickets for these concerts were extremely cheap. The music was world class, including the classical singers. An attractive and friendly woman sitting next to me introduced herself as Karin Peters, the wife of the leader of the second violins in the Staatskapelle, Klaus Peters. We had a drink together in the interval and exchanged contact details. She was friendly, but I was chary. I suspected she might have been a plant, placed next to me on purpose, to cultivate me. She introduced me to her husband after the concert: he was also open and welcoming. They did not contact me again, but a couple of months later the embassy organised a concert, in one of East Berlin's gorgeous little churches, for an Australian classical music ensemble sent to Berlin under a cultural relations fund, and I invited Karin and Klaus Peters to come.

A little while after the concert they invited me to their home; it was instructive to see inside an East German apartment and how a family like this lived. I put aside my suspicions of them, and a lifelong friendship grew. They had a neatly furnished three-bedroom apartment in a walk-up building in Pankow, where they lived with their two children, Katharina and Nils, then aged five and ten. The small living room had comfortable chairs and a coffee table which could be extended to become a dining table. They welcomed me into their family, and I sympathised with them through their stories about the difficulties of obtaining building materials for a small country house – they used the Russian word 'dacha' – in the little village of Lanke, a little way out of Berlin where they could maintain a garden, grow vegetables and spend summer weekends. Since all construction materials were committed by the state under the official 'five-year plan', the common economic planning device in communist countries, materials for unplanned, unofficial constructions like the dacha had to 'fall off the backs of trucks' or be procured through devious exchanges or in return for certain favours. Life in the 'people's paradise' was managed through small and larger acts of official disobedience and corruption. A current wry joke said that the most important tool for fulfilling the five-year plan was a pencil. Good clothes had to be smuggled in from West Berlin by visiting relatives. Young westerners wearing jeans and fashionable sneakers while making day trips to East Berlin were often approached by young East Germans offering to buy their clothes. When I left Berlin at the end of my posting, the wife of one of Klaus Peters' colleagues in the orchestra bought my warm sheepskin coat: I wouldn't need it in Australia. The Peterses never asked me for any favours, however.

I spent time with the Peters children and visited Katharina's school open day with Karin. I visited the Sudetenland, over the border in the Czech republic, with them one weekend, to help clear out books from a house which had belonged to a late German friend of theirs. That part of Czechoslovakia had previously been part of Germany. They took me to the town of Goerlitz to visit Karin's mother and gave me plants from her garden for my own garden in Berlin. We had lovely dinners and outings and spent New Year's Eve together at a dinner in their home, with other musicians. If they were reporting on me, I didn't care. It was a risk I took. It felt like a real friendship, and I was learning a lot about everyday family life in the GDR.

Everyone was cautious and suspicious about their neighbours and work colleagues. Who knew whether they were spying on you and reporting your activities to the Stasi? The Peterses suspected that others living in their building might well work for the Stasi. I always parked my car some way distant from their home.

I was convinced that my own house was bugged with secret listening devices, and my boilerman-gardener confessed quietly while we were planting a flowerbed together that he was 'a holder of official secrets' (*ein Geheimnistraeger*). Despite being over the retirement age, when citizens were allowed to make visits to the west, his official security classification meant he was not allowed such travel. I suspected he was responsible for either installing the bugging devices in my house or letting in those who did so.

I should write a little about the geographical and political framework which faced us in our work at the embassy. At the end of World War II, in 1945, the defeated Germany was divided into four zones, each occupied and administered by one of the victor allies – Britain, the United States, France and Russia. The capital city, Berlin, was similarly divided into four sectors. These arrangements were meant to be temporary. But as the Cold War hardened, the four occupation powers failed to agree on the creation of a new, united Germany. In 1949, the three western powers went ahead and united their three zones, forming the self-governing Federal Republic of Germany with its temporary capital in Bonn. In the east, the Russians established the communist state of the GDR with its capital in East Berlin. The whole city had been heavily bombed during the war, and fighting by the Russians as they moved into the city to finally defeat Hitler caused more destruction and disruption. Considerable postwar rebuilding in both parts of Berlin took place, but the city remained scarred. In West Berlin one church remained as a ruin, stabilised but not rebuilt, on the smart street, Kurfuerstendamm, as a memorial. East Berlin contained many of the original important city buildings, including the Museum Island in the Spree River, the Staatstheater on the main avenue Unter den Linden and the famous Brecht theatre, the Berlin Ensemble. On the western side, through the Brandenburg Gate, was the bombed-out parliament building and the large houses, abandoned or in ruins, which had housed many of the pre-war foreign embassies.

In the middle of East Berlin the Russians had flattened and paved over a large area to create Berlin's Mitte, the desolate and windy heart of the capital. A contemporary joke had it that the GDR had created a new job category: men and women to walk about and promenade in Mitte to create the impression that it was a crowded capital city. A modern television tower had been built in the middle of Mitte, which was the butt of more jokes. Ironically, a crucifix style cross was formed as the setting sun reflected on the circular glass windows on top of the tower, which was the centre of the agnostic state. Another joke circulating described how Erich Honecker, the GDR's Communist Party leader, was working in his office in the television tower at dawn. He heard a voice: 'Good morning, dear Erich, you hard-working Communist Party leader!'

'Who is speaking?'

'It is I, the sun, and I will shine and warm you throughout the day, as you work away for the good of the people'.

Honecker thanked him profusely. At sunset, he was still in his office, working away, and as the sun was going down he called out, 'Thank you, sun, for looking after me and warming me all day'.

The sun replied, 'Piss off, arsehole! I'm in the west now!'

The City of Berlin, the historical capital, was some 180 kilometres from the nearest point of the West German border and completely surrounded by the GDR. People think that the Berlin Wall merely divided the city into East and West Berlin. In fact, the wall surrounded West Berlin, creating a western island within the GDR.

In the early days, the inhabitants of both East and West Berlin could move freely around the city and between the GDR and the rest of the world, and movement within the four sectors of Berlin was relatively easy. But as the economy of the capitalist western state of the Federal Republic of Germany and its lifestyle freedoms grew, in contrast to those of the communist-controlled economy of the GDR, the outflow of population from east to west became stronger. By 1961, the people who had moved west numbered 3.5 million. Most of these were skilled workers, professionals and members of the intelligentsia. To arrest the flow, in 1961, the East Germans fortified their western and southern border with the Federal Republic of Germany and constructed an aggressively defended wall around West Berlin.

Diplomats posted in western embassies in East Berlin were able to pass through the wall at will, using a specially designated crossing at Bornholmer Strasse. We were not searched, and we had diplomatic immunity, so we could shop and carry personal goods in each direction freely. All other westerners had to face the long queues, extensive questioning and examination, and compulsory currency exchange at the infamous Checkpoint Charlie.

The Communist Party and government of the GDR were fixated on the dangers of overthrow or undermining of the state by hostile western powers. The East German state was paranoid about the enemy without and the enemy within. It was sure that the whole western world was out to undermine it and to influence its citizens to work within the state to disrupt and destroy it. Therefore, it set up an extraordinary structure to protect the state: the *Staatssicherheitsdienst* (State Security Service), which was often shortened to 'Stasi'. The Stasi's power, reach and impact on everyday life were pervasive and have become well known since the reunification of Germany and access to the former Stasi headquarters and files.

Anna Funder, in her book *Stasiland*, suggests that the network of collaborators and informers comprised one in six of the East German population of 17 million.[7] The Stasi had 97,000 employees, or one Stasi operative for every sixty-three citizens. The Stasi network was one-and-a-half times the size of the regular GDR army. Of course, these details were not known during my time in Berlin – such figures were well-kept state secrets.

I always assumed that, as an active western diplomat based in East Germany, I would be a target of Stasi interest. My fluent German, capacity to move about freely, skill in developing friends and contacts and relatively young age for a senior position in the embassy were grounds for suspicion.

The Stasi's files became available upon the reunification of Germany, and thousands of Germans and many foreigners, like me, were able to seek access to them. So, in 2006, thirty years after my posting, I applied to the German government agency responsible for the files of the former Stasi for access to my file. In 2008, they confirmed that they had indeed located a file on me – 900-odd pages – and that they would send photocopies by post, for a very reasonable charge to cover costs. This fascinating parcel arrived in Perth in early 2009. The file has provided a unique insight into the actual workings of the Stasi, into the thoughts and assumptions of those reporting on me, on the extent and assumed expense of maintaining a three-year-long watch on me, and on who, surprisingly, was *not* reporting on me and why.

Many people, I know, on reading their files have felt enraged, betrayed and shocked at the contents, which in some cases have caused a serious blight on their lives. In many cases, GDR citizens suffered as a result of Stasi interference. Jobs, promotions and access to higher education for children were denied. As I read my own file, I was once more convinced about the need for extreme care before authorising any state-sponsored surveillance of citizens, how easy it is to reach wrong conclusions and make false assumptions based on incomplete information and context, and how many lives were blighted by pure malice.

In my case, I was not shocked. I had known I would be under surveillance and had been confident that I was doing nothing in secret and nothing which could cause harm. I was going about my legitimate business as an Australian diplomat. I am an open character, and my job, as with any posting, was to try to understand the workings of the GDR and, indeed, the Eastern bloc, to identify the Australian interest and to advance it by open means. In the embassy I was responsible for political and economic reporting and for the press and culture programs. During absences by the ambassador, I was the chargé d'affaires and in charge of the whole embassy. I was not a spy.

But the GDR was not a society like Australia, in which, relations between people are usually based on trust – people basically trust each other until there is evidence to question such trust. East Germans were very careful and mistrustful of each other until they were absolutely certain that a relationship of trust could be established. German society overall is more formal than Australian society. Even close friends, work colleagues and long-time neighbours use the formal forms of address – 'Sie' rather than 'du'.

Every member of western diplomatic missions posted to the GDR was seen by the Stasi as a potential enemy of the state, and it was illegal for ordinary East German citizens to have contact with western diplomats without authority. Knowing this, I assumed from the outset that I would be under surveillance and that any

East German with whom I could build a relationship was likely to be reporting on me. I also assumed that my relationship with diplomats from other embassies would be noted, that my phone would be bugged and that my friendships and private life would also come under scrutiny. So, I did not feel hurt or betrayed by what I found.

The Stasi was very organised and bureaucratic in its files. My file opened with reference to the exact provisions of the GDR law which authorised the operation against me and a statement of the objective of the operation. The trigger cited for the operation against me was 'her great activity in making contacts'. The material in my file is all in German. Translations used here are mine. The purposes of the operation were stated as building up a complete personal picture of me, establishing whether I was conducting intelligence activity on behalf of my own country or on behalf of another intelligence agency (such as the CIA), identifying and clarifying my contacts and contact activity, identifying activities in the cultural and journalist areas, and finding out my own ideological position and attitude towards the GDR.

My file identified a number of people (by code names) I had made contact with through my work early on, who were authorised to pursue a relationship, to report on the above matters and to receive payment for this work. Two members of the Australian Embassy's local staff were identified who had to report on my movements and travel plans. They were the ambassador's driver, Walther Pflaum, and our receptionist, Fraeulein Partsch. In fact, all the embassy staff were provided to us by the East German authorities, the *Dienstleistungsamt*, through which we paid their salaries. My file was full of detailed records of my conversations with these and many other people with whom I came in contact. From my own recollection of the conversations, the transcripts were mostly accurate, and my interlocutors were not hostile. It was quite enjoyable and interesting to rerun conversations from forty years earlier.

Because I had worked part-time for the *Daily News* in Perth for four years I had felt comfortable with the press, and many of my contacts in Berlin were journalists. Through developing contacts with them I could build up my knowledge and understanding of the GDR's foreign policy and international activities, as well as an understanding of how the press and society in the GDR worked. I met regularly with the deputy editor of the GDR's foreign affairs newspaper, a journalist from the daily newspaper *Berliner Zeitung* and the editor of the women's newspaper *Für Dich*. My closest friends became the British Reuters correspondent in East Berlin Mark Brayne and his German wife, Jutta. He later transferred to West Berlin as the BBC correspondent but still covered the same beat. I also looked for opportunities to place material in the press which would help GDR readers learn about Australia. Through discussions and press material I tried to broaden knowledge and understanding among these possibly influential opinion-formers. I gave them foreign journals and publications which they could otherwise not access, either from an ideological point of view or because of the cost, in hard currency, which their newspapers' budgets could not afford. My journalist contacts saw professional and personal advantage in building a relationship with me and accepted that the cost to them was the obligation to report to the Stasi on me and on our discussions. I knew this, and they knew that I knew. So we were all relaxed about it.

My contacts clearly liked me and reported on me in surprisingly positive terms, contributing to the central picture being built up by the Stasi. They were not portraying me in negative terms or as a class enemy. My Stasi profile said I was of above-average intelligence, had wide general knowledge and was well educated. I was polite and knew how to bring personal matters into the conversation in order to develop trust quickly. My questions were well formulated and to the point, and they emerged very naturally from my own openness. I knew how to establish friendly relationships quickly. I loved life and made contacts easily. I liked good food and could cook, had housewifely talents, was interested in the theatre and literature, was observant and quick thinking and seemed to be professionally ambitious. The overall impression I made was described thus:

> [She] appears uncomplicated, open and empathetic [*sympathisch*]. She is single, dresses well, is interested in men, has a lot of male friends, but does not seem to have a particular boyfriend. She is at ease in men's company...She enjoys food and eating, but does not drink much. But this is not from a prudish point of view, as borne out by the jokes she tells.

They got the last bit right: I am known as a joke-teller. In both languages.

The file reported that I played sport, including squash in West Berlin and attended an exercise class within the US Embassy. The file assumed I played squash in a club in West Berlin; in fact I played with members of the British military posted in the former Olympic stadium in West Berlin, where there were courts. The Stasi failed to pick up on my close friendships with members of the British Commanders'-in-Chief Mission to the Soviet Forces in Germany (BRIXMIS), which regularly roamed at will throughout the GDR, much to the irritation of the GDR authorities. Britain did not recognise the GDR and still treated it as the Soviet zone as defined under the Four Power Agreement, under which the allies had full travel and access rights, and they took full advantage of them. The GDR tried to stop this and erected large signs in German, English, French and Russian declaring access was prohibited to members of the foreign military missions. The Brixmis officers, in full uniform and in army troop carriers, flouted these prohibitions, took down the signs and gave them to people like me – in my case, as a farewell gift at the end of my posting. A prohibition sign was an invitation to the Brixmis troops to check what was going on. They were splendid young officers with huge energy, full of derring-do and a taste for adventure. They were great theatre and concert companions. One of my nicest memories is a winter dinner with them in their Potsdam residence, which was beside a lake. We watched an old couple with a lantern, in wooden skates and long coats, skating arm-in-arm on the frozen water under a full moon.

In my file I found that Stasi recorded my family background and my education, as well as my father's job and those of my siblings. They knew I voted Labor but observed how carefully I carried out my official duties when the government in Australia changed and I skilfully avoided discussions on domestic Australian politics.

All of my interlocutors commented on my good German, some saying it was perfect and others picking up a slight unattributable accent.

As well as recording the detailed subjects of our conversations, my interlocutors offered analysis of them. After my second conversation with the female deputy editor of the main East Berlin newspaper, the *Berliner Zeitung*, she commented on the relatively little focus on political matters and the wider coverage of personal matters in our discussions. I talked about my impressions of Berlin and my relationship with the current boyfriend, and I asked about her personal interests and her family. She concluded that I was possibly just a single woman, new in town, who needed a woman friend. She became such a friend.

In the record of conversations with the editor of the largest women's magazine, *Für Dich*, she wondered at my apparent great interest and friendliness towards her husband, whom I had met, and whether I was after him. She later chided me gently for using the familiar '*ihr*' in my Christmas card to them, which suggested to her employers (who read her mail and interrogated her about it) that they had an overly familiar, unauthorised relationship with me.

My file revealed that the deputy editor of the foreign affairs newspaper, a man I saw most frequently, had received Stasi permission to invite me to his little weekend dacha, in the country, and to meet his wife and son. He recorded amazement at the short time I took to establish a good, open relationship with his wife, to the extent that we were calling each other '*du*' and using first names within an hour. I asked for my bicycle seat to be lowered before we went for a ride together, but he was astounded when, after knowing his wife for such a short time, I said to her, jokingly, 'Otherwise, it might ruin my prospects of having children'.

Towards the end of my posting, I gave this same fellow a copy of George Orwell's *Animal Farm* to read. My file included his full report on the content of the book. He wondered, at the end, whether it might be seen as a 'critique of socialism'.

My Stasi file contained exhaustive lists of my friends and contacts among diplomatic corps staff, journalists and members of foreign military missions based in West Berlin, as well as a long list of many, but not all, of my other East German contacts.

As I have mentioned, my closest friends were the Reuters correspondent Mark Brayne and his wife, Jutta. A large section of my file was taken up with transcriptions of telephone conversations between us. We knew our phones were bugged and never talked about anything really sensitive over the phone, so the content of these conversations was not very meaningful. But the reports concluded that Mark was my main source of information. Mark has since told me that in his Stasi file, I was given to be *his* main source of information. His file, by the way, was much larger than mine. I have remained close friends with Mark and Jutta, and I am the godmother of their second son, Alastair.

In the file there were amusing detailed reports from Stasi operatives who were shadowing me on visits to towns outside Berlin. I visited Magdeburg and the following report is in my file.

> She arrived at the edge of town at 8.30 and drove to the main hotel, arriving there at 8.38. She drove down a one-way street the wrong way, twice, which made it hard to shadow her and showed her unfamiliarity with the town. She parked the car in front of the hotel, took out a brown suitcase, and checked in. She received the key to room 335. She went up to her room and came down again five minutes later. She walked around the

town square, looking at the buildings and the shop windows, not seeming to be looking for anything in particular. She bought a postcard, and sat down on the town hall steps to write it, then posted it in the postbox in front of the town hall. Here is the postcard.

The postcard was addressed to my parents and read,

Here on a day and a half visit, to talk about Australia. The town used to be the Krupp HQ before the war, and was therefore bombed almost out of existence. This Cathedral and one or two other buildings are almost all of note which remains. The rest is quite modern. Love, Sue.

Not much subversive here!

My shadow's report continued,

She went into a telephone box and looked up a telephone number in the phone directory. I could not see the name, but she found the number on page 183, and the last digits she dialled were 3 and 4. Later examination showed that this number belonged to Schmidt but there had been no answer...

She went for a drive outside the town, and stopped frequently to consult a map. I was forced to overtake her during these stops, in order not to look as if she was being followed, and lost her on a couple of occasions – but eventually picked her up again in the next village.

I was in Magdeburg to give a talk to a small English-language conversation group that evening and had been invited by the convenor of the group, who issued the invitation during a personal call to the embassy in Berlin. The file contained four separate reports on my talk. The first was a transcription of the event, recorded secretly from outside the room. The Stasi operator confessed that the recording was not the best, given that the recorder malfunctioned, that the battery ran out and that the recharger also malfunctioned. In addition, as he was located outside the room, he could not tell who was speaking. Also, he did not speak English. The three other reports were by members of the conversation group who participated in the meeting. None, apparently, knew that the others were reporting afterwards. They were pretty accurate reports of what went on, which was totally innocuous. I showed two short films on Australia, one of which concerned the lifecycle of the kangaroo and the other a short tourism promotion. I gave a short talk. All the reports noted that I made no comment on political matters, whether in Australia or the GDR, and handled all questions appropriately. Nothing to worry about there! Except that, apparently, the nice fellow who had invited me was not, in fact, authorised to do so: my file did not reveal what happened to him. After the event, he invited me and a smaller group back to his private apartment for more talk over a few drinks, but there were no reports of the conversations which took place there.

There were a number of such reports made by someone tailing me in a few visits I made to towns around the GDR, all equally painstakingly observed and clearly revealing nothing of any consequence. I have to confess to having been unaware at the time that I was being tailed. They did it very well, even, on one occasion, tailing me and my companions on a narrow path into a forest, where we stopped in a clearing, put down a rug and had a picnic; the report detailed what we ate and drank, including the label of the wine.

At an official reception for cultural attachés in Leipzig, I connected with a woman who was the resident people's artist at an agricultural cooperative. I later paid her a visit at home, in the cooperative. She showed me her studio, and we talked about her work, about art in general and about the role she played in the cooperative. We walked around a little. We seemed to get on, and I asked to visit her again, which she seemed to welcome. On my second visit, however, though she was just as pleasant and hospitable, she asked me not to come again. She said she was sensitive, as an artist, and she found my conversation, about places and events she could never visit and experience, made her feel like a bird trapped in a cage. The feeling was unbearable, and she had to ask me not to visit again. I quite understood, and I was always careful, in my contacts with ordinary GDR citizens, not to do anything which might be uncomfortable for them or get them into trouble with their own authorities.

However, on reading my Stasi file, I discovered that after my first visit she had been interrogated by a Stasi agent who had asked her about our conversation and the circumstances of our meeting. What she was reported as telling the agent matched my own recollection – she had been truthful. The agent had then asked her to develop our association and to report on me, which she had declined to do, saying she had no interest in the association: I did not really know much about art, I had no family, and we had nothing in common. So, that explained what had really gone on! It also revealed that citizens had a choice: it was possible for people to decline to cooperate with the Stasi.

One of the amusing stories in my file was a record written by a man who was a guest one year at my birthday party at my home. He listed everyone who was there, to the extent he could. He thought it was very odd that there were no formal introductions of guests to each other, quite a lot of drink and little food. A new Reuters correspondent, Mark Wood had recently arrived in Berlin and was also at the party. He had engaged this other guest in conversation and taken him on a tour of my art collection. They stopped at an antique cash register that I had found in Portugal, and Mark demonstrated how the register worked and how, in turning the handle, the drawer was made to open, to the sound of a bell. He turned the handle several times to demonstrate. The Stasi reporter thought that a camera was hidden in the device and that each time the handle had turned he had been photographed!

Halfway through my posting, my file revealed that Stasi reviewed the purpose of spying on me. They assessed that I was *not* an intelligence officer but that, because I associated with people who were still suspected of working for foreign intelligence agencies, particularly in the British, US and West German diplomatic missions, the surveillance of me should continue.

The East Germans were surprised when I asked for a year's extension of the two-year posting. And there was an effort to discredit me to my own government: they planted a story in Canberra that I was having a secret affair with a professor at Humboldt University. Had this been true, it would have resulted in my withdrawal from the post. But the plant did not succeed, largely because of my excellent relationship of trust with my own ambassador.

In reading my file, I was struck by the number of people who were *not* included in it. Earlier in this chapter I wrote about my artist friend Gigi and our holiday together on the Baltic. She appeared only once in my file, as the hostess of a small, impromptu gathering at her flat after my official farewell party.

My closest East German friends, Klaus and Karin Peters and their children, were nowhere reflected in my Stasi file, except as guests at the birthday party. In 2006, when I revisited Berlin on holiday, I spent a lot of time with the Peters family including their then grown-up children and grandchildren. We visited the dacha at Lanke, and we played in the garden.

Klaus, who was first violin in the Staatskapelle, told me that, years earlier, the Stasi had approached the director of the orchestra, noted that they had frequent international tours and asked that members agree to spy for the Stasi. The director had resisted vigorously, arguing that the orchestra earned a strong international reputation for the GDR, as well as a great volume of hard currency, through the excellence of its artistic performance. Orchestra members were sensitive artists, whose performance would be compromised and negatively affected by any such association with the Stasi. He therefore recommended strongly that no such approach should be made. Klaus said that the orchestra members and their families were thus exempted and protected; and that is why there was no reference to them in my file. He told me that after the fall of the Berlin Wall the whole orchestra had met, reaffirmed the importance for the performance of the orchestra of full mutual confidence and trust. The orchestra leaders had asked whether any member had been working for the Stasi. Just one junior administrative officer owned up and promptly resigned.

Another significant omission from my file was Frau Helga Precht, the embassy interpreter. As all of our local staff were provided to us by the GDR authorities, we assumed all were required to report on us. Frau Precht was extraordinarily friendly and helpful to us, as was her husband. At one stage she suggested that I would enjoy visiting her father and stepmother, who lived near the picturesque town Seiffen, in the Erzgebirge – the Ore Mountains. This was the centre of traditional German woodcarvings of children's toys and Christmas decorations, and she thought it would be especially interesting to visit in the winter, during Advent, when there were special Christmas displays in all the towns and villages there.

I drove to Seiffen with Margaret Johnson, another Australian staff member of the embassy. Herr Hedewig and his wife were extremely hospitable and welcoming, and they gave us delightful old handmade Christmas carvings from the family's collection. We had an adventure on the way there, when my orange Volkswagen Scirrocco had a puncture. We had to spend Friday night in a small town at the foot of the snowy mountains. I was reluctant to drive into the icy mountains in the dark and without a spare, and the puncture could only be repaired the following day. There was no hotel, but we were welcomed into the home of the garage owner and his family. They shared their traditional Advent meal with us and then took us with them to a special concert and party in the local castle. Later, they made up sofa beds for us in their home. The next day, on departure, Margaret and I gave them gifts in gratitude – chocolates and food-stuffs unobtainable in the GDR. They were very surprised; they had not realised we were foreign diplomats but had assumed we were visitors from Czechoslovakia. All this was very natural, warm and genuine. None of it was reflected in my Stasi file.

I met up with Frau Precht during my 2006 visit. She had clearly enjoyed working with Australians; we had liked each other and there had been mutual respect between us, and we had maintained regular contact.

She shared with me her own Stasi file, which had shocked her and made her very angry. It revealed that the Stasi had considered enlisting her as an agent when she was a student at Leipzig University, which specialised in foreign language studies. The plan would have been to send her to spy abroad. However, it was also noted that her father was a significant senior member of the community and held an important position in business in the Erzgebirge. The Stasi assessment was that he would react badly to the sudden and permanent disappearance of his daughter. The file recorded that the Stasi judged he would be very angry if attempts were made to enlist his daughter. So she was left in peace.

In 1975 when she was appointed to our embassy she had declined to collaborate with the Stasi. A large number of new embassies had opened around the same time, and the authorities had been stretched to recruit enough appropriate staff for them, so they had needed her: she had been able to set the terms.

During my visit Frau Precht introduced me to an old university friend, then working as a tour guide in Dresden – they had studied together at Leipzig. The friend had been a teacher and had also refused to collaborate with the Stasi. They had tried various means to force her, including suspending her from her teaching position. But she had used the provisions of the GDR's own laws to resist and had succeeded. They had been forced to reinstate her in the teaching profession. She said there had been a battle, with personal costs, but she had won. This was again interesting information on how it was possible for citizens to resist pressure from Stasi.

However, Frau Precht had got her comeuppance for her close collaboration and friendships with the Australian Embassy staff.

After the Australian Embassy to the GDR closed, in 1986, the government agency for the employment of local staff for foreign embassies – the *Dienstleistungsamt* – transferred her to a poor developing country Asian embassy, which she found a much less congenial place to work.

In 1976, Gough Whitlam, by that time the former Australian prime minister, paid an official visit to the GDR. Ambassador Malcolm Morris was sure this was because of the importance of the decision Whitlam had made to recognise the GDR and open the embassy. The ambassador envisaged a program of official visits with current leaders and Communist Party officials. I suspected, from my previous personal contact with Whitlam and from his extensive interest and knowledge of ancient civilisations, that the real purpose of his visit was to see the Pergamon Museum and all the historical treasures in Berlin's other museums. When I crossed to West Berlin with our driver to pick him up and take him through the checkpoint, he looked at his program in dismay and asked, 'But when am I going to see the Pergamon Museum?' Luckily, we had reserved a whole free day in his program for just that purpose. He dutifully went through the official program, but his great joy was to see the contents of the museums. Morris and I both went with him on these visits. Whitlam had an encyclopaedic knowledge of ancient history and was able to speak at length about each exhibit and its context. He enjoyed educating us. He was very content with his visit to East Berlin.

Soon after my first meeting with Whitlam, as prime minister in 1974, I had developed a close friendship with the economic adviser to one of the Labor ministers in Whitlam's government. Whitlam knew of this relationship and approved of it, and I acquired the status of a trusted insider. He was easy in my company, which made this visit and our encounters in future postings very comfortable.

My economic adviser friend was a member of the small group of urban planners that in 1972 took advantage of the newly elected Labor government's pursuit of variety in urban design. The group sought alternatives to the traditional suburban pattern of single houses on large blocks and embraced the then new concept of cooperative housing schemes which promoted good neighbourliness, intergenerational living and creative play and recreation space but which nonetheless respected individual ownership and privacy. This led to the ground-breaking creation of Urambi Village in the Canberra suburb of Kambah. Urambi is a 72-unit development which over time proved successful and true to the vision of the founders translated by the architect Michael Dysart. I liked the concept, bought a small unit and joined up in 1974. Urambi became my base in Australia and my home until 2003. My neighbours were the stable core group of friends whenever I returned from my various postings. A decisive practical attraction for me was that the credit union which underwrote the project guaranteed finance to each new homeowner. At the time, the banks were refusing to lend to single women, which made me furious. My bank manager was condescending and recommended I continue to share apartments: 'You can't be that difficult to live with'. Having shared already in Canberra and lived by myself overseas, I wanted a home of my own.

At the end of my East German posting, in 1979, I was recalled to Canberra and was genuinely sorry to leave the GDR. There were slight beginnings of a new openness: modern music did not respect national boundaries, and nor did radio broadcasts. West Berlin was a constant showcase of what the rest of the world had to offer. But controls on GDR citizens were still tight, and those trying to cross the wall and escape were still being shot by the border guards. That made us all very sad. I could not imagine how the necessary change could come from within.

On an official visit for cultural attachés to the mountainous area of Thuringia in East Germany, I had sent a postcard to my parents extolling the beauties of the area. But then I wrote,

Last evening, drove across the border to West Germany for the evening. What a contrast! Everything much more prosperous looking and well kept and the people looked so different – so confident, unsuspicious and <u>normal</u>. This place gets to you sometimes. Our guide was a typical, colourless, unhealthy looking party arse-licker here in the GDR.

In another card sent to my parents, in June 1978 from Magdeburg, I wrote,

Here again, on a special excursion organised by the cultural section of the Foreign Ministry, to see how well they have renovated their national monuments. At the moment we are being subjected to the usual lecture full of clichés about the workers and peasants and their achievements, and meaningless statistics. I could have written the speech before we came!!

These postcards went back to Canberra in the diplomatic bag.

A card I sent from Paris in July 1978 included the line, 'It's hot here, but a great change from Berlin. So open, free and uncomplicated'.

The 155-kilometre Berlin Wall was in place throughout my posting and was not breached and demolished until 1989, during the dramatic implosion of the GDR and the formation of the new, united state of Germany, in 1990.

The GDR imploded, and all that the Stasi and the Communist Party had tried to protect – at great expense and considerable harm to its citizens – came to naught. But the Stasi archive files remain, protected by the new, reunified Germany, and people are still making surprising and shocking discoveries.

7

United Nations, New York, 1981–84 and a short stint in Washington DC in 1985

Arms Control, peaceful uses of nuclear energy and of outer space, a zone of peace in the Indian Ocean. The beginning of the end of the Cold War and Australia's modified position under a new government.

I was in New York from 1981 to 1984 as a member of the Australian delegation to the United Nations, under ambassadors David Anderson and then Dick Woolcott. The work of the United Nations General Assembly is divided into six subject committees, covering the main work of the organisation and each member of the delegation focusses principally on one of these committees. I was responsible for the First Committee and so took care of disarmament and arms control, international security, the peaceful uses of outer space and of nuclear energy and the ad hoc committee on the Indian Ocean Zone of Peace. My colleagues in the delegation, also posted from DFAT, covered the other five committees, which were concerned with economics and trade; social, humanitarian and cultural questions, including human rights; special political questions and decolonisation; the budget and administration of the United Nations; and legal questions. The Deputy Head of the Mission covered the United Nations Security Council and the UN Specialised Agencies.

In the First Committee Australia's special interest was the Comprehensive Test Ban Treaty (the CTBT): a treaty which would, if adopted, ban the testing of nuclear weapons in all environments – in the air, on land or in water.

Picture a table on the pavement outside a hamburger joint in New York near the United Nations in October 1983. Australian foreign minister Bill Hayden, Australian United Nations ambassador Dick Woolcott, a minister from the Australian Embassy in Washington, DC, and United Nations First Committee Australian delegate, me, are all sitting around a small table of the hamburger joint on the pavement on Third Avenue, close to the Australian delegation office and the United Nations Headquarter building. The subject of discussions was Australia's key disarmament resolution at the United Nations on a comprehensive nuclear test ban treaty.

In March 1983, the Australian Labor Party won the federal election, and Bill Hayden, formerly the party leader, became foreign minister. Australia had long been an ally of the United States, and the ANZUS Treaty was the fundamental cornerstone of Australian military defence strategy, sacred doctrine. It provided that the United States would come to the aid of Australia if needed. Following World War II it had replaced Australia's previous reliance on the United Kingdom. At the United Nations General Assembly Australia had, under the previous Liberal–National coalition government, always voted in line with the United States on a range of disarmament and arms control resolutions. Harold Holt, the conservative prime minister, had assured visiting US president Lyndon B. Johnson that Australia was 'all the way with LBJ'. But times were changing. The Australian electorate, along with many in the rest of the world, was extremely nervous at the prospect of nuclear war. Newlyweds were asking whether they should bring children into the world at this risky time. People were building nuclear shelters. It was an electoral issue the new government had to address, the tiger it had to ride.

The major international treaty covering the topic was the Nuclear Non-Proliferation Treaty, and this was becoming increasingly less reassuring as a means of avoiding the proliferation of nuclear weapons, and possible nuclear war, at the height of the Cold War. The March 1970 treaty was based on an international deal. The five states which already possessed nuclear weapons – the United States, the Soviet Union, France, the United Kingdom and China – undertook to reduce and eliminate them. Other states, in turn, undertook not to acquire nuclear weapons. But it was becoming clear that a number of states were in fact developing these weapons, despite their earlier pledges, and there seemed to be evidence of nuclear weapons testing by those states. Successive review conferences of the Nuclear Non-Proliferation Treaty failed to reach consensus. The general public was less and less confident that nuclear war could be avoided. Australia's ally the United States was a nuclear weapon state.

Australia and New Zealand were leading the international demands for a comprehensive nuclear test ban treaty, an important step to control a nuclear arms race. Without nuclear testing, it was unlikely that states could progress to build and stockpile nuclear weapons or test the continuing potency of weapons they might already possess. Australia and New Zealand each year jointly introduced a resolution to the United Nations General Assembly, via the First Committee, looking to persuade more UN member states to agree to negotiate such a treaty and to bring increasing pressure on both the declared nuclear weapon states and those states which might have been moving towards nuclear weapons. The wording of the resolution each year was always a delicate balancing act, as Australia and New Zealand sought to keep their ally the United States engaged. The United States argued that the nuclear weapons it possessed in fact acted as a deterrent to nuclear war and mutually assured destruction. In order for its weapons to remain viable, the United States claimed that it needed to continue to test them periodically. Australia's overall defence strategy relied on the US nuclear umbrella, while the Australian public was increasingly anxious.

The Australian delegation to the United Nations in New York serving the new Labor government thought that the time was ripe for change. It was in Australia's interest to be more assertive in the United Nations on arms control questions. Australia could be both an ally of the United States and a country committed to bringing about a world without the danger of nuclear war. A comprehensive nuclear test ban would be a significant step. Australia had its own row to hoe, independent of the position the United States was choosing to adopt. Australia wanted the United States, like all the other nuclear weapons states, not to conduct any further tests. It was in Australia's interest, the delegation in New York argued, to have a more independent stance and to pursue a resolution with stronger wording than hitherto. The United States would not like this, of course, but the delegation maintained that the bilateral relationship was strong enough to tolerate a bit of disagreement. It recommended that Australia should change its voting at the United Nations and strengthen its commitment to a comprehensive nuclear test ban.

On behalf of the delegation I sent these arguments off to DFAT in Canberra for consideration as a change of policy and copied it to our embassy in Washington, DC, and to the Australian mission to the United Nations in Geneva, where substantive arms control negotiations took place. The embassy in Washington did not like the initiative at all and argued that, as it would be unacceptable to the United States, it should not be pursued.

When foreign minister Bill Hayden arrived in New York in late 1983 for the United Nations General Assembly, he had all the papers with him. He was interested in our proposal and asked Ambassador Dick Woolcott to invite a senior member of our embassy in Washington to join us in New York for a full discussion. So we four found ourselves eating hamburgers on a pavement at lunchtime, considering a change to Australia's position on nuclear testing and ways to strengthen the way Australia's policy was presented.

I set out my arguments, and the contrary case was raised by the Minister from our Embassy in Washington. Apart from arguing against the merits of the case he denigrated my relatively junior standing, my youth and my gender. Hayden was having none of this and told him firmly to 'play the ball and not the woman'. He had listened to the arguments and decided that the New York delegation's proposal was sound, and that was how that year's resolution and vote would be crafted.

This was a significant shift in the way Australia conducted itself in disarmament matters. One of the immediate initiatives the Labor government had taken to meet the Australian public's nuclear fears was to create the new position of ambassador for disarmament. Richard Butler was appointed to this role and posted to the Australian mission to the United Nations in Geneva. Our resolution was adopted by the United Nations General Assembly in 1983 and opened the way for the delegation in Geneva to capitalise on the momentum and in 1984 to reinvigorate the issue, open up actual negotiations with member states and have the Comprehensive Nuclear Test Ban Treaty adopted by the General Assembly in New York in 1996. The treaty was signed by all five nuclear-weapon states. This was a major achievement.

I tell this story as an insight into the way policy shifts sometimes come about. It gave me great satisfaction as the Australian delegate to explain our changed position to the whole membership of the United Nations in the General Assembly that year.

A New York taxi driver once asked me, 'So waddya do at da United Nations, lady? You a secretary or something?'

I replied coolly, 'Actually, I negotiate arms control agreements'.

The ambassador was Australia's permanent representative to the United Nations and had overall authority for looking after Australia's interests. When Australia was elected to the Security Council, the delegation staff was augmented to deal with the additional workload. The Security Council is one of the six principal organs of the United Nations. According to the United Nations Charter, it is charged with maintaining international peace and security, co-operating in solving international problems, promoting respect for human rights and to be a centre for harmonising the actions of nations. It has five permanent members (who are also the five nuclear weapons states) and ten other members, each elected for a two-year term. There is strong competition for these positions. Australia was elected for 1946–47, 1956–57, 1973–74, 1985–86 and 2013–14.

The mission is a collegial team, and full delegation meetings on Monday mornings provide a chance to maintain an overview of the work and to ensure all the angles are covered. After the formal meeting, a very social period often ensues, with exchanges of reports of the weekend's activities, restaurants discovered, theatres and shows seen, places visited, topics discussed.

Alongside the permanent missions and their staff, the United Nations Secretariat is a large and complex international bureau-cracy, with units of staff dedicated to supporting each of the six main committees, the Security Council and all the organisation's special projects. These include peace-keeping operations. It also looks after some of the UN Specialised agencies such as the United Nations Children's Emergency Fund (UNICEF), UN Women and the UN Human Rights Council. Other specialised agencies such as United Nations Development Programme (UNDP), and the World Health Organization (WHO) are primarily responsi-ble to another of the UN Charter Organisations, the Economic and Social Council. The Australian delegation staff all maintain close working relationships and sometimes friendships with Secretariat members.

The United Nations can only exercise power and authority to the extent that member states are prepared to delegate and fund the programs and activities carried out in the name of the organisation. There is competition for the positions of influence and staffing in the Secretariat. It is a highly political organisation with circumscribed power. Member states of the United Nations are all independent countries and each is cautious about allowing a multilateral organisation to encroach and exercise independent power.

In 1982 the newly elected secretary-general Javier Pérez de Cuéllar established a new group within his office to monitor world events so that he could intervene and take pre-emptive actions to head off an emerging crisis, rather than having to wait until the crisis actually happened and then crafting a suitable intervention and finding funding for it. I was flattered to be invited to join this group but I declined the invitation. If I had wanted to remain in New York for a longer period and to be seconded from DFAT to take up the job, it might have been an attractive option, but I saw my role as continuing to work directly for Australia rather than as an international public servant in a highly politicised multilateral body.

Every country in the world has a mission at the United Nations, from the smallest to the largest, each with an equal voice and vote. Our colleagues were all highly intelligent and great characters. One of the responsibilities of the First Committee delegates was to cover the Ad Hoc Committee on the Zone of Peace in the Indian Ocean, which met a few times each year, to prepare its report to the General Assembly, in the form of a resolution. At one meeting a new Pakistani delegate appeared. He was unfamiliar with the landscape. Seeing an opportunity, the Indian delegate quickly put up a new proposal that would have disadvantaged Pakistan. The Pakistani sought the floor. 'Mr Chairman, I am new to this committee and am covering for the usual Pakistani delegate, who cannot be here today. There was little time for him to brief me, but the one thing he said was, "Anything India proposes you must oppose". Mr Chairman, I don't know why I must oppose this new Indian initiative, but I must oppose it'. Everyone was very amused.

Our Pakistani colleague Riaz Mohammad Khan (not the delegate just mentioned) was single and a good friend during my time in New York. He was actually a mathematician and had worked on Pakistan's nuclear programs before becoming a diplomat. He went on to become Pakistan's foreign secretary from 2005 to 2008.

In 1982, the United Nations held its Second Special Session on Disarmament. A preparatory committee made up of delegates from interested member states was established to pave the way for the full Special Session, and met a number of times in New York in the run up to the Special Session. I was the Australian delegate in the preparatory committee. At the end of each day's session, the Indian chair Ambassador A. P. Venkateswaran (known familiarly as Venkat), would say, 'Well, gentlemen, I think that concludes our business for today. I declare the meeting closed'.

After a couple of days of this, at the end of the meeting I interrupted the chair and asked for the floor. I said, 'Mr Chair, the women delegates at these meetings are getting extremely tired: each day you close off work only for the gentlemen. So we women have been in continuous session. Could I ask that you close off the work for the whole committee?'

Ambassador Venkat replied, 'I apologise to the most beautiful, most charming lady delegate of Australia. But when I was at school, we were taught that "man" embraces "woman" unless otherwise specified'.

Quick as a flash, and for this I am quite proud, I replied, 'Sir, I am sure that your school also taught that gentlemen do not embrace ladies unless specifically invited'.

We had a good laugh and no further sexist language!

New York was then the gay capital of the world: several of the delegation members and staff were gay, and there were many holiday visits from gay colleagues posted elsewhere. Through these friends, I learned a lot and became much wiser about their world. Homosexuality had been forbidden, illegal and hidden for so long; in New York it was all out there. The Australian staff bought Ambassador Dick Woolcott a birthday cake from the Erotic Bakery, with corresponding cake decoration. He said he wasn't sure where decently to make the first cut.

The busiest time at the United Nations was the Annual General Assembly, in November and December. All the preparatory work and negotiations which had taken place during the year came to a head with the presentation by each committee of the many draft resolutions on the very wide range and number of topics on which the international community was asked to vote. The Australian delegation, like most, was augmented with additional specialist staff for this period. Two members of the federal parliament joined the mission for this period each year. In my time one of these members was appointed chief government whip by his party in Australia during his absence in New York, and I accompanied one of my gay colleagues to scour the sex shops to find a suitable whip to present to him. I had not visited a sex shop before and was amazed by the range of things available. My gay colleague was embarrassed when I asked for explanations of some of the devices. The social period after the Monday morning delegation meetings was sometimes enlivened with reports of visits to gay bars, bathhouses and sex clubs.

After a while, following the wave of euphoria and liberation, the terrible reality of HIV-AIDS dawned, and the freewheeling sexual behaviour changed. Sadly, a much loved member of our own delegation was affected, and died all too young. I attended his funeral service in Canberra; it was packed with grieving colleagues, family and friends. He was hugely popular and an excellent foreign affairs officer.

Working at the United Nations and living in New York gave me a real buzz. It really is the city which never sleeps. I had a small rooftop penthouse apartment on Park Avenue, at 39th Street, in Murray Hill, near the United Nations. I lugged bags of soil up there and, in garbage cans and planter boxes, established a rooftop garden, growing small trees, moon and other flowers, tomatoes, herbs and vegetables; runner beans raced up the water tower.

The apartment had views of both the Empire State Building and the Chrysler Building. In renting it, I insisted that blinds and curtains be installed on the windows on three sides. The real estate agent expostulated, 'Whaddya want koitins for? This is the penthouse, for God's sake. Ya think they're gunna climb up the wall and look in on ya?' I got the window treatments. The agent had shown me several other apartments with no kitchens. 'Kitchen? Kitchen? Whaddya want a kitchen for? This is New York. You're not goin' to be cookin' in – ya gunna be eatin' out!' My penthouse apartment had a nice, small kitchen, and there was plenty of cookin' in. It was the perfect place to entertain my new international friends and get to know and understand them better.

Dan, the neighbour in the other penthouse, chartered a sailing boat for summer weekends and was generous in inviting friends to sail with him on Long Island Sound. The friends provided the food and wine. This was delightful. Dan was a social worker at the men's shelter on the Bowery, a disadvantaged area in Lower Manhattan, and his wife Jewell worked in the civil human rights area. She did not like sailing. Their son Dan was a law student. They were generous neighbours and shared insights into New York with me. Jewell died, sadly, while I was living there, and after a time, Dan was using personal ads to find a new companion. Rich widows were abundant, and Dan got lots of responses. Those he brought home were paraded for my approval under the pretext of coming over to borrow some milk. None of them made the grade. People were amazed that I was friendly with my neighbours and socialised with them. Most New Yorkers were jealous of their privacy and deliberately avoided having much to do with the people they lived close to. Knowing Dan and Jewell and their family was part of the rich tapestry of my New York life.

New York is an arts wonderland. Sessions at the United Nations and follow-up and preparatory work often lasted well into the evenings, which left little time to enjoy what the city had to offer, but I crammed in as much as possible. My passions are opera, classical music and theatre, but in New York you could not ignore modern dance or wonderful musicals. A long-time New Yorker advised me at the outset to focus on a few areas of the arts. 'If you try to see everything you will end up knowing nothing in depth'. These were wise words.

My cousin Tessa Trench worked for the Australian conductor Richard Bonynge and his wife, the Australian opera singer Dame

Joan Sutherland. When Dame Joan was singing at the Metropolitan Opera in New York, Tessa arranged for me and my opera companion Joe Thwaites, who was also at the United Nations, to go backstage to meet her. Dame Joan was in a floral housecoat and slippers – a complete change from her elaborate on-stage outfit.

While we were there, an Italian tenor who had made a musical slip on stage came around to apologise. 'Scusi, donna, scusi!'

She was gracious and forgiving. 'Don't worry about it, mate. It happens to all of us sometime', she said in her wonderfully broad Australian accent. She was beautifully Australian and was interested in what we were doing at the United Nations. I spent some time with Tessa and the Bonynges again at their home at Les Hauts de Montreux, in Switzerland, when I was working at the United Nations in Geneva for a short time the following year.

New York moves fast, and we also lived fast. We Australians crammed a lot into our lives, in order to experience as much as possible. Our spare time was taken up with wonderful restaurants, museums, art galleries and clothes shopping. Women arrived from Australia with a certain casual way of dressing and poor haircuts, and within about three months they had dramatically changed their clothing and hair styles. New York was stylish, and like everyone else I soon fell into line. My long-time friend Sheri Salzberg lived in Brooklyn; she took me in hand and showed me the places to shop for stylish clothes with little money. Our favourite shop in Brooklyn carried a wide range of discounted designer fashions and had a large communal changing room. Everyone commented on the clothes others were trying on.

'Oh, take that off! That colour is terrible on you!'

'That outfit could take you everywhere!'

'Those pants make your tush look huge. No!'

'That dress makes you look terrific!'

Hairdressers were open all hours: I frequently had my hair cut and styled at 10.00 pm.

The United Nations ski club left the United Nations building late Friday afternoons in winter, and members travelled in a coach to the various ski resorts in New England for the weekend. There were also group excursions to snowfields further away, including the American Rockies and in Canada. For two winters I also joined Geoff Dixon, his wife, Dawn, and their young son, Ben, in renting a ski chalet together for alternating weekends at Killington, in Vermont. Geoff was the Australian information officer with the mission to the United Nations and the Australian Consulate in New York. He was full of fun, drive and energy. On return to Australia he was drawn into business and in due course became chief executive officer of the airline Qantas.

Winter skiing was a great joy. I awoke one Sunday morning in New York to an uncharacteristic quiet and looked out on a pristine city blanketed in deep snow, which had fallen overnight. On my cross-country skis, I skied up Park Avenue to Central Park. Mine were the first tracks in the snow. Vehicles and snow ploughs had not yet come out. It was glorious gliding quietly through the bare winter trees silhouetted against the white.

In summer, staff formed syndicates and rented houses on Fire Island, off the coast of Long Island, New York to escape the city for the steamy, hot weekends. My group included Spanish, Australian and German colleagues. Eating dinners and lunches in common was fun, but breakfast was a different matter. Each nationality wanted its own way to start the day. The Australian friends wanted full cooked breakfasts – egg, bacon and lamb chops. This totally disgusted the Spanish, who only wanted strong black coffee, while the Germans brought cold meats, cheeses and black bread. There is no United Nations on breakfast food.

In 1984, soon after Ronald Reagan's second term election, serious negotiations began between the United States and the Soviet Union to reduce the number, style and capacity of existing nuclear weapons. These talks had been strongly supported by the international community, and this was reflected in a series of resolutions adopted that year by very large majorities in the United Nations, including most of the United States' strategic allies. Australia was, of course, vitally interested in these active negotiations to reduce the stockpiles of nuclear weapons. The place where we were able to learn from the Americans about actual progress was Washington. The Australian Embassy officer there responsible for this liaison went on urgent sick leave at a crucial time, so rather than returning to Canberra directly at the conclusion of my New York posting in December 1984, I was diverted to Washington, DC, for two very cold and icy winter months, to join the Australian Embassy and pick up the reins. It was all fascinating stuff. It really seemed that a significant breakthrough to end the Cold War was imminent. But my colleague came back to work in Washington, and, reluctantly, I went back to Canberra for another complete change, to become director of Personnel Development in DFAT.

I should confess to making a mistake while at the UN. I always told my staff that while I expected them to do their best, the odd mistake was inevitable, and the important thing was to learn from the mistake and not to repeat it. Most mistakes were not terminal.

The new comprehensive nuclear test ban resolution, sponsored by Australia and New Zealand, passed through the First Committee in 1983 with no complications. There were two other draft resolutions each year on the same topic, with different emphases – one sponsored by Mexico, with the support of the neutral and non-aligned group, the other by the Soviet Union and its Allies. Both resolutions contained provisions and language which Australia could not accept, notwithstanding the support in general for nuclear disarmament. In these circumstances, Australia would abstain in the vote while, of course, voting for our own. However, unusually, when our resolution came up in the full General Assembly in 1983, the Soviet delegation asked for the floor and, before the vote was taken, denigrated our resolution, urging member states to support theirs instead. This was dirty pool! I was incensed and quickly penned some words to read out in retaliation before the Soviet resolution came to the vote. As per my instructions from DFAT, I said that we would abstain in that vote.

Voting in the United Nations General Assembly is by machine. There are three buttons on a dashboard before each member state: 'Green/Yes', 'Red/No' and 'Yellow/Abstain'. The chair of the General Assembly announces each resolution and invites delegations to vote, and they then press the appropriate button. A large electronic scoreboard records graphically how each delegation has voted. The chair asks delegations to check their votes and then announces, 'The machine is locked'. In my excitement, I had pushed the wrong button and voted 'No' on the Russian resolution, instead of abstaining. Delegations are seated alphabetically and this year we were located near the front of the General Assembly but the New Zealanders' desk was at the back of the hall. They were the main co-sponsors of our resolution but their delegate could not get to me in time to help me correct my vote. It was up there, locked and wrong! I took the floor and made an 'explanation of vote after the vote', but everyone knows that what is said after the vote is not included in the official record. So my glaring error stood, glowing red instead of yellow. I felt terrible. All my First Committee colleagues saw what had happened. What could I do? I reported, apologetically, to my ambassador, who was understanding. I then wrote up the formal report, which as a matter of routine, was sent to Canberra, gliding over my error, knowing full well that the item reports were scarcely ever read. I heard nothing from Canberra, as I had expected.

There, I thought, the matter rested. But no! In April 2008, I was invited to attend Prime Minister Kevin Rudd's 2020 Summit in Canberra, specifically for the 'critical policy area of security and prosperity, including foreign affairs and trade'. At the dinner for those invited to the Summit for their contribution to international relations I found myself sitting next to an Australian National University academic specialising in disarmament. He asked when I had been at the United Nations and brought up the aberrant Australian vote cast in the General Assembly in 1983. He gave a lengthy special explanation for that vote, saying it had been cast in the light of convoluted developments in the disarmament field at that time, which he claimed had affected Australian policy. I smiled inwardly, knowing that there was no policy reason whatsoever for the vote: it was a plain mistake on my part!

Our initial training in DFAT did not formally study negotiation, which was a key element in our professional skills. While in New York, at the United Nations I had quickly discovered that highly competent negotiation skills could be learned. All children are born negotiators, as parents soon find out, and we know the importance of negotiation in all aspects of our lives. The Harvard Negotiation Project began in 1980 and 1981 and the initial publication arising from this work, *Getting to Yes* (1981) by Ury and Fisher published by Penguin, was having a major impact in the United States. I had never had formal training in negotiation skills and had found at the United Nations that many of the other delegates were extremely competent, particularly the Russians, French and British. I wished I had had the same training as them.

Happily, I was able to do something about it. In Canberra I became director of Personnel Development and could introduce formal negotiation skills training for all staff in DFAT. The existing courses on offer in Australia were all focussed on the commercial business environment, and none was suitable for the skills needed for international diplomacy. So, I consulted widely within the department, researching in detail significant international negotiation exercises in which senior staff had been involved. Our consultant Bill Nicholls and I worked together closely to design and pilot a course specially tailored to the needs of the Australian foreign service. International negotiation skills training remains an element of the foreign service program for new recruits.

8

Bangladesh, 1986–89:
floods, golf and aid

High commissioner in Bangladesh, floods, development cooperation and leadership challenges, golf diplomacy and gold smugglers

Bangladesh has a strong oral arts tradition, including Bengali group poetry sessions, where each in turn continues where the previous poet left off. The Bengali language has one particularly well-known writer, in the Nobel Prize winner Rabindranath Tagore. Bengalis love telling jokes and stories, often involving animals. Their language is important to them, a political statement, an innate part of the culture and a distinctive language in a subcontinent of many languages. 'Bangladesh' is sometimes translated as 'the country of the Bengali language'.

I was posted in Bangladesh as the Australian high commissioner from 1986 to 1989, a challenging but satisfying and enjoyable couple of years. The main business of the Australian High Commission in Bangladesh was development cooperation. It was a small mission, with a staff of thirteen, posted from DFAT in Canberra, including specialist AusAID staff. Our sizeable aid program included health, education and agricultural development. It was a great post to see aid programs in action and develop a real body of knowledge and understanding. This stood me in good stead in later postings and in my post-retirement work with non-government development organisations in the Pacific and in Australia's remote northwest.

Not all of Australia's aid projects were successful. One project provided wells to villages, so that women did not spend hours each day carrying water from the nearest river and family health and hygiene would improve. The project provided a small business opportunity to an operator of a truck equipped with an auger, used to drill the wells. But the operator of the equipment found more profitable uses for the truck, and the well project was not rolled out as quickly or as widely as originally planned. Also, there had been poor research on the social impact of the wells. They were drilled on the land of the most important family in each village, and this strengthened the family's power, at the cost of the already poorer village families. And to crown it all, the wells brought up water from a water table contaminated with arsenic, the presence of which had been hitherto unknown.

The content and shape of the Australian Development Country Program were decided by the Australian Government in close partnership with the Bangladeshi Government, which was responsible for deciding what its country needed and how partner countries might best work with it, taking into account their particular skills and capacities. Bangladesh's plans and policies for economic and social development were reviewed each year at a World Bank international meeting in Paris.

Australia's international aid agency AusAID led the delegation from Canberra to this meeting, and I was always included. The annual Paris meeting reviewed Bangladesh's development plans and needs and was the coordination mechanism for the many international donor countries and agencies that wanted to help Bangladesh to meet its current immediate needs for support for the poor at the same time as helping it to build a better social and economic infrastructure for the society's long-term needs.

Bangladesh is one of the most densely populated countries in the world, extremely poor, with very low per capita income. The country is physically very beautiful. It is mostly agricultural, with fabulous shades of green from vegetable crops and flowers, the predominant rice paddy fields, jute plantations and tea 'gardens' that covered the hilly province of Sylhet. The villages are built of locally procured materials; the houses have thatched roofs, and some more permanent structures are built of locally fired clay bricks and corrugated iron. At the time I was there, village life was simple and villagers worked hard. Schools and health posts were thinly spread. Not every village had a well, and in many cases the women spent hours each day carrying water from the nearest river in clay pots balanced on their heads. The many boats on the rivers were made of wood, with large sails. The country was originally part of Pakistan when India was divided on religious grounds in 1947, at independence. Bangladesh emerged as an independent nation in 1971, breaking away from Pakistan in the Bangladesh Liberation War. Islam is the predominant religion. There are also sizable Christian, Hindu and Buddhist communities, each with their own places of worship. Rural Bangladesh was very pleasing to the eye, though for most Bangladeshis it was a hard place in which to live.

The country's wealth remains agricultural: rice, jute, tea and, formerly, fine muslin. It is a deltaic country, formed by centuries of silt laid down by the rivers and floods, and has very little natural hard stone. Bricks were baked and then broken by armies of women accompanied by their small children, working on the roads with hammers. Health workers promoting birth control and community health found it best to reach the women while they were at this arduous work.

There are only a few historical buildings in Bangladesh, since low-temperature-fired bricks decay and crumble easily in the humid climate. The country has 700 rivers, part of the Padma (Ganges), Brahmaputna, Jamuna and Meghna river systems, all flowing down from the Himalayas through Bangladesh into the Bay of Bengal.

It is a crowded country, and growing, and there is great competition for land and other resources. One story I heard, which seems to reveal something of Bangladesh, tells of a farmer tilling his field when the plough hits and breaks open an old terracotta jar. Out springs a genie, who has been imprisoned for thousands of years. In gratitude, he offers the farmer one wish but warns that whatever the farmer wishes for himself, the genie will give twice as much to his neighbour. So, the farmer thinks long and hard. Wish for a bumper harvest? But no, the neighbour will get twice as much. A good marriage for his daughter? But then his neighbour's daughter will get an even better marriage. Eventually he says to the genie, 'Blind me in one eye'. I tried in each country of my postings to find what the local jokes were. They tell you a lot about the culture. Folk tales are also helpful, even in translation.

I learned early in my career to ask questions and not assume that different was inferior. At the first reception at the High Commissioner's Residence soon after I arrived in Dhaka, the capital, I was puzzled. I had discussed the arrangements with the staff, but as each guest arrived, they were asked individually what they would like to drink, and each drink was prepared and presented separately. This took time. I thought that guests would be offered a tray of varied drinks on arrival. I asked one of my new Bangladeshi friends about this. He explained that there was a hierarchy in the community of the domestic staff of diplomats, and the Australian high commissioner's staff ranked highly. They drew their ranking from me. As high commissioner, I was expected to have the ingredients of any drink my guests could desire. By offering a few specified drinks I would lose face, as it indicated that I only had a limited range. My reputation would be damaged, along with that of my staff. They were protecting me as well as themselves.

In 1974 Bangladesh established Petrobangla as the national mineral resources company and, in partnership with international players, in the 1980s it had discovered oil and gas, both onshore and in the Bay of Bengal, and this was beginning to provide income for the government and the small private business sector. However, each of these economic activities provided opportunities for corruption, which was a pervasive and growing concern, right along every supply chain. It was easier to cream money off the aid programs, through legitimate and corrupt means, than to really create entrepreneurial activities to grow wealth. Growing personal wealth by those in a position to do so predominated rather than government capacity to really respond to the needs of the community.

Bangladesh did not present a perfect picture by any means, and working there brought emotional as well as professional challenges. The status of women was paradoxical. In the villages, women and men both worked hard physically, the women bearing and bringing up the children, keeping house, gathering and preparing food and, often, water, and looking after the animals. In the 1980s the growing garment industry provided employment in Bangladesh's cities, which affected the status of women so employed. Educated, upper-class women were frequently employed outside the home. Two of Bangladesh's prime ministers have been women. Bangladesh being a Muslim society has had a profound impact on the status of women. In 1987 I was deeply depressed by the murder of a young lawyer who worked for a local non-government organisation which sought to educate women on their rights under the Koran, including marital rights. The ideas she was giving the village wives infuriated their husbands, a group of whom killed her. This was shocking.

On the ground, we enjoyed a great range of experiences. Australia was a large supporter of the World Food Program in the country. Australia's contribution was in wheat, of which we grow a surplus. Bangladeshis prefer to eat rice, so the World Food Program would monetise the donation: they would sell the wheat and buy rice. In addition, the aid program supported the creation of bakeries, so the donated wheat could be turned into bread, which was a desirable food, and also generated employment and small business development.

A large project was the Save the Children's mother and child health program, which had its own specialist hospital focussing on the needs of children. It was headed by Dr Sultana Khanum, who developed a significant career in the World Health Organization.

Australia was a long-term supporter of the International Centre for Diarrhoeal Disease Research in Bangladesh. This conducted key research into cholera and also maintained a longstanding vertical population research survey: they collected information on the life and medical history of the population of a specified area, over the years. Many of the researchers were international doctors on whom the high commission could call in case of emergency. There were no private health providers in Dhaka. The health clinic at the Australian high commission was staffed by a remarkable, experienced and multi-talented nurse practitioner, Carmel Sullivan. It was established to look after the Australian High Commission staff, but was made open to the whole diplomatic community.

During my posting about ten diplomats, including me, suddenly developed odd symptoms – large, inflamed bumps which appeared on random parts of the body and then subsided, only to reappear somewhere else. They were accompanied by flu-like respiratory symptoms. Carmel thought that the sudden appearance of ten patients with the same symptoms was odd, and her research revealed that all ten had been guests at a dinner held by one of the Australian High Commission staff, at which raw fish had been served, cured in the Pacific islands way, with lime juice and coconut milk. She discovered that the fish was a Bangladeshi river fish which was infested with a parasite, *Gnathostoma*. Humans are not normally part of its life cycle, and so the parasite tried to eat its way out through the soft tissue in our bodies. Each attempt at escape produced the lump-like inflammation. Two of the guests and the host, who had eaten a lot of the fish, became very sick and were sent to the hospital in Bangkok. One British diplomat was medevaced to the London School of Hygiene and Tropical Medicine. Carmel collaborated with the researchers at the International Centre for Diarrhoeal Disease Research in Bangladesh to unravel this mystery, which the team wrote up for a medical journal. They asked if they could photograph my bumps to illustrate the journal article, which is why photographs of my left breast and right buttock accompany a widely circulated medical journal article on a rare case of gnathostomiasis!

My personal little parasites must have found some way out, as the bumps and other symptoms subsided. We were lucky. There have been cases of blindness caused by these parasites. A lack of sophisticated medical facilities is one of the hazards of a diplomat's international life, and we were fortunate on this occasion to have medical researchers to help us. We all survived.

I travelled widely in Bangladesh, checking on the various Australian aid projects, in the high commission's trusty 4WD vehicle with our magnificent driver, Durbar. Durbar came from the brave and warlike Gurkha people of Nepal who had been recruited since 1857 in large numbers for service in the British and Indian armies. Durbar had driven tanks in the British army in India, and nothing fazed him. Because the courses of all the rivers and streams frequently changed after each flood season, there were few decent roads or permanent bridges in Bangladesh, so visiting more remote areas or making field visits to aid projects presented challenges. On some visits, Durbar crossed rivers by driving our 4WD onto makeshift pontoons of boards strapped over a couple of small boats. I always stayed safely on land until the vehicle had driven off the pontoon, but my heart was in my mouth each time. Sometimes, we got bogged and had to seek help. On one occasion, the men travelling with me got out of the vehicle and tried to dig it out. Being a no-nonsense, egalitarian, practical sort of woman, I was about to get out and help too, but the men firmly resisted, saying they would all lose face if they let me join in the work.

After one particularly bumpy journey early in my posting, I developed bad chest pains and saw a doctor, worried I might be headed for a heart attack. He reassured me that the pains were muscular – I have good-sized breasts and needed a better support bra! My mother sent some over in the diplomatic bag, the fortnightly despatch of material from DFAT to the high commission. This was a challenge probably not faced by my male diplomatic colleagues, who at the time made up all bar four of our head of mission posts globally.

Gillian Mellsop, the high commission's splendid aid officer, and I once visited St Martin's Island, in the Bay of Bengal, where a new Red Cross monsoon shelter and food store had been built with Australian funding. The government boat picked us up at high tide at the Government Rest House on the coast, but by the time we returned, in the late afternoon, it was low tide, and there was a kilometre of mudflat to be crossed. The men jumped overboard and, tucking up their trousers and lungis, waded up to their knees in mud to the shore. They ordered Gillian and me to wait for a while, and they returned pushing a rowing boat over the mud. We were then ceremoniously and cleanly handed into the boat, which was pushed back, sleigh-like, over the mud to the grassy shore. Gillian is a very stylish and caring woman, with attitude. She always wore silk garments and high-heeled shoes. My preferred style was a cotton *salwar kameez* and flat shoes. Of the pair of us, Gillian was often taken to be the high commissioner. One of my Bangladeshi women friends told me I should wear more make-up and jewellery, and more ostentatious clothes, so I would *look* like a high commissioner. I retorted that I *was* a high commissioner! I was quite capable of dressing up and looking the part on appropriate occasions. But maybe they were right. What you wear does send signals.

Gillian and I had a great personal as well as professional relationship and visited most of the Australian aid projects together, many of them in remote parts of the country. The only way to visit one community development project in the north was to go as pillion passengers on motorbikes – an unconventional way for a high commissioner to travel. There were sometimes government rest houses where we could stay, but the accommodation was rudimentary. It was usually better to stay with the project managers in their accommodation, and this made it easier to get to know them and find out about the project, as well as demonstrating a real interest in what they were doing.

We ate local food – excellent curries – and carried supplies with us, always including green coconuts, which provided sterile drinking water. Our hosts preferred to eat with their hands, but I never found this easy and generally carried a fork and spoon in my handbag, as well as a small, wet towel in a plastic bag. Also in my bag were two more plastic bags, for when I had to use the toilet. The local people cleaned themselves with water, but it was easier for me to use toilet paper. However, you could not leave the dirty paper behind – that would have been very bad behaviour. So, into one of my plastic bags it went, until I could dispose of it discreetly in a fire. Finding toilets along the way was difficult. There were few petrol stations. We identified government schools and guesthouses in advance of any trip. It was very hard to go behind a bush, because there were few bushes along the way, and Bangladesh was a crowded country. Everywhere we turned there were people within our field of vision. And we were within theirs! A parked Land Cruiser with a white woman trying to squat discreetly nearby was an obvious source of curiosity. There were times when Gillian and I had to hold up fabric shawls or blanket screens for each other.

In 1988, the Australian television program *60 Minutes* made an episode on women heads of mission and I took up their invitation to travel to Kathmandu, in Nepal, and join our ambassador there, Diane Johnstone to appear in the program. We were two of only four women Australian heads of mission at that time. At the end of the filming, the interviewer asked me, 'Is there anything a male ambassador can do that a woman ambassador can't?'

I replied, 'Yes: pee standing up'.

They didn't use that in the program. What a pity.

People often ask whether I found it difficult being a woman in the predominantly Muslim country of Bangladesh. There were many times when it was actually advantageous. The two political leaders of the opposition parties at that time were women. They welcomed me wholeheartedly. Sheik Hasina, who led the Awami League, was the daughter of the first prime minister of Bangladesh,

Sheik Mujibur Rahman, a national hero and the founder of Bangladesh. He had been assassinated on 15 August 1975, along with Sheik Hasina's brothers and sisters, as part of a coup. Rather than focussing on governing and developing Bangladesh, she seemed preoccupied with preserving her father's memory and gaining revenge on his murderers. The second opposition party, the Bangladesh Nationalist Party, was led by Begum Khaleda Zia, the widow of Bangladesh's president Ziaur Rahman, who had also been assassinated, in 1981. She was also preoccupied with seeking justice for the killers of her husband. Neither woman nor their parties seemed at that time to have concrete plans for how to govern the country in the interests of its people. Since my time, both women have actually won elections and have served as prime minister in Bangladesh for considerable periods of time.

In 1986 I presented my credentials as Australian high commissioner to President Hussain Mohammad Ershad, who was a former officer in the Pakistani military forces of the united Pakistan, before the partition of the country in the civil war of 1971. He became president of Bangladesh in 1983. He knew that my grandfather had been commandant of the military staff college in Quetta, where most of the leaders of Bangladesh had trained. He said that I should regard myself as a 'daughter of the regiment' and that the Bangladeshi leadership would be very happy to support me during my posting.

Soon after I arrived, I learned that from the president down, almost all the top leadership of the country played golf, as did most of my fellow ambassadors, and I was advised that most high-level decisions were made on the golf course. I was not then a golfer, though I was in general a good sportswoman and ready to learn. The Australian community was keen to help me and a visiting businessman brought from Australia all the equipment I needed: golf clubs, bag, shoes, gloves and balls. Kurmitola Golf Club was first class and beautifully maintained, within the Dhaka military cantonment. But there was no golf pro or pro shop, so everyone had to import their own equipment.

The caddy master selected a caddy to teach me the game. Hassan became my permanent caddy, and my coach, and was paid A$100 a month, with a tip after each game and a bigger tip if we won – good pay in the local economy. I learned the game quickly and was soon proficient enough to be invited to play with local Bangladeshi members, other ambassadors and business leaders. Most of my golf companions were men. They bought their equipment on visits outside the country, in Thailand or in western countries. The few women golfers were mostly expatriates. President Ershad was also president of the golf club; the home minister, General Mahmudal Hassan, was vice-president; the chief of the naval staff, Rear Admiral Sultan Ahmed was the club captain, and so on. After a short while, they made me the ladies' captain.

I made a lot of friends and excellent contacts through the golf club and was able to encourage a few local women to take up the game, with the support of their husbands. Some tried to play in saris, but the *salwar kameez* was more practical. Office hours in Dhaka were 7.00 am to 1.00 pm. So, after lunch and a short nap, it was generally off to the golf club with my sparkling clean shoes and clubs, where Hassan would be waiting. The course was a green and peaceful oasis, away from the overcrowding and clamour and traffic of the rest of Dhaka. It was flat, with mango trees and palms. There were few sand bunkers; strategically located water ponds – known as 'tanks' – were the main hazards. Each was attended by a tank boy, whose job was to dive down and retrieve any balls which ended up in the water. The trouble was that there was a fixed fee to be paid on retrieval, but the tank boy would get twice as much by selling the ball to the club. I always left my caddy to negotiate with the tank boy, and there was no tip for Hassan at the end of the round if the balls had not all come back.

Corruption was rife in Bangladesh, and at one stage the president decreed that the golf club subscriptions for foreign golfers should be increased by an unreasonable amount. This was allegedly to cover the increased costs of maintaining the course. The foreign community resisted and, as a body, agreed not to pay subscriptions until this demand was reversed. After a month or so, I received a phone call from General Hassan, the vice-captain. 'High commissioner, we have a problem. Members are not paying their subscriptions and golf club is running out of money. What to do?'

I suggested that the club committee should be convened and the accounts presented, after which the committee could decide what should be done.

'High commissioner, madam! President is president of golf club and president of Bangladesh. Bangladesh is not a democratic country and golf club is not a democratic institution! What to do?'

The conversation ended with me promising to discuss the matter with the other ambassadors. The American ambassador had a private chat with General Hassan, and they came up with a face-saving compromise involving new categories of membership. So, golf went on.

Cheating in competitions was not unknown, so they made the caddies wear canvas shoes during tournaments so agile bare toes could not surreptitiously move badly placed balls to a better lie! One of the more audaciously corrupt senior government golfers was nicknamed the Thief of Baghdad, and this seemed in no way to shame him.

To celebrate the Australian bicentenary, in 1988 the high commission held a special golf tournament, which the president opened. A young Australian pro golfer from Perth, Andrew Wynne ('Wynne Every Time!') came to help us. Qantas covered his fare, the ANZ bank lent him a company house, the golf club provided his meals, and he kept all the money he received for coaching and lessons. We had no resident pro, and Andrew was in great demand, including from the president. He was also surrounded at every lesson by the caddies, eager to learn from him. Two golfers from Shenzhen in Southern China came especially to play in the bicentenary tournament. The Special Economic Zone of Shenzhen was in the process of designing its first golf course, and the visitors recruited Andrew to go and advise them. The king of Bhutan's brother and several members of the Bhutanese nobility also came to play and went home singing the praises of Australia. Australian companies working in Bangladesh donated the prizes, including clothing and cans of powdered milk. During my leave in Australia before the tournament I bought Australian bicentenary merchandise, including a special house brick bearing the bicentenary logo. This became the booby prize, carried off by a Danish golfer, who later incorporated it into the brickwork of his home in Copenhagen. So, the influence of the golf day spread far and wide.

One of the better golfers, Kaiser Rasheed, was a retired Bangladeshi diplomat who had served in Australia, and he and his wife, Kurshid, and their family went out of their way to help me settle in and enjoy the posting. They were from a large and prominent family from the hilly province of Sylhet, the tea-growing area of Bangladesh. They invited me to visit the region, to join a duck-shooting party, and, with some of the other guests, I stayed in one of the tea garden guesthouses belonging to their family. These were splendid colonial-style houses with wide, shady verandas and colourful flower gardens. Kurshid could not join us and remained in Dhaka with their young son. Well! The British ambassador's wife Molly, who had not been with us in Sylhet, was a waspish woman who never passed up an opportunity to score a point against Australia. She started putting it around in Dhaka that I was having an affair with Kaiser Rasheed! I told him this, and he agreed that this poisonous behaviour was potentially damaging, to both of us, and needed to be arrested. So, the next time we were both in the golf clubhouse, sharing a post-match lime juice with President Ershad and other leaders, I asked, 'Have you all met Kaiser Rasheed, my lover?' There was an immediate shocked silence. So I said, 'Well, that's what Molly, the British High Commissioner's wife, is putting around. As she's the High Commissioner's wife, she must be right, eh?' They all got the point, I spoke directly to Molly, and there was no more scandalous gossip.

As a woman, I actually had wider access across society in Bangladesh than the male ambassadors. There was a lot of hospitality offered, at all levels of society, but it was not customary for wives to be present when non-family males visited Bangladeshi homes. When the visitor was a female ambassador, however, the women of the family were also welcomed in.

The cool dry season was the time for many weddings, which were expensive events for both families. There were generous amounts of food and drinks, served in two separate, highly decorated marquees, called *shamianas* – one for the men, the other for the women. The women were all brilliantly clad in brightly coloured, new saris, with all their jewellery on display. My male ambassador colleagues could only, of course, enter the men's marquee. I, on the other hand, was welcome in both tents: Australia was a major donor to Bangladesh, and everyone wanted to be in the company of the captain of that cargo vessel! And she was fun as well. My gender was irrelevant and, uniquely, everyone accepted my free access.

Most of my professional contacts were with male political and business leaders, but behind the scenes, women influenced many decisions. I had access to many women of influence, from the president's wife down. In 1987 the journalist Shireen Rahman founded the first women's magazine in Bangladesh, *Jogajog Barta*, and asked me to join the advisory board. She brought together eight educated, intelligent and gifted women, including Shahnaz, the wife of Riaz Khokhar, the Pakistani high commissioner, a woman member of parliament, the founder of an influential non-government aid organisation and the wife of one of the government ministers. These women became my eyes into Bangladesh society, and we shared stories and learned about each other's challenges and lives, including domestic violence and navigating individual freedoms, as we came around the board table and worked on the magazine together.

The woman member of parliament invited me to accompany her on a visit to her coastal constituency. I shared her bedroom in each place we visited, so I was able to see, close up, how saris were secured and worn. (Despite being urged by many, I never wore a sari. That was the dress of the subcontinent, not of senior Australian officials. People expected me to look Australian. Besides, western women who know how to move elegantly in saris are very rare – most look awkward. And you need special jewellery.)

The MP had, of course, an ulterior motive for asking me to go with her. She took me to visit a school founded by her father, which needed funds for new classrooms. The amount asked for seemed modest and well within the limits of our head of mission discretionary aid fund. But my mental arithmetic had never been good, and in translating the crores of Bangladeshi taka I was out by a factor of ten. All those noughts!

To be effective in Bangladesh it was especially important to understand the women and their roles. Women are fundamentally the most important members of most societies. They are the carriers of the culture, the force for civilised behaviour, the guardians of the common good and the fiercest defenders of family welfare. Development programs which work through and empower women are the most effective. Employment is a key issue. Garment manufacturing was just beginning in Bangladesh when I was there, using cheap labour but also providing valuable income. Women working in the garment industry were also having fewer babies. With no maternity leave provisions, maternity affected a family's income. As significant breadwinners, women now had greater power within the family and the persuasive capacity to enforce family planning.

Professor Rokeya Rahman Kabeer, a well-known social researcher in Bangladesh, introduced me to the rural women's development organisation Saptagram Nari Swanirvar Parishad (Seven Villages Women's Self Reliance Movement) which she had founded in 1976. The name Saptagram means 'seven villages' in Bengali. Rokeya's philosophy was that very poor women can better their lives by joining forces. Since its foundation, the organisation has grown exponentially, in 2019 covering 900 villages and reaching 22,000 targeted members.[8] Rokeya invited me to a village some way from Dhaka where Saptagram had started a project ten years previously. The village women had no cash, but each agreed to contribute one handful of rice per month from the meagre family food store. When they had pooled a kilogram of rice, they sent one of their husbands to sell it for them in the local market. (Custom did not permit the women to go to the market themselves.) With the money they bought chicks. As the chickens grew and multiplied, the families were provided with eggs – important protein supplies. And on special occasions, like the major Muslim festival of Eid-ul-Fitr, at the end of the fasting month of Ramadan, they could eat the meat of some of the hens. They sold the surplus eggs and chickens in the market. With this money, they bought a few goats, and so the chain of growth continued. The health of the village improved, the women grew in self-confidence, and, ten years down the track, I had been invited to open a small garment factory they had built. This not only would supply the village but would also produce garments for the wider market. All from just a few handfuls of rice.

The Bangladeshi banker Muhammad Yunus was at the time I was in Bangladesh promulgating his ideas for microfinance, finding that groups of village women banding together to win and service loans for community projects were highly successful and having a real impact on local development: female empowerment, lower infant mortality rates, better community health and higher rates of school attendance. His influence was spreading. He founded the Grameen Bank, and in 2006 both he and the bank won the Nobel Peace Prize. He was a personal inspiration.

Following some pre-departure language lessons in Canberra I had enough Bengali for simple conversations – I could ask basic questions but could not understand the answers fully. But it helped, and the women were welcoming. One woman seated next to me on a mat on the ground in one remote village I visited said that this was the first time she had met a white person. Early in my posting, I had been greatly embarrassed when a poor village I visited put on a veritable feast for me. I knew how poor they were and really did not know how to handle the situation. But a wise

Bangladeshi friend advised me to accept the hospitality, which was offered with pride. They told me to just eat a little and express appreciation, and to know that as soon as I had left there would be many hungry mouths fed as a result of my visit.

Bangladesh is prone to floods, as the Himalayan snow melts and overflows the delta's rivers. The floods replenish the soil but are a great inconvenience and danger to the people, who have to crowd onto the small areas of higher ground – like the river dykes – with their animals and a few key possessions. The flood of 1986 was particularly high and long lasting and was combined with a large tsunami, which lifted naval vessels from the port of Chittagong and deposited them several kilometres inland. The high commissioner's residence was sandbagged, but the garden was flooded, and small wooden boats from the country had crowded into the city. Early each day the domestic staff would tuck up their lunghis and wade out to hire a country boat to carry me to work. The boat would be cleaned and I would be handed in, wearing my yellow gumboots and carrying my briefcase, and escorted through the floodwaters to the nearest high ground, where our driver, Durbar, would be waiting to take me to work. President Ershad invited me to accompany him in his helicopter to visit the flood-affected areas and victims and see the needs for myself. There was, of course, full media coverage, including pictures of me in my yellow gumboots. People noted with appreciation that the Australian high commissioner was on the job.

The golf course was under water, the fish had swum free from the tanks, and for a month there was no golf for the caddies. One or two tees were on raised mounds, as were a few greens. So to cheer everyone up, and provide some income for the caddies, some of the golfers mounted a mini-tournament, with all shots being played from boats, which the caddies held steady. The caddies also dived down into the floodwaters to retrieve the balls, while the boats were paddled to the correct spots for the next strokes. Tees to hold the balls were forced into knotholes in the boats' planks. It was a lot of fun, and friends made a little video of the events.

On the more serious side, a community of nuns from the Catholic Marist order, including two Australians, ran a small hospital some way out of Dhaka. They were flooded out. The patients were accommodated in boats tied to trees around the hospital, and their medical drips were also suspended from the trees. The nuns slept on the flat roof of the hospital under tarpaulins. In the maternity ward, the delivery bed was raised on bricks, clear of the floodwater. One emergency maternity case arrived from a distant village by boat. When they got the patient up onto the bed, a snake emerged from her clothes: all the animals were also looking for dry, safe ground. The nuns tucked up their saris and painted their legs with gentian violet, to protect against fungal infection as they worked in the floodwater. An Australian television news team was in Dhaka to cover the floods and was persuaded to fund the donation of a larger boat chartered to carry medical and emergency food supplies for the sisters and their hospital. It all made great television back in Australia, especially Sister Jenny Clarke standing up in a small boat and shouting in Bengali to a crowd which had gathered in a flotilla that these were only medical supplies – not food flood relief.

I invited Sister Jenny to stay at the residence for a few days' rest after the flood crisis, and just before she left I asked whether there was anything we could give her to take back. She responded that she had already had the greatest gifts from us: a dry, comfortable bed, hot water, airconditioning and peace and quiet. The nuns in their hospital had none of that. And they also put up with harassment from increasingly militant Muslim neighbours, including deliberately loud calls to prayer and long readings from the Koran over loudspeakers, day and night.

Working in a country like Bangladesh built especially strong relationships between members of the high commission staff, many of whom were extremely competent women. Whenever I made visits out of town, I took some of the support staff with me, as well as the diplomatic members. It was good for everyone to see at first hand what Australia was doing in Bangladesh; and, culturally, our hosts appreciated a larger delegation. There were some very funny times. I visited an Australian volunteer who was introducing farming studies into a school on a mission station a little way from Dhaka. The high commission party arrived about midday after a long and uncomfortable ride. We went along the footpath to the school via the church. The path was lined with schoolchildren throwing rose petals. The procession was led by the priest, the volunteer and me. The third secretary, Pat Duggan, and the head of mission secretary, Ros Jackson, walked behind, as the rose petals fell. I was already finding the situation amusing when Pat, in a loud whisper, said, 'I don't know about you, Ros, but I feel like a bloody bridesmaid'. It was hard to stay serious.

The group of us who served together, which we called the 'Dhaka mafia', has held strong, with frequent reunions both in Australia and in countries of our subsequent postings, including China and Fiji. The predominance of competent women in the high commission was remarkable, and this presented me with some difficult management and leadership challenges. The men called the corridor outside my office Petticoat Lane.

This was my first head of mission job, and there was a lot to learn. Margaret Johnson, who had served with me in Berlin and was widely experienced in DFAT, warned before I took up my new post: 'At all your previous postings, Sue, you have been in the thick of it all and knew everything that was going on. Now you are the ambassador, you'll be the last to know. People won't want to bother you, and they will try and keep things from you'. This proved to be true.

One of the lessons I learned is that if you have an incompetent, difficult and disruptive member of staff and all efforts to remedy this fail, it is better to move the misfit on. As Jim Collins, the management and leadership guru, emphasises in his influential book for leaders *Good to Great*, you need to have the right people on the bus and in the right seats.[9] One particular staff member was racist, legalistic and not a team player. He came to physical blows with another Australian staff member in front of the local staff.

The crisis came to a head shortly afterwards while he was taking part in the Hash House Harriers run with other expatriates and some Bangladeshis. The HHH was an informal running club, made up largely of expatriates, which was established in several Asian capitals. The club in Dhaka had both men and women members, who would run through parts of the city, clad in skimpy jogging shorts and singlets. I had already warned that I thought these activities were culturally insensitive in Dhaka. The Australian staff member had made some particularly critical remarks about the country while on the run, which exceeded acceptable limits and provoked a group of the Bangladeshi runners to beat him up badly. This could have been the trigger to get him removed from the post, but I did not use it. I should have done so. But I felt sorry for him and for his wife and children. I consulted the other staff about what I should do, and reactions were mixed. But in the end I should have followed my own judgement. He remained difficult, litigious and disruptive, and difficult to manage.

The process to get staff recalled from a post is laborious, difficult and time-consuming to the leader and results in a disproportionate amount of time devoted to the less competent staff member at the expense of the more productive members of the team. At an overseas post, compared with Canberra, and particularly at a hardship post, everyone is part of each other's lives, personal as well as official, and the leader is responsible for them all.

In a post like Dhaka, the staff were also extraordinarily close to members of the wider Australian community, a situation encouraged by the decision to share the high commission social club's swimming pool, tennis courts and clubhouse with other Australians and their families working in Bangladesh. Each expatriate community had its own club – the Canadian club, British club, French club and American club, as well as the Scandinavian embassies' club – and these were refuges and centres of expatriate social life. While I was there, a few members of the Australian community were going through the complex process of inter-country adoption, and the club swimming pool was a haven for them and their children.

At that time, there were just two good hotels and only one safe, decent restaurant in Dhaka. Most entertaining was done at home, where the staff were well trained in hygienic food preparation. Nepal was a short flight away and offered a cooler climate, fascinating historical cultural offerings and fabulous shopping opportunities. But staff often came back to Dhaka with gastro-intestinal infections after eating in the attractive local restaurants there.

Naive Australian travellers sometimes do silly things and end up needing consular assistance from the local embassy. In 1986, three very young Australian men were among a group of foreigners who ended up in Dhaka gaol after attempting to smuggle gold from Thailand to Bangladesh by air – they had met someone in a Bangkok bar who had paid them several thousand dollars each and convinced them that the scheme would be risk free and profitable. Unfortunately, Bangladesh had just tightened up its border controls, and all three had been caught and sentenced to twenty years' detention. Of course, the Australian consul in the high commission was involved and ensured that the young men received good legal advice and representation and were not treated badly in gaol. But Dhaka gaol was no paradise. Their case received wide attention in the Australian media, and the father of one came to stay in Dhaka to try to help his son. Our minister decided that, because of the media interest, rather than leaving the case purely in the hands of our consul, the high commissioner should go and visit the young men in the gaol. So I did, with interesting consequences. One of the men had found god and was convinced that his divine purpose was to spend his life in gaol, preaching and seeking to convert the other prisoners, most of whom were Muslims. He did not want to have his sentence reduced or to be released. I was the first woman the prisoners had seen since their incarceration, and another of the Australian prisoners fell desperately in lust with me. I was bombarded with increasingly graphic pornographic letters from him. I got our consul to speak to him with understanding and to arrest the flow. The third prisoner was a sweet young man and just grateful for anything the high commission could do for him. It was agreed that the consul should be the only high commission officer to continue to visit the gaol.

After two years, the British were able to procure a pardon and early release for two of their gold smugglers. Heartened by this, I approached the home minister General Hassan on the golf course to discuss what might be done for the Australian prisoners. He invited me to his office to discuss the matter, and there I met his architect and was shown the plans for a small hospital in his home village. He suggested Australia might assist through its aid program by funding the construction of one ward. This was a reasonable proposition which fitted within our development policy guidelines, and so our foolish young gold smugglers were freed and sent home.

The foreign ministry frequently invited the diplomatic corps to the airport to meet visiting VIPs. Pope John Paul II visited Bangladesh in 1986 (see picture insert figure 14) and the high commissioner's cook, James, who was a Catholic, was asked by the papal nuncio – the Vatican's ambassador – to join his staff for the visit and prepare food for the pontiff. He felt very honoured, and I was happy to let him go for the duration of the visit.

Mother Teresa came from Calcutta to join the Pope in Dhaka. Mother Teresa produced in me the very strong feeling that I was in the presence of someone extraordinary. I felt the same when meeting Sir Edmund Hillary, New Zealand's high commissioner resident in New Delhi. He made regular visits to Dhaka, and I always invited him and his partner to dinner. Although he was immensely modest, he had an indisputable charisma. This was the first man to climb Mount Everest, and he had dedicated his life thereafter to work for a better life for Nepalese Sherpas, the people who live around Everest and derive their living – and often their deaths and injuries – from supporting foreign mountaineers determined to tackle the great mountain. The New Zealanders did well to appoint him their first high commissioner to India, Nepal and Bangladesh. In the foreign service, you meet a lot of famous people and high achievers in their fields. A few really stand out and make an impact.

Mike Lightowler, a DFAT deputy secretary was a welcome visitor when he paid a useful visit during my posting in 1987, reviewing the high commission's performance – which passed muster. The immigration program was the major challenge, managed by the consul. He was overburdened and under-resourced, and there was an unmanageable backlog and unrelenting flow of immigration applications. The local press would carry a story that Australia was taking more migrants, and the high commission gates would immediately be thronged by hundreds of would-be applicants. The consul tried putting up a notice denying any change to the migration regime, but that was pulled down. So he printed off hundreds of individual handbills and gave them to our security guard to give out. But then he discovered that the security guard was selling them! The Department of Immigration eventually designed a workable system, and the flow was brought under control. The problem was that most applicants from Bangladesh did not have the skills Australia was seeking. Australia was obviously an attractive migration destination for educated Bangladeshis, and when a Bangladeshi cricket team played an international match in Australia, half of the Bangladeshi supporters' group who were granted visitor visas disappeared into the community on arrival and became illegal immigrants. Apart from the DFAT official's performance review trip, however, there was not exactly a constant flow of official Australian visitors to Dhaka. The foreign minister and other Australian ministers had no reason ever to visit the post, and Dhaka was hardly on parliamentarians' must visit list. The National Party backbencher Tim Fischer was the only parliamentarian who made the journey while I was there. He came over in December 1987 and joined the high commission party for the New Year's Eve celebration at the Sheraton Hotel.

Tim was a railway fanatic as well as a war veteran, and he planned to travel to Chittagong by train to visit the Common-wealth War Graves cemetery. The trains in Bangladesh were dirty, overcrowded, unreliable and unsafe, and nobody of any standing used them. In making conversation with members of the Bangladesh parliament, Tim was astonished to find that none of them was interested in Bangladesh's trains or had travelled on them. The foreign ministry refused to sanction Tim's rail travel plans, on the basis of security. So, the faithful Durbar drove us to Chittagong together. There are a large number of Australians buried in the cemetery, victims of the Burma campaign, some of whom had been friends with my mother in Calcutta. I was pleased to make the journey in Tim's company and to lay flowers on their graves. The high commission staff were all delighted to be visited by an Australian member of parliament, and Tim impressed them by remembering their names and showing genuine interest in what they were doing. He behaved in a similar fashion during his visit to one of my later posts, Vietnam, where he was equally welcome.

Overall, I was impressed with the resilience of the Bangladeshi people in the face of poverty, flooding and the challenges of daily family and community life. People essentially got on with life, doing the best they could. Children were on the whole oblivious of their economic and social status and played happily, swimming in the rivers and dams, making their own toys and behaving like children everywhere. But poverty and the desire for a better life, indeed for survival, drove increasing numbers of people off the land and into the cities and towns, where living conditions were hard and jobs scarce. There was nonetheless growing employment in small manufacturing and service industries, which capitalised on abundant cheap labour which could be well trained. Working conditions for the predominantly female labour force in the garment industry were a constant concern, but the economic and social benefits flowing from their employment were remarkable.

As high commissioner, how did I deal with the challenges of living and working in Bangladesh? The task sometimes seemed overwhelming, and the havoc wrought by the floods and the huge displacement of people were heartwrenching. In the case of the floods, the whole country responded. Those with resources cooked food for those displaced and went personally to deliver the meals to people seeking refuge along the dykes. As part of their religious duty, Muslims must contribute to charity, and the Muslim aid organisations provided considerable relief and assistance in resettlement. International United Nations agencies such as the World Food Programme and the Development Programme and non-government agencies like the Bangladesh Red Cross, the Red Crescent Society and the Save the Children Fund all provided assistance. Official Australian emergency relief aid was mostly channelled through these agencies, which had good governance and worked in an accountable manner. This minimised the chances of the aid being delivered corruptly and made sure it reached those for whom it was intended.

There were well-designed and well-executed projects which were clearly working to advance the status of women, help end poverty and provide development opportunities. Many were small projects, helping a limited group of people but with the capacity, through them, to help more. I think about the small project which, year after year, trained traditional midwives in safer assistance practices at births, in an attempt to help tackle the extraordinarily high infant mortality rates. I remember larger projects developing and delivering flood-resistant rice varieties which grew fast, keeping pace with the rising water. Qantas helped Bangladesh's national airline, Biman, by training maintenance crews who could work on the aircraft in Bangladesh. Some of those, of course, by virtue of the training, qualified for migration to Australia and were lost to their mother country, at least for the time being. Australia's aid program provided concrete ways to help, providing good assistance in the health and education fields, but the focus moved increasingly to institutional strengthening, providing high-level education and training and helping national structures work more efficiently.

In personal terms, the support and friendship of fellow high commission staff and several members of the wider international community helped me cope and do my job. There was a small group of especially close and supportive Australian friends with whom, when it all got too much and I was in a 'fuck Bangladesh trough' I could hunker down and share feelings and frustrations, along with some good Australian wine. My friends also had difficult times, and we supported each other. I was grateful for the professional friendship and wisdom of experienced diplomatic colleagues, including Swedes, Indians, Pakistanis, Canadians and Americans, and, most importantly, of the many Bangladeshis working in the field. Some have proved to be lasting friends, long after our time together in Bangladesh.

9

Bhutan, 1988: the Dragon Kingdom

A short visit to the Dragon Kingdom, one of the early visits as it cautiously began to welcome foreign visitors

Flying in to Bhutan was terrifying. Druk Air's small aircraft took off from Dhaka and flew over the flat Delta of Bangladesh and then, suddenly climbed up into the Himalayas. It flew along the first valley, so narrow that you felt that, if you had perched on a wingtip, you could have reached out and touched the trees and the rocks. At the end of the first Himalayan valley, it rises suddenly and steeply, over a mountain, and down into the next, higher valley, and then into the next, climbing progressively upwards towards the capital, Thimphu. Ros, who was afraid of flying anyway, clutched my thigh for the whole journey: five distinct bruises. Roslyn Jackson was the head of mission's secretary at the high commission in Dhaka and had been keen to join me when two rare tickets became available to fly to Bhutan for a week's visit.

Bhutan's national airline, Druk Air provided regular direct flights from Dhaka to the Himalayan mountain kingdom, but visas were hard to come by in the late 1980s. The king, or Druk Gyalpo, Jigme Singye Wanchuk, had only just decided that it was time to open up the kingdom a little, but there were worries that a large western tourist inflow would impact on the national culture and nature of the kingdom. The king's brother-in-law Sangay Dorji had attended a foreign service training course in Australia. One of the king's brothers, Benji Dorji, accompanied by other nobles, had played in the Australian bicentenary golf tournament in Dhaka in 1988, and invited me to visit his home country, Bhutan and play golf with him there. With his assistance and that of Bhutan's ambassador in Dhaka, Ros and I were given visas and flew off on a one-week visit in the autumn of 1988.

Bordered by India on one side and China on the other, the kingdom is perched high in the Himalayas. Our high commission in New Delhi had formal accreditation to the country and visited a couple of times a year. There was a small Australian aid program there, and the Australian company Snowy Mountains Engineering Corporation (SMEC) had a resident presence of two engineers working with Bhutan's hydroelectric scheme. Australia also had a sheep and wool development project at Wabthang, 3,353 metres above sea level in Central Bhutan.

On arrival at Paro airport, we and our four fellow western passengers from Dhaka were formed into a group, introduced to each other and given a guide and minibus for the duration of the visit. Luckily, we all got on. Taschi, our guide, was dressed in the traditional Bhutanese men's way, in a *gho*, a knee-length, red plaid, woven wool wraparound coat with large, white linen cuffs, worn with long argyle socks. He also wore a white silk scarf. We discovered that the colour of the scarf indicated the wearer's rank: white was for a commoner. Taschi briefed and looked after us for the whole week. We had no formal program, no information on what we would see each day, where we would visit or what hotels we would stay in. But all was looked after perfectly.

It was a stunning place in cold, clear, mountain, autumn light. Bhutan is a Buddhist country, and each district was dominated by its own *dzong*, a single magnificent fortress building which was placed in the centre of its valley and served as the administrative offices as well as a Buddhist monastery and training centre for young Bhutanese boys (we did not see any evidence of schools for girls). Each *dzong* was artfully decorated with carvings and with painted and decorated scrolls. The *dzong* in Thimphu also houses the parliamentary chamber.

I asked our guide to contact the king's brother to arrange the promised game of golf. He was reluctant to make this contact – there were protocols governing contact between commoners like himself and the nobility – but I insisted and made clear who I was. It eventually happened, and a morning of golf was arranged for us. The course comprised nine holes on the rough, magnificently green cow pastures surrounding the glorious Thimphu *dzong*, and Ros and I were welcomed by the king's brother Benji Jorji and the local United Nations Development Programme representative, who made up our golf foursome. We met at the beautifully constructed little clubhouse, which was architecturally in harmony with the *dzong*. We were invited to sit on the king's throne inside the clubhouse and to use the king's bathroom, if needed. Refreshments of freshly squeezed lime juice were served, and the game began. On a regular golf course there are separate places designated for men and women to tee off. Here there were no women's tees, so a relatively flat piece of ground cleared of cow pats and stamped down, a little forward of the first tee was allocated to us.

A large number of young boys were accompanying us. We each had a caddy, to carry our clubs and advise us on the game, and also a fore-caddy, whose job was to locate the ball after each shot. But Ros and I wondered about the functions of the other boys. We discovered that the first green was actually made of oiled sand, and one boy's job was to mark and remove our balls, pull a jute bag over the green to smooth it, then replace the balls before each of us putted out into the small cup in the centre. Another boy held the flag, and it turned out that there was only one flag, as the boy ran ahead as soon as we had putted out to mark the next hole.

This was one of the most special games of golf we had ever played, and the highest, at nearly 2,000 metres. But we understood why the king's brother and his friends liked so much to fly down to Bangladesh and play with us on our beautifully maintained course at Kurmitola, in Dhaka.

On the first evening, Ros and I explored the main street of Thimphu. It was an unmade road lined by simple stores which were all open to the street and lit by kerosene lamps. Each store displayed piles of building materials, tools and machinery, open bags of cereals and spices, and vegetables. There were also long wooden counters, behind which were shelves of fabric and drawers with a variety of stock. At the back of one dimly lit store we spied a gorgeous red silk blouse and went in to investigate. The storekeeper greeted us. 'Hello! Damn fine evening, isn't it?'

We agreed it was.

'Which damn country are you from? Australia? Damn fine country! What do you think of Bhutan? Damn fine country, isn't it?'

After half an hour of this sort of conversation, during which we found out quite a lot about Bhutan, I said that I'd like to try on the red blouse.

'No damn point', he said. 'It won't fit. You're too damn fat'.

I discovered that Bhutanese conversation was often just as frank. When we visited one *dzong*, we observed a large number of small boys, dressed in red robes, chanting their lessons. They were supervised by a red-robed monk, who carried a long whip. I asked our guide what the whip was for and was told, 'It's to hit the boys on their bottoms when they don't pay attention to their lessons. And if I were you, I wouldn't go too close, as your bottom is so big, the monk might be tempted to use it on you!'

My penchant for telling jokes was derided by our guide, who described this to Ros as 'childish'. Stories were for children. Adults discussed philosophy and serious matters. And he advised both Ros and me that, at our age, we should consider entering a nunnery and prepare for the next life. Indeed, it turned out that in Bhutan the nunneries serve as homes for older women once their childrearing and family responsibilities are over. But I was only forty-one!

The SMEC team was made up of Geoff Percival and Wyn Carnie who invited us to dinner in their house. It was a great, relaxed evening with good Australian wine and western food cooked by the engineers. They had been told of our visit by the SMEC representative in Dhaka, John Cooney, and had gone to some trouble, erecting a welcoming banner outside the house and composing a joke menu in which yak meat and rancid butter purportedly featured in every course. But what they did provide were fresh asparagus and strawberries grown in Bhutan, and magnificent cheese – foods which were unobtainable in Dhaka. All accompanied by wonderful conversation and stories. One of Bhutan's major resources was hydroelectricity, which is why SMEC was there. Australia also ran an agricultural research and development program in the country. Chillies featured strongly in Bhutanese cuisine, and on the roof of almost every house were mountains of chillies drying in the sun. One Bhutanese vegetable dish consists entirely of chillies. Ros loves chillies and was in her element.

During the week, we visited stunning temples high up in the mountains, outside which were strings of prayer flags hanging in the mist. We climbed up the highest road pass in Bhutan, Chele La, at nearly 4,000 metres, then down to the bottom of the steep footpath leading up to the Paro monastery known as the Dragon's Nest. A couple of intrepid members of our party climbed all the way up, while the American artist in our midst, known as Peter the Painter, captured the scene and I stayed behind and enjoyed the view. The cold, thin mountain air was affecting the asthma from which I sometimes suffered.

On the second day, we were lucky enough to coincide with a great festival at the Wangdue Phodrang *dzong*, which provided extraordinary photographic opportunities ranging from colourful dragon and spirit dances to shy, beautiful children and colourfully and carefully dressed local onlookers in their best traditional clothing: *gho* for the men, colourful woven *kira* for the women. We seemed to be the only outsiders. This was a truly local festival. There was also an archery competition and games of darts.

The houses we saw throughout our stay were all distinctive, rather like Swiss chalets, in timber and stone, decorated in orange, yellow, black and white colours and painted with dragons or lions. We were invited into one house and climbed up a steep, wooden, exterior access stair to be greeted in the kitchen at the top by an old lady who was preparing traditional Bhutanese tea for us, finished off with rancid yak butter. The addition of cooked rice, which absorbed some of the oil, made it slightly more palatable. But this was a nourishing meal. She used an open wood-fired stove; the kitchen was blackened by the smoke.

At one *dzong*, Ros and I needed to visit the bathroom and were directed to the communal toilet facilities in the basement. There, we found that the building straddled a rapidly flowing river channel. Cement platforms and pillars had been built close to the channel, and it seemed you had to do your business balanced over the running stream while clinging on to one of the pillars. The naughty Ros took a photograph of me in action, which has since been confiscated!

As we travelled around the villages, we passed mobile United Nations Development Programme clinics, vaccinating and treating children. We saw beautifully dressed Bhutanese in their *ghos* and *kiras*, and the most engaging children.

Bhutan has been notable for setting up its Gross National Happiness Index, against which every government initiative is measured. The index is used to measure the collective happiness and wellbeing of the population. It was enshrined in Bhutan's constitution in 2008. Elements of the index include community vitality, ecological diversity and resilience, living standards, health, psychological wellbeing, time use, education, and good governance. Tourism was still controlled and limited, to minimise its impact on the Bhutanese way of life, but many more people were able to visit the country. We were very lucky to be among the earliest westerners to arrive as tourists. I understand that visits to monasteries were soon after taken off the tourism itinerary. The only objects then for sale in the market were fabrics and objects needed by the Bhutanese for daily life, including exquisitely woven storage baskets, some of which I bought and enjoyed using. There was nothing when we visited that was made expressly for outside visitors.

I would have loved to have visited Bhutan more often, to get to know more of the country and understand the politics. It occurred to me while I was there that it would be logical, and good for us in Dhaka, for DFAT to transfer responsibility for Bhutan from New Delhi to Dhaka. There were regular direct flights from Dhaka, and New Delhi had a full workload in looking after our relations with India, whereas we had limited responsibilities in Dhaka and could handle the extra load easily. But when I floated this idea with Canberra, it was quickly shot down by our more experienced high commissioner in New Delhi, Graham Feakes.

I have not been back to Bhutan but I have seen advertisements by travel companies revealing a much more developed and prosperous Thimphu, with paved streets, well-built stores selling fabrics and accessories, with helpful staff. The markets look well stacked with fresh produce. I have horticultural inclined friends who visit the more remote parts of this stunning Himalayan kingdom to study the rare plants. I have met impressive Bhutanese students undertaking postgraduate studies in government administration, development studies, health and education on Australian scholarships at Perth's universities.

The carved slate that I bought in Thimphu, shown in the artwork insert (see artwork insert figure 6), depicts a fable about the animals of the jungle, who were arguing as to who knew the tree best. The elephant claimed that, as the largest animal and with his exploring trunk, he was able to know the tree best. The monkey disputed this; he could move about easily through the highest branches, and therefore he knew the tree best. The rabbit chipped in: he had nibbled at the grasses at the foot of the tree as the sapling grew and, being so intimately involved in its development, he knew the tree best. The bird sang out that as she had dropped the seed from which the tree grew, she had known it the longest and therefore knew it best. Having heard each other, the animals agreed that only collectively, as a team, could they claim that they knew the tree. This image appears frequently throughout Bhutan's *dzongs*, and the country has taken the tale as the inspiration for its national philosophy: a useful way to look at things for a country that has adopted the Gross National Happiness Index.

10

The foreign service, 1990–94:
at home and abroad

The foreign service at home in Australia, working
in Canberra and Sydney, running public affairs
during the first Gulf War, forging links with
business, working very closely with ministers.

The telephone rang at home in Canberra very early on Thursday
2 August 1990. Iraq had just invaded Kuwait, and the Australian
media were demanding information. What was the Australian
Government's reaction? Would Australia send in troops? Were
there Australian civilians in Kuwait? What was Australia doing
to protect them? I was the Foreign Affairs spokesperson and the
first point of contact for the media. I needed to find out what was
going on and field the continuing barrage of press demands.

The Public Affairs staff started work early in the office each
day, and when I arrived we set about finding the answers and
responding to the press gallery journalists. The DFAT division
responsible for the Middle East, the minister and his staff, the
prime minister and his staff, the secretary, the minister and the
Department of Defence were all involved in what turned out to be
Australia's involvement in the first Gulf War. It was a busy time
for Public Affairs.

The Australian mission in New York was instructed to work
with the United States and other sponsors on a United Nations
resolution condemning Iraq and calling for immediate and

unconditional withdrawal from Kuwait. Speedy work led to the adoption of the resolution on the same day. Australia joined the international force, contributing army, navy and air force personnel, ships and planes to what became known as Operation Desert Storm, launched in January 1991. The international coalition force included ninety warships, more than 100 smaller and amphibious craft and 800 aircraft.

Once the government had decided on Australian participation, the Department of Defence assumed major carriage of media relations on the operational aspects. A particular focus for us in Foreign Affairs was the small group of Australian civilians taking shelter in Kuwait as the oilfields were torched. They were in hiding but had contacted us, and their protection was the department's consular responsibility. Concern for their safety was affecting public opinion about Australia's military involvement. It is easier to identify with, and feel for, Australians with names and faces as compared with the complex reality of a war.

The invitation to appear on an early morning television break-fast program with a daily update on the situation was welcome – an efficient way of getting information out to the general public. This job fell to me. I woke at four each morning, showered and dressed carefully, choosing suitably smart but conservative clothes and jewellery, and then went to the department to read the cables, be updated on overnight developments and work out a clear media line. Then I went into the breakfast studio in Parliament House. I was very aware that we had an audience of thousands of concerned Australians, and I was careful to look and sound reliable and reassuring. I was most sensitive to the reaction of Gareth Evans, the foreign minister, who unfailing phoned just after the broadcast each day with a vigorous reaction to what he had just watched, frequently suggesting other words I might better have used. The Australians were evacuated safely from Kuwait, and the level of public support for Australia's military involvement rose. The need for daily breakfast television updates on the situation passed.

A career in the foreign service includes stints at home. In my total career, I spent twenty-three years representing Australia overseas, working in seven diplomatic missions abroad, and eleven years in total back in Australia, working in a variety of jobs in DFAT headquarters, in Canberra, and three years in the state office in Sydney.

Time spent working in DFAT in Australia is an important part of the professional experience. It is there that policy is made. Service at home keeps you grounded in the Australian reality, up to date with domestic political and public service developments and what is going on in the Australian states and territories away from Canberra. It is easy to get carried away with the importance which comes with your positions overseas. It is also easy to forget that it is Australia's interests that come first, not those of the country where you are posted, no matter how fond you become of it or how much you grow to understand it. 'Localitis' is a common disease among Foreign Affairs officers. Some foreign services leave their ambassadors in place overseas for years; Australia does not. I had a continuous stint of ten years overseas up to my retirement, albeit in three different posts, but this was unusual.

In an earlier chapter I have already written about my first period at home, after Portugal, when I was placed in two political sections, West Europe and then South East Asia, focussing largely on East Timor. When I returned to Canberra from Bangladesh, in 1989, Dick Woolcott had become head of DFAT, and on the basis of our work together in New York he asked me to take on the Public Affairs role in DFAT. This section, which reported directly to the Secretary, was responsible for the department's contact with the news media, for briefing the ministers in preparation for Question Time in Parliament and writing speeches for the ministers. It included being the Foreign Affairs spokesperson. The Public Affairs team scoured the morning news media and the daily flow of reporting from our overseas posts and alerted the departmental leadership and the ministers' offices to the major issues of the day – the issues likely to attract media attention and possible questions of the minister in Question Time on parliament's sitting days. The team worked with the appropriate branches and sections in the department, the ministers' offices and often the prime minister's staff to prepare briefing material each day. We served both the Minister for Foreign Affairs and the Minister for Trade.

Constant questions came from journalists in the Canberra press gallery, and press releases were often prepared and released. Our minister for Foreign Affairs, Gareth Evans, made clear that *he* was the spokesman for the media, and that was true for key matters of emerging policy, but the department fielded a wide range of questions on policy, as well as consular matters, affecting the welfare of Australians abroad. The journalists in the press gallery were on the whole focussed, competent and hardworking, up against tight deadlines and keen to get the story right. As a former journalist, I understood all this.

Public Affairs was a terrific job. There were long hours, but staff worked across all areas of public and foreign policy, knew what was going on in the department and our overseas posts and got to know the journalists in the parliamentary press gallery. It was a position of authority. The Public Affairs team members were experienced and knew their jobs well. Outstanding was Jim Dollimore, a senior and experienced journalist who had also started out in West Australian newspapers in Perth. For years he had been the chief contact in DFAT for the media. His integrity and helpfulness, along with his genial courtesy, had earned the trust of the press gallery as well as that of our ministers. Jim well earned his posting as ambassador to Syria, in 1995.

I had worked in Public Affairs during my second stint at home in DFAT, after returning from East Germany in 1979 I was then the Parliamentary Liaison Officer, working with branch head Kim Jones as he briefed our ministers, first Andrew Peacock and later Tony Street, for Question Time. The Minister for Foreign Affairs was a member of the House of Representatives, but there were often questions asked in the Senate. One minister was designated to represent the minister there and deal with those questions. I sat at the side of the Senate chamber, with reference material to pass to the minister should he be asked a question related to Foreign Affairs. At the end of each parliamentary sitting day, staff collected the official daily records of Question Time in the Senate and in the House of Representatives and sent relevant material off by cable that night to those overseas posts which needed to be kept up to date with the most recent parliamentary discussion of matters of Foreign Affairs interest. In later years, all this was done electronically, but in the late 1970s, it was very much laborious pen-and-paper work, with people running back and forth between the department and the old Parliament House.

Fred Chaney, a senator from Western Australia, was always welcoming and ready for a chat when I had to wait for the Senate's daily records of an evening. He went on to nationally significant roles affecting Aboriginal policy, and it was good to have the chance to get to know him. This was especially useful later when, after retiring from DFAT in 2003, I went on to work with Aboriginal communities in the East Kimberley and Pilbara regions of Western Australia.

In early 1980, Sir Garfield Barwick, the chief justice of the High Court, hosted an international conference in the newly opened High Court building, inviting fellow chief justices from countries of the region. He asked for a Foreign Affairs liaison officer: I was given the job. As I have written earlier, when I met the chief justice, he told me my task was to look after the wives of all the visiting judges, to 'help them with their hair appointments and so on'. I did not see this as an appropriate role for a professional Foreign Affairs officer and shared my reluctance with my branch head, Kim Jones. He provided sage advice: 'Take the job and turn it into the job you want'. So I did. *Retro sed ultro – backwards yet forwards.* Working at this high level conference turned out to be extremely rewarding. My job was principally to assist the future governor-general Sir Ninian Stephen, the judge who was actually doing all the work for the conference. While the conference was under way, a coup occurred in the home country of one of the international chief justices, and he was unable to return home. And there were a number of other international issues to be sorted out as the conference proceeded, about which I was able to advise Sir Ninian and the chief justice or the visiting judges. This was all good experience, and Sir Ninian remained a kind mentor and advocate throughout my career. I learned a valuable lesson. And no-one asked me to help with a hair appointment.

I also worked with the Senate Standing Committee on Foreign Affairs and Defence under its long-time and experienced chairman Western Australian senator Peter Sim. Australian Parliamentary delegations attended the annual meetings of the Inter-Parliamentary Union which were held in different cities overseas. As the liaison officer I went as adviser to the delegations to the meetings held in Athens, Berlin and Oslo and to a meeting of the Commonwealth Parliamentary Association in Lusaka. This latter was a similar organisation, but confined to members of the Commonwealth. These meetings discussed matters of relevance to the respective parliaments but were principally an excellent international networking opportunity for the members. Places in the delegation were decided by the political parties and were eagerly sought. The Inter-Parliamentary Union meeting in 1980 was held in Havana, Cuba, and I attended it on my way to take up my new job at the United Nations in New York later in the year.

The United States had a long-standing embargo in place against the communist country of Cuba. The US Congressional delegation had to get specific presidential approval to attend, and it arrived later than the other delegations, in a US military aircraft. The members of the US delegation were some of the very few senior US officials to have contact with Cuba at that time, and they endured with us a two-hour-long speech by President Fidel Castro. There were private meetings in the sidelines of the Inter-Parliamentary Union meeting between the Americans and Cuban officials, which we understood explored ways in which bilateral relations might be improved. We were all lodged in a very grand and well fitted-out old hotel, and one afternoon we relaxed at Veradero beach, where each delegation had been given a large 'sugar baron' beach house as its base and changing room for the day. Before the Cuban Revolution in 1953–59 which brought the Communist Party and Fidel Castro to power, Cuba's economy was largely based on sugar, an industry dominated by the wealthy. The main customers for Cuban sugar were in the USA, so the trade embargos imposed by the USA from 1961 hit Cuba hard. These families had large, luxurious beach houses, as a retreat from the heat of Havana. After the revolution, these were taken over by the communist government and used as government rest houses.

I stayed on in Havana for a couple of days after the other international delegations left. Going down for an early morning swim in the hotel pool on my first morning alone, I found it had been emptied, and all the pool furniture had been removed, as had all the taps, showerheads and other plumbing fixtures. These were scarce and precious in Cuba and had to be safeguarded so they could be installed to impress the next foreign visitors.

The Canadian Embassy looked after Australian interests in Cuba, and I went to see them. A Cuban policeman tried to stop me entering. With my long, dark hair I looked quite Hispanic, but my Australian passport opened the path. The Canadians provided a very good briefing on the current political, economic and social situations in the country, including the effect of the US embargo. Chris Pala, the *New York Times* correspondent who had covered the Inter-Parliamentary Union meeting and also stayed on in Havana, knew the city well and introduced me to the Cuba Libre, a rum and mint cocktail, and took me around. The city was architecturally and historically interesting, if shabby and poorly maintained. There was a vibrant, joyous and fun-loving spirit among the Cubans we met in the cafes, bars and nightclubs, as well as people on the street. Whatever the official American embargo attitude – and this clearly had a negative effect on the economy – the people of Cuba had impressive energy and spirit.

My next period in Canberra followed my return in early 1985 from the postings at the United Nations in New York and Washington, DC. I took over the Personnel Development Section, which was responsible for the training and development of the staff of DFAT.

At that time, personal computers were being gradually introduced into the department, and there was an emerging need for staff training in the use of the new technology. A core business of DFAT is communication, and the new computers made a radical change. Developments in communication systems and information technology had the greatest impact on changes to the day-to-day workings of the foreign service. They altered the hierarchical nature of the organisation, streamlined processes, led to greater productivity and eliminated whole job categories.

When I joined, the department proudly possessed a single huge, central computer, housed and protected in the basement and staffed by professional computer operators and communicators. No natural light penetrated the basement, so there was a program which delivered changing colours and intensity of electric light, which was designed to mimic the diurnal light cycles outside. Officers' interaction with the communicators was via a small, cave-like, subterranean window where we went, twice a day, to collect our cables, printed and sorted, with their various security classifications. We then lodged our own carefully typed cables for despatch to overseas missions. The actual typing of the cables was done by secretarial staff in the typing pool. One of the necessary skills for us was being able to persuade the dragon-woman who controlled the typing pool that our work had priority. She was in a very powerful position, so being able to type myself, bypassing the typing pool, was a great advantage. The typing pool soon disappeared. Modern keyboard equipment made creating and amending documents easy, as well as enabling seamless transitions from original compositions to their despatch and appearance at the desks of users in our embassies overseas.

At overseas posts, there were laborious systems for encryption and decryption of cabled reporting. I started in Portugal in 1971 with the very basic one-time pads, which I have described in an earlier chapter. On arrival in Canberra, the messages were decrypted, typed up and passed to the designated action officers and others with a need to know. Classified instructions were received at posts via similar telex tape. This took a long time, and each post had a dedicated Canberra-based communicator on the staff.

By 1985, personal computers were being gradually introduced into the department. The Personnel Development team started training staff in their use and rolled this out through the whole department. Many older senior officers were resistant and refused to use the new system, relying on their personal assistants to perform their keyboard work and to sort the paper cables for them. There was an intrinsic reluctance to welcome new processes, but a shift in power structures in the office was taking place. The departmental secretary decided that it was possibly too hard for the older senior officers to learn the new skills, and the path of least resistance and overall efficiency was to allow them to continue to rely on personal assistants for an interim period. But by the time I retired, in 2003, almost everybody in the department had keyboard skills and worked online, and secretaries were disappearing as job classifications. Personal assistants, better paid with a wider range of responsibilities took their place

All the work of journalists at the *Daily News* in Perth in the 1960s was done on typewriters, so I learned keyboard skills early on and thereafter always used a keyboard for my work. As a woman with keyboard skills I had, in the early days, to endure the joking attempts of some male staff to denigrate me by treating me as their secretary, and even trying to get me to do some typing for them.

'Please take a letter, Miss Boyd'.

'Please get knotted, Mr Smith'.

As everybody eventually caught up and learned keyboard skills as a necessary tool of trade, this ceased.

Our team in Personnel Development also trained the annual intake of diplomatic trainees, and it was good to get to know the new graduate entrants, fresh from their universities, and help them to learn how to be productive members of the department and successful diplomats. I shared with them my own experiences and ways of coping. I followed closely the careers of many of those I helped recruit and train as they moved up the ladder and out to a variety of postings.

Experience in Canberra in the periods between overseas postings was invaluable. It provided a solid understanding of the working of the whole of government and the interaction between our elected representatives and the public service bureaucracy. What was missing was an understanding of the workings of state and territory governments and the important role in Australian life of the business community. This was remedied for me in the period from 1991 to 1994, when I learned more about working Australia by being the DFAT representative in New South Wales, in our Sydney office. There were DFAT offices in each of the Australian states and in the Northern Territory. In New South Wales the DFAT domain included the central office, on William Street, as well as separate passport offices in the coastal town of Newcastle, at the then growing city centre of Parramatta, in the Sydney central business district, and a trade promotion office in Edgecliff, not far from the centre. Most of the staff saw themselves as permanently employed at the Sydney offices and felt little allegiance to DFAT as a general entity. Canberra was the enemy. Canberra-based staff rarely sought postings to the state offices. And, for their part, most Sydney-based staff were not interested in being posted overseas. There was a very different office culture from the one that I had experienced in Canberra. The Sydney staff all worked hard in their individual jobs in the office and willingly worked longer hours when needed. They were mostly god-fearing, conservative people, who watched their language. Many came from culturally and linguistically diverse communities, whose original settler families had worked hard to provide a better life for their children. There was none of the colourful, profane language common in ministerial offices and the press corps in Canberra. While in Canberra, I had blended in to the political life, giving as good as I got. I had to learn to behave differently to earn the respect of the Sydney staff.

I worked to integrate the state offices better with the main-stream department in Canberra, arranging short-term job swaps and experiential training exercises which developed team skills and awareness of the wider entity of DFAT. We also made sure that Sydney staff were rewarded by inclusion in several department-wide recognition programs. Several of the Sydney staff applied successfully to take up overseas postings, and over time, a couple of years in a state office came to be seen as worthwhile and highly desirable by policy officers returning from an overseas post.

In Sydney I built up the business liaison program, which brought the resources of DFAT and our overseas posts and ambassadors to Australian international business development. Many businesses were already internationally active, but many more were looking to establish themselves in markets overseas. The office helped them in building their international knowledge and pathways to assistance from Foreign Affairs, successfully introducing regular breakfast briefings to top business leaders at our long conference table in Sydney by Australian ambassadors when they were on home visits. This was of practical service to the businesses, who told us the briefings were very valuable, and they also helped build a powerful domestic political constituency of support for DFAT. Businesses could learn at first hand what DFAT was doing and our value to them in facilitating and supporting export opportunities. They appreciated the confidentiality and productivity of the meetings. In writing an evaluation of this innovative program I asked the business leaders involved to assess the value of our service to their businesses. The chief executive of one large company, who was a regular at the briefings, said we knew what his salary was and how many hours he spent with us each month; these could be taken as an indicator of the value he placed on the time he spent with us. The breakfast briefings became a model adopted in all the DFAT state offices.

I was often the only woman at many boardroom business lunches outside the office. At first it was hard to break in to the groups of men, who seemed uncomfortable when I joined them and introduced myself. I wondered why that was. Were they just not used to women peers? Or maybe they assumed I must be a junior staffer? Or, worse, somebody else's wife? I found it a useful tactic to enlist a male champion who would introduce me. 'Have you met Sue Boyd yet? She is doing some really useful work for us in business here – I'm sure you will find her very helpful'. Introduction by a respected peer seemed to work well until I was better known and could make my own way. A few of the senior business leaders were committed to better gender diversity and were happy to help when I explained my situation. Business cards and name tags were also useful, so they could see who I was.

Austrade was the separate government agency dedicated to promoting international trade and investment. Its staff worked directly with Australian businesses, in Australia and on the ground overseas. There were Austrade officers within the embassy in Vietnam, in Fiji and in Hong Kong. In Sydney, I worked closely with my Austrade colleague Geoff Gray and with Jonathan McKeown from the Chamber of Manufactures of New South Wales, to establish a common export support centre in Parramatta, in the geographic centre of Sydney and convenient for many smaller businesses. The New South Wales chamber invited me to join a trade mission visiting Singapore and Jakarta, looking for export opportunities for small businesses, including veterinary products for caged birds, smart men's ties and business directories. This was priceless experience of business in action.

The Sydney office of DFAT provided advice and information to the New South Wales Department of Development, the premier, Nick Greiner and the mayor of Sydney, Frank Sartor, on matters of international importance. The Sydney-Florence Sister City Committee included the women's fashion designer Carla Zampatti, other significant business and political leaders of Italian origin and the retired Gough Whitlam. Meetings were always lively. The mayor gave a farewell dinner for me in the town hall on the eve of my departure for Vietnam, at which Whitlam gave one of his splendid, amusing and very warm speeches.

I was DFAT's representative with the Sydney Olympics bid organisation, which successfully brought the highly successful 2000 Summer Olympics to Sydney. There was widespread scepticism in the Sydney community and in the department about the prospects for winning this bid, and fears of widespread negative consequences for the city and its inhabitants should it be successful. I was staying with John Dauth, our high commissioner in Kuala Lumpur, the night the winner was announced. The decision was due at 2.00 am Kuala Lumpur time, and of course I waited up. John was firmly of the sceptical view that we could not win. 'How much more Coca-Cola will be sold in Sydney as compared with Beijing?' he asked cynically and insisted on going to bed. I took great pleasure in waking him up violently to share the news of Sydney's win immediately after it was broadcast on the television.

The 2000 Sydney Olympics reflected their success on the whole country. And the large number of first-time volunteers meant that the local community was actually very enthusiastic. Before the games took place I was posted to Fiji – a sports-mad country with a significant Olympics team – and was able to share the excitement from there. It was a pity that heads of mission were specifically banned from returning to Australia to experience the Olympics firsthand. We had to stay at our posts.

Chief Executive Women, then a small group of very senior women in business in Sydney, invited me to join them – the first member recruited from the public service. It was a welcoming and rewarding network of women leaders. As part of the group, I agreed to be shadowed in Sydney for a week by a Year 7 high-school girl student. This smart young woman accompanied me on all my work engagements and wrote a report on the experience at the end. She said she had found the most impressive event was the meeting with the New South Wales premier Nick Greiner. I asked about our meeting with Gough Whitlam. 'Is he someone important?' she asked, innocently. I was shocked – she attended a very good school, and Whitlam had been such a major political figure for our generation and for me personally. I had regarded our meeting with him as the highlight of the week. But then I realised my shadow had been born after his time in politics, and she was the child of recent migrants from Hong Kong. Australia was changing.

The initial Australia-ASEAN-Women's Leaders Telstra Business Forum, in Singapore in July 1994, was an opportunity to network with women business leaders in the region. There was an impressive line-up, and among the most impressive was the princess who was a business leader from Brunei. Australia's diplomatic missions in the region had been asked to identify women business leaders to be invited to the conference, but the high commission in Brunei had said there were none there. Luckily, however, one of the conference organisers had delved more deeply than our high commission in Brunei. When I asked the Brunei delegation why these women were not known, they responded that they did not join the local business associations, as the men treated them so badly and expected them to make the tea. As a result, they just went about their businesses independently, and very successfully, and did not come to the attention of foreign embassies.

Such conferences, and my work with businesses in Sydney, set me up very well for my later postings to countries in the Indo-Pacific.

11

Being a woman, and some ideas
on career progression

**Managing as a single woman, particular challenges
overcome, changing the status of woman and
making the workplace better for everyone.**

This might be a convenient juncture to write a little about the
experience of forging a career in what had been very much a man's
world and what I learned. As I previously mentioned, when I joined
the Department of External Affairs in 1970 it was a conservative
organisation which had very few women in positions of authority.
Diplomacy is an ancient profession, though the Australian foreign
service was relatively new, having emerged in the 1940s.

How was it, as a single woman, pursuing my career? I moved
a lot, lived in a number of different cities, learned a range of languages, managed my way through different cultures and faced
difficult personal, policy and staffing decisions, all without a
significant other to lean on or talk through the difficult issues
with. I've maintained my Australian family relationships. Keeping
up with friends from university in all the far-flung places I have
lived and worked in has been important. Many of them have been
welcome visitors in my various homes.

The new friends made in each posting have kept me balanced
and sane. I have been fortunate to find a special individual or
couple who were not members of the embassy staff, who were on
the same intellectual and educational wavelength and who were

prepared to befriend me as an ordinary woman, aside from my official status. Mostly, these have been fellow Australians whom I have been able to trust and rely on and who are not wary of a powerful woman. They are the ones who, when the going gets tough, provide the necessary personal support.

I have also been a consultative leader, sharing problems and issues with staff, where appropriate, although there are still many things I had to deal with alone and could not share with anyone. And, in the end, the decision is yours.

Some of these personal relationships became extremely close and intimate. The peripatetic nature of the foreign service made it very difficult to convert such friendships 'with privileges' to long-term close relationships. Just when the time comes to face up to the inevitable difficulties in a relationship and decide whether or not to work seriously on making it lasting, it's time to move on, back to Canberra or on to another posting. Many of these friendships have nonetheless endured the disruptions.

As the Australian head of mission, you live in a glasshouse. Everybody in the community is watching you, and you are on duty twenty-four hours a day. In 1999 I was talking to some children at the Australian International School Hong Kong. They asked if there were any downsides to being the Australian consul general. I said there were: I could never be naughty. Then, of course, they asked what I would do if I could be naughty.

Once, in Bangladesh, I invited a new male friend home to the residence for dinner. As my bearer, Punu, served the meal, he asked wickedly, 'How many for breakfast tomorrow, madam? One or two?' How to put off a potential lover!

Over the years, I was asked frequently why I never got married. My joking reply was, 'the good ones have all already been taken'. Adi Kuini Speed, deputy prime minister of Fiji in 1999 when I arrived there, suggested that might not be applied to her husband. Clive Speed was an Australian, and we all shared the same ironic sense of humour. When I returned home to Perth in 1972, on holiday during my first posting, a hairdresser assumed that I was able to tell her tales about a life abroad because I was accompanying my husband on his job overseas. She was shocked when I told her that it was my own job we were talking about and that there was no husband. 'Not many women your age are still single!' I was all of twenty-six!

When I joined DFAT the extent of the gay community was not realised. Homosexuality was illegal, and many of the nice single men I knew were either very discreet or in denial or underground. With the need for discretion came the opportunity for blackmail, so everyone was very careful. I had a particular long-lasting relationship with a very talented and fine man who eventually told me he was gay. Having taken the monumental step to come out, he thought that nothing had changed in our relationship. But it had changed fundamentally for me. I no longer thought our friendship could become something more permanent. The man against whom I had compared and had found wanting each potential new partner had transformed into just a very good friend. He remains so, and I am now good friends with his husband as well.

My experience is that men are in general chary about a personal involvement with powerful, strong women. Older, more experienced men find us less challenging, and I continue to enjoy many and varied friendships.

I always say that there is such a shortage of suitable men around that women who are lucky enough to have found one should be ready to share them with the rest of us. Don't jump to conclusions! That sharing is not necessarily sexual; there are lots of things that single women enjoy in the company of men, as well as in the company of women friends: going to concerts or movies; discussing books; sailing boats and travelling; skiing and walking; playing golf; sharing professional experiences. The list of normal pursuits is endless, and it is great to share many of these with men, even if you are not in a permanent relationship.

The question of children became important to me when I turned thirty. When my sister was asked as a child what she wanted to be when she grew up, she always said that she wanted to be a 'mummy'. My childish goals varied but included being a research scientist, a diplomat and a flight attendant. The careers counsellor in one high school thought I would make a good secretary. It was never my goal to be married and have children. I observed my mother's life and did not want one like that – dependent on a man, with no independence of income and a life of constant domestic negotiation. And as my siblings each married, had children and then divorced, I saw how much pain and trauma that caused everyone, and I didn't wish it for myself. But in my early thirties I looked seriously at the question of children. Did I really want a child? If so, I had better get on with it. Of course, I could have one and be a single parent, but that path seemed fraught and not the best for the child. No, it had to be the full family thing with a shared responsibility or to continue happily alone.

I did enjoy friendships with married couples and families, who seemed to be well adjusted and in harmony with each other, and with whom there was plenty of warmth and room to be shared comfortably with friends, but these were rare. I was prepared to just see what happened. I enjoyed children. I had four godchildren and six nephews and nieces, and I loved them all and liked being the loving, eccentric and exotic aunt. I did not yearn for a man of my own; I already had a quite satisfactory life. As the first post-Pill and, for a time, pre-AIDS generation we had great freedom in relationships.

A sense of humour is probably the most important asset when negotiating life through the challenges of the traditionally male world. Women were not really welcomed at first in External Affairs. The department and our embassies abroad had been worlds for so long, in which women had been supportive, self-sacrificing wives or junior support staff. The men expected that women would perform less well than their male peers, and there was a sense of surprise when they found that, actually, women could do the job extremely competently. We worked our way gently into this environment, making allowances for the egos of our workmates, many times swallowing both intended and unintended slights or sexist remarks and trying not to 'frighten the horses' unnecessarily. But we still had to stand up for ourselves and work to hold our own and carve out a better workplace for everyone. The women worked hard to help the department address all the issues which underpinned and brought about a less-than-equal workplace.

It was often helpful, when working with men, to be able to talk about sport, which is on the whole men's safe topic of conversation. In countries like Fiji and Hong Kong, rugby union is the national passion. When I was in Hong Kong I attended each year the annual Hong Kong rugby 7s tournament. I was invited into the various private boxes which were sponsored by Australian businesses, which were excellent networking opportunities, and it was fun being with my 'tribe', seated close to the game, with beer and pies, rather than exotic canapés and champagne. In Fiji, after one rugby tournament, the whole Australian Wallabies rugby team came to where I was sitting and thanked me for being there. Fiji is rugby mad. People noticed that the New Zealand high commissioner did not get similar treatment from the All Blacks.

I suffered the same as most women when I was the sole woman in a workplace meeting. The men talk over you: their ears are attuned only to male voices, and the gentler, higher pitched women's voices often fail to penetrate and sometimes irritate. All the women I have worked with have had the same infuriating experience of making a contribution in such a meeting only to have the idea ignored but then voiced a little later by one of the men – and the idea being praised and taken up seriously. In DFAT leadership course participants, men and women, were all warned of this phenomenon and how it meant that discourse would be the poorer for its failure to take the ideas of all participants into account. To make the most of women's potential input to a team, the training courses encouraged the chairs of workplace meetings specifically to ask the women participants to voice their ideas. If they were reluctant to speak out during the meeting, chairs could usefully seek out these women afterwards to check whether they had any particular additional points to make. The same phenomenon started to appear when people from culturally and linguistic diverse communities began to join the department. Somehow, the women were seen to be deficient and had to make the effort to muscle in; the default setting was overwhelmingly masculine.

After I'd been in DFAT for a while a neighbour of mine in Canberra, Margaret Byrne, a workplace relationships researcher, told me of her interesting work into all-male and all-female work meetings, which found that the processes in each were distinctly different. The all-male meetings were hierarchical, with each speaker being heard out when they managed to get the floor. Those who failed to get the floor or found that the subject had moved on by the time they had been given a chance to make their contribution left meetings feeling disgruntled. They felt no ownership of the decisions made. On the other hand, the all-women meetings were less structured, people jumped in to make their points, and often side-discussions ensued. To an observer, it all looked a bit chaotic. But in the end, though the all-female meetings might take longer than those with all men, everybody's voice and ideas were heard, and the chair drew together the consensus decision which emerged. After all-female meetings, women said they were happy with the process and the outcome, for which they took ownership.[10]

We women had to learn to speak out when we found ourselves not heard or ignored, and to speak out for another woman in the group, but to do so in a style which made the men receptive rather than hostile. We danced the constant dance of upsetting the men as little as possible so that they became allies rather than adversaries. The balance between being assertive and being aggressive is difficult to find, and, while it was okay for men to be aggressive, woe betide the woman who exhibited the same behaviour. But often one has to be firm, insistent and self-promoting. A mistake I made early in my career was to trust the department to recognise and judge how best to use my talents. I was comfortable going along with the flow. In the early days, that served me well: I was happy with the postings they gave me and my assignments in the department. I was seen as a can-do, fix-it, reliable sort of person: a safe pair of hands. I did not assess each assignment for where it placed me in my career. As Sheryl Sandberg wrote in *Leaning In*[11], we now know that for women it is not so much a career ladder as a jungle gym: a piece of children's playground apparatus. You jump or climb up, move sideways along the rails, grab the rings and swing up, pull yourself up the rungs, and sometimes fall into the sand, dust yourself down and start again. It is not necessarily a smooth, upwards journey, especially in Foreign Affairs, with such a range of possible assignments and, for many, the desire to fit in partners and children as well.

Sometimes, what seems a backward or sideways step actually takes you forward. *Retro sed ultro.* When they posted me to Bangladesh in 1986 as a rather young female high commissioner, the department was under pressure to have more women heads of mission, and sending me helped meet this goal. At that time, the job of deputy head of mission at our embassy in Jakarta was also on offer, and, with the wisdom of hindsight, in career terms, I should have taken that. It would have given me more experience in policy work in a country firmly in Australia's area of major interest, I would have learned from a more experienced head of mission and experienced work in a larger embassy, with staff from a range of other departments, in addition to DFAT. Learning more about Indonesian culture was also central to DFAT's needs. But I was keen to have an embassy of my own, and I do not regret the experience at all.

But at a certain point, I noticed I was lagging in the promotion stakes. Men I knew were being promoted over me, when my service had been no less meritorious. What I was doing was valued less. My curriculum vitae was lacking a demonstrable policy track record, and those being promoted had proved their talents in posts with policy focus or in ministerial offices. This was the juncture at which I decided to take my career progression seriously. I am forever grateful to two younger colleagues, Jack Heath and

Martine Letts, with whom I had worked in DFAT and who had moved from the department into the commercial workforce. In Sydney in the early 1990s, they told me they were shocked that I had not been promoted when I so patently deserved it and that I was being overtaken by my male peers. These two became my 'upwards' mentors, coaching me in writing a compelling promotion application and then in performing well at a promotion interview. They helped me focus on the selection criteria and made me aware that every question put to me was an opportunity to show how well I met a particular selection criterion. They also underlined how the promotion committee was not about rewarding past experience: it was looking for how well I would perform at the next level. In the next promotion round in 1993 I was at last successful: I jumped from being a Foreign Affairs Officer Class 4 into Band 1 in the second division, a significant step. That opened up more challenging and satisfying job opportunities, with plenty of scope for policy work.

In 1994 I threw my hat in the ring for a posting as ambassador to Vietnam, in Hanoi and got it. And I did the job well. Three years later, I applied for promotion to the next level up, band 2, and successfully got the Hong Kong posting. I heard that the DFAT secretary, Philip Flood, was describing me as 'the feisty Sue Boyd'. That was okay.

At overseas posts, a single head of mission was expected to shoulder the practical obligations usually managed by a couple. I had to run the residence and organise the residence staff as well leading the embassy. Indeed, without good and loyal domestic staff, it would have been much harder. Tasks included managing the guest lists, menus, seating plans, shopping and flowers for dinners, lunches and receptions at home, as well as ensuring that the conversation flowed well, every guest felt happy and the whole event fitted into the government's policy agenda. When a single male ambassador succeeded in putting on a stylish meal, everyone thought how clever he was. It was taken for granted when single women did the same.

As a woman, I was expected to dress well and wear 'real' jewellery, with appropriate shoes, handbag and, sometimes, hat. Men could get away with a couple of suits, some good shirts, ties and shoes, and a pair of good cufflinks. When I was in Bangladesh, safari suits were de rigueur for men, while colourful open-necked cotton 'bula' shirts were the male business uniform when I was in Fiji. Both are much easier to manage than a woman's wardrobe. One advantage, however, was that wearing a bright and stylish outfit attracted more media attention than a grey suit. It provided better opportunity to be visible and show your personality. People noticed the Australian high commissioner. What you wear matters and needs to be appropriate to the job. After retirement I have been working as an executive business coach, with senior business leaders, male and female. I advise clients to observe the details of what senior, successful people in their organisation wear to work and to aim for that standard. To women, I say, 'Don't come to work in "Fuck me" clothes. Wear "Fuck you" clothes'.

While I'm on the subject of clothes: I learned always to travel in an outfit suitable for my professional engagements on arrival. In my experience, airline staff treat well-dressed women passengers better. Also, luggage gets lost, and you cannot always easily buy suitable clothes quickly at your destination. I lost my case en route to Damascus and Athens once, and the only clothes I could buy at short notice were caftan-like long dresses in a souk. The ambassador's wife in Athens very generously lent me a professional outfit from her own wardrobe for the conference I was due to attend.

At a post overseas, the wife of a male head of mission would often take care of befriending the other ambassadors' wives and looking after the families of embassy staff. As a single female ambassador, I had to do all that plus the head of mission's job. I had difficult cases of postpartum depression and extreme culture shock to look after. Over the years, as more women became heads of mission and males increasingly had partners with professions and careers of their own, social secretaries were appointed so that the ambassador could concentrate on the main job and spouses were free to pursue their own interests. Community liaison officers, usually one of the spouses, were also employed to look after the staff families. In Fiji our CLO, Colin McKenzie, was invaluable in helping manage the disruption to staff families, who were evacuated out of Suva during the Speight coup in Fiji in 2000.

People often assumed that the ambassador would be a man. I had to learn how to deal with that. At one reception I was introduced as the new Australian high commissioner to one rather pompous fellow who clearly did not listen carefully and proceeded as if I was the wife of the new high commissioner. 'Oh yes', he started. 'I met the new high commissioner just a little while ago. Nice fellow'.

Wickedly, I asked, 'Oh yes? And what did you think of him? What did you talk about?'

After letting him talk himself into a hole, I reiterated clearly that *I* was actually the high commissioner, then left him to his own discomfort.

Early in my posting to Bangladesh, in 1986, I made a long and uncomfortable journey to inspect an aid project some way out of Dhaka. The man greeting me on arrival, as I got out of the car bearing the Australian flag said, 'Oh, couldn't the high commissioner come? We will really miss him'. I was irritated, and he felt extremely embarrassed when he discovered my position. On subsequent occasions, to avoid such situations, I always made sure that my staff had made clear to my hosts ahead of time that the high commissioner was a woman.

My first deputy in Bangladesh, a man, originally travelled with me to some functions. He got out of the car before me and proceeded to shake hands with our hosts while leaving me trailing, as the hosts invariably assumed he was the ambassador. He was not helpful in disabusing them. So I stopped taking him with me.

The introduction of part-time work, flexible working hours and paid parental leave in DFAT made a great difference to both men and women who had to balance family responsibilities.

DFAT established a fully licensed in-house child day-care centre, which was a great boon. For overseas postings, better allowances for families with children eventually ensued, for single as well as partnered parents, and there were more funded reunion visits both to and from postings for children in boarding school.

These measures, and with time a welcoming rather than a tolerance of women, made it possible for more women to move around the career jungle gym and forge satisfying combinations of work and family or other interests. It was possible for men as well as women to fit career breaks in when they worked best for them and to look after their families.

There are two particular behavioural traits which I think are worth addressing. One is the imposter syndrome – the inward feeling that you are really not as good or as knowledgeable as you are projecting and that one day 'they' will find out and you will be exposed. No matter how much you prepare your presentation or a discussion, you feel that it hasn't been enough – and 'they' will pick up on that. In my coaching work, I have discovered that men also experience this syndrome, but they just go and brave it out. All I can say is that I had these fears, but in a 34-year career the worst never happened. 'They' never saw through me. At least, not that I noticed. The danger is that this fear can stop you taking the plunge. Just acknowledge it and go on nonetheless. The allied situation is when someone offers you a job and the immediate female response is to discount your competence to do it. You don't have the experience yet. It's outside your field of interest. All sorts of excuses. I'm ashamed to admit that I reacted this way when I was invited to take up business coaching, after retiring from DFAT in 2003. I had to be persuaded that I did, in fact, have the necessary experience and skills. Most men don't react like this: they just go and take the job.

While DFAT was busy changing the workplace making it a better, more enjoyable and more productive place to spend a good chunk of our lives, similar processes were going on elsewhere in the public service and in business. In other countries it was happening at a greater speed than in Australia. Then, the concern was the balance between life and work. Good businesses now think about life in its totality: life includes work; the two are not separate. Those who manage the 'working' elements of our lives have to accommodate the range of duties and responsibilities we all have, as well as the ways in which we ensure balance between work and play. Society has changed, as have perceptions of gender and gender roles. Men as well as women have parenting responsibilities and responsibility for ageing parents. Everyone has ways in which they make wider contributions to their societies, whether in sport, philanthropic activities, schools or bringing up the next generation. Our children need male and female role models to learn how to be good men and women, good citizens and to play their full part in the lives they lead.

In the 1970s, work was tightly demarcated as separate from our private lives. 'Private' phone calls were frowned upon in work time, and flexitime was only adopted in the workplace reluctantly. All staff had to sign in and out of work, and a terrifying woman came to the External Affairs sign-in counter twenty minutes after the official starting time in the morning and gleefully ruled a thick blue line on the sign-in page of the register so those who were late were noted and penalised. Flexitime, when introduced, accommodated both women and men who had to get their children off to school before they could go to work. It also allowed them to remain at home with sick children or in case of family emergencies. Previously 'making allowances' was the key concept. It assumed that the male-dominated, hierarchical, rigorously organised workplace was the proper norm and had total priority in people's lives. The growth in numbers of women in the workplace and in positions of power has led to a workplace revolution – admittedly not yet perfectly or uniformly implemented.

When coaching I see workplaces which have, as the norm, a nine-day working fortnight, giving staff a full day to attend to private or community matters and much greater flexibility in working hours on the remaining nine days. Fathers are playing a fuller role in parenting and family matters. It is as common for fathers as for mothers to drop the kids off at school and then pick them up at the end of the school day, and to share household management jobs like shopping, laundry and cleaning. Hired help is now more commonly used to get the household jobs done, from nannies to cleaners, freeing up quality family time. Or couples may agree that the male partner take on the major domestic leadership and management roles, giving the female partner the opportunity to be the major breadwinner in the family. The modern workplace seeks to celebrate and accommodate male and female qualities. Both are seen as equally legitimate and valuable parts of the whole. None of this was foreseen when I joined External Affairs.

There are still enterprises finding out how to run an efficient and profitable business with a fully flexible workforce. Men and women occupy this space together, sharing the benefits as well as the challenges. I hope that the work the women did throughout their careers and their pressure for change have made a major contribution to a more equitable workplace and greater flexibility in how we see our genders and gender roles.

The practise of diplomacy has changed considerably since the 1970s. Revolutionised communication systems, the greater politicisation of the public service, including the foreign service, the greater ease of international travel, which brings the foreign minister, the prime minister and other ministers frequently to play a direct role in diplomacy at overseas posts, have brought about major changes. But in an ever changing world, with challenges to international security and international events impacting more on domestic daily life than before, there is even greater need for skilled teams on the ground, with the right contacts, detailed understanding of what is going on, resources and nous and the capacity to find the right path – teams who know what is going on, what it means for Australia and what Australia needs to do about it.

I was privileged to have played a part as an agent of many of the changes. I was heartened to receive a message on my birthday in 2019 from Pat Duggan, who was third secretary at the high commission in Bangladesh. She went on to an interesting career in international aid. Pat wrote,

> When you are young, you don't always recognise how significant events or people are...You, Sue, were one of the handful of women in Canberra making a real go of it, working very successfully in a male professional environment. I certainly didn't recognise just how significant your achievements were then...We didn't have many role models to look up to (and to gain support from when dealing with a largely male dominant culture) – you were certainly one. You are significant![12]

At a farewell party at the end of my DFAT career, in 2003, David Irvine, one of my oldest friends and colleagues, gave a speech describing my accomplishments at DFAT.

> [Sue achieved success by] making her point, not by stridently burning her bra outside the secretary's office, or by insisting on pedantic political correctness, but through professionalism and humanity over a long and successful career, providing a role model for women in diplomacy. Young women entering DFAT today with firm expectations of a bright career, unencumbered by the glass ceiling, do not always appreciate the debt they owe to Sue Boyd and a number of other women of her generation in blazing the trail the young now follow.

He also described me when we were student friends at The University of Western Australia:

> Sue was the gregarious, intelligent, funny, serious, determined and above all the warm and loving person that she remains today. Sue has done a great job for Australia. Her personality has won us many friends. Her advocacy has helped promote our nation.[13]

Frances Adamson, who became the first woman to head the department, in 2016, said at an Australian Institute of International Affairs meeting in Perth in 2017 that I had been a mentor and role model for most of the women in DFAT.

12

Vietnam, 1994–98: the best posting

'Mrs Shoes-On Boy, Ambassadress Extraordinary and Plenty
Potential of the Republic of Australia' My favourite posting.
The right political juncture for Australia to shine and the
ideal time to be ambassador. Using all my skills as the
country opened up and looked for international partners.

Đặng Thị Khuê was selected for the 1996 Asia Pacific Triennial of
Contemporary Art at the Queensland Art Gallery. Her story helps
explain the Vietnam I was working in as ambassador from 1994 to
1998. Khuê was an art student at the Vietnam University of Fine
Arts at the time of the Vietnam War (1955–75). The whole country
was focussed on winning the war, and money for art materials was
scarce. The Communist Party supplied artists with materials and
art school education, but their art had to serve Vietnam during
the struggle against the French, the Chinese and, latterly, the
Americans and their allies. A large body of propaganda art was
produced, and through this artists were able to develop their skills.
But there was no free rein on creativity. The mid-1990s, however,
saw a burgeoning of artistic creation in Vietnam at the same time
as an energetic explosion of economic and social activity. With
the reunification of Vietnam, the end of the war, peace and the
adoption of the Đổi Mới ('new way' – economic renovation)
policies, artists were free to create as they wished, and materials
became available on the open market. Several Australian artists
went to Vietnam during this time to experience the new openness,

see the rapidly growing body of new art and make friends and contacts with Vietnamese artists. The local artists were thirsty for foreign contact after years of repression and isolation. They soon realised that foreigners were prepared to pay good money for local art.

In this emerging cultural exchange was an opportunity for art to play a role in Australian diplomacy. The Australian organisation Asialink funded a studio and a series of residencies for young contemporary Australian artists at the Hanoi University of Fine Arts in 1993. The new Asia Pacific Triennial, at the Queensland Art Gallery, supported by Griffith University, searched for good contemporary Vietnamese artists to be represented there in 1996. The three Vietnamese artists selected for the second Asia Pacific Triennial in Brisbane were Đặng Thị Khuê, Mai Anh Dũng and Vũ Dân Tân. I got to know these artists and bought works by each of them.

Anh Dũng was a young man from Ho Chi Minh City (formerly Saigon) who lived and painted in a tiny garage space otherwise occupied by his motorbike. At night he took his motorbike inside and slept on the floor next to it, while his completed artworks were suspended from the roof. During the day he earned his living making finely detailed Vietnamese lacquer crafts in a small factory in Ho Chi Minh City. When I offered to buy one of his paintings, he was reluctant to sell. He said it was not a very good painting, as he was only a young artist and needed to paint more to improve. But he needed money for art materials, so he reluctantly agreed. I was pleased to be able to support this talented and determined young artist. He was focussed on the Chàm people, a minority who had been pushed south by the majority Viet people as they in turn were pushed south by the invading Chinese. The remains of the Chàm kingdom are inland from Đà Nẵng, a coastal city 765 kilometres south of Hanoi, and their distinctive stone sculptures can be viewed in the Museum of Chàm Sculpture, from Đà Nẵng. The painting I bought from Anh Dũng was of a Chàm priest.

Woman artist Đặng Thị Khuê, in her early forties when I first met her in 1994, lived and worked in Hanoi. She had long served as secretary of the artists' association, helping support and develop younger artists, at the same time as bringing up her own family. She was newly free of these commitments and for the first time free to paint what she wanted. The other two artists chosen for the second Asia Pacific Triennial were installation artists and needed to be in Brisbane in person. Khuê's work was less difficult to hang, and she had not been invited to attend the exhibition. She dearly wanted to go. So we agreed to exchange the painting for a return air ticket to Brisbane (see artwork insert figure 7). She came back to Hanoi after the triennial enraptured by installation art, which she had not encountered before, and immediately set about creating an exhibition centred on women in Vietnam.

A pleasant surprise on arriving in Vietnam was to discover Toh Hock Ghim as the Ambassador of Singapore. We had been together on the foreign service training course in Canberra in 1970. He had then gone on to an internship in the Australian High Commission in Nigeria. He and his wife went out of their way to make me welcome in Hanoi, show me the ropes and expand my understanding of Vietnamese politics and culture. He was an avid art collector, both for his government, which was establishing new art galleries in Singapore, and on his own account and he introduced me to the artistically interesting aspects of Vietnam, as well as to the newish Hanoi golf course. On the first game we played together, he observed that there were few countries where you could bet in thousands on each hole. Wouldn't it be fun to play for 1,000 Vietnamese dong per hole? This was still A$100, but, gulping, I agreed. We both played hard but ended up quits, much to my relief. I'm still not sure to what extent he played diplomatically!

Before Vietnam joined the Association of South East Asian Nations (ASEAN) in 1995, I played golf a few times with the Vietnamese Foreign Minister Nguyễn Mạnh Cầm, who was learning the game, knowing it was useful in diplomacy. He was also working hard to learn English. I told him that Australia could help him in a number of ways to prepare for the coming ASEAN debut. There were four informal requisites for success in ASEAN: playing golf, speaking English, wearing coloured shirts and singing karaoke. We could assist with the first two.

He paid an official visit to Australia in February 1997 and called on Prime Minister John Howard, who was initially reluctant to receive the communist leader. Cầm insisted on conducting this conversation in English, without using the interpreter. The prime minister sent him a note after the meeting, congratulating him on the level of English he had achieved.

When the embassy in Hanoi was first established, in July 1973, it was staffed only by single officers or couples without children, due to the difficulty in finding appropriate accommodation and the challenging living and medical conditions. After the Vietnam War, food was scarce in Vietnam, and supplies for the embassy were sourced from Bangkok via a fortnightly bag run. This regular visit to Bangkok, primarily to collect the diplomatic bag of documents and mail, rotated among the embassy staff. The original embassy had been housed in rooms in the landmark hotel, formerly called the Thống Nhất (Reunification Hotel), which was then very run down. The first staff occupied four hotel rooms which doubled as official offices. Jan Forrester and Richard Rowe, both early staff members, told me that they kept their cipher pads under their pillows. The official vehicles were bicycles. Jan reported that the hotel courtyard was thick with rats, and staff kept their feet high as they rode their bicycles into the hotel grounds at night.

Conditions had improved over the years and when I arrived in 1994 the embassy was occupying a cluster of old French villas on Lý Thường Kiệt Street, which were historically charming but not really suitable for a modern embassy the size of Australia's.

By 1995, Australia had a new embassy compound, with good offices, staff apartments, a swimming pool and children's play facilities. There was an international school and clinic in Hanoi, other good accommodation and an adequate local food supply.

The 'no children' policy was abandoned, and the first children were very welcome. For the first time there was a normal bunch of men and women professionals serving Australia's interests in Vietnam – some single, some married, some heterosexual, some gay. The newly built embassy buildings included areas which could be opened up for large receptions and served well as art exhibition spaces and other gatherings. We were less concerned with embassy security in those pre-9/11 days and welcomed visitors freely, after minimal security checks. This was an ideal place for exhibitions like Đặng Thị Khuê's installation.

My initial introduction to the art scene in Hanoi came through my long-time colleague and friend Graham Alliband, who had been ambassador in Hanoi a few years before me (1988–91) and had stayed on for a time as a business consultant. His whole career had been focussed on Vietnam. He spoke the language fluently and had worked in Vietnamese refugee camps in Hong Kong following the Vietnam War. He tucked me under his arm and took me around Hanoi soon after my arrival, introducing me to the city and its eating places and to his friends, including his artist friends. Among these was Bùi Hữu Hùng, an artist who used the traditional Vietnamese lacquer techniques for expressions of modern art. I loved his work. Graham left Hanoi for a while and I gave a farewell party for him. He and I and the domestic staff converted the embassy residence, in Lý Thường Kiệt Street, to an art gallery for Bùi Hữu Hùng and invited all the embassy friends and colleagues we thought would be interested in the art. When I revisited Hanoi a few years later, his work was heavily collected, and pieces were selling for US$15,000 and up. He was well and truly launched.

Graham took me to the home of Professor Nguyễn Thu, the retired head of the Vietnam University of Fine Arts, which was founded by the French in 1925. Like many older Vietnamese, Professor Thu spoke French, so we could talk to each other easily, without needing an interpreter. The embassy had worked with him in setting up the Asialink Australian studio at the university, where young visiting Australian artists could work. We had a riotous lunch in his home with his wife, who belonged to one of the minority ethnic communities. The lunch was lubricated with her very potent homemade black rice wine; we drank quite a lot. After lunch I looked through a portfolio of Professor Thu's own works, which included several exquisite works on silk – a traditional medium. One evocative piece I admired showed Vietnamese soldiers crossing a country bridge in misty conditions, regarded by an inquisitive lamb. Professor Thu offered to give it to me: I refused the gift and insisted on paying. Eventually, he accepted payment of one sou for him and ninety-nine sous for his wife. (The sou, a French unit of currency, was worth one one-hundredth of a franc: very little. It was symbolic for an actual payment of A$100.) We became friends, and he told me he could not possibly call me Bà Đại Sứ, my formal title as ambassador, which literally translated means 'grandmother ambassador'; I was far too young. He would call me 'Em Đại Sứ', which means not only 'little sister ambassador' but also 'darling ambassador'. This caused great amusement locally, and he called me this throughout my time in Vietnam.

There are no terms for 'me' and 'you' in Vietnamese, and it is polite in Vietnamese culture to address each other with family terms which would be appropriate to your relative ages, were you actually family members. But it is a mark of extra respect to go up one notch – so I was 'grandmother', rather than 'aunt' or 'older sister'. It is impolite to use the name of the other person without preceding it by 'sister', 'brother', 'uncle', 'aunt' or 'grandchild' where appropriate. This is why the first question Vietnamese people ask is 'How old are you?' which in western culture seems impertinent. They just need to know what to call you.

A stream of Australian artists was coming through Hanoi at that time. Joe Furlonger, an established and award-winning Australian artist, spent six months painting frenetically in Hanoi, accompanied by his wife, Heidi, also an artist, and their children. He donated a large artwork to the embassy in appreciation of the support we gave them and also one privately to me. His work reflected the hectic life on Hanoi's streets, as well as the tranquil countryside.

I encouraged Australian businesses in Vietnam to buy examples of the works of each visiting Australian artist and to donate them to the embassy, where they were displayed with credits to the donors. We thus began a permanent collection in Hanoi. Having visitors like these artists opened up new perspectives for us, and we helped them understand Vietnam and make linkages. By the time I left Hanoi the embassy collection included works by Joe Furlonger, Julie Shiels, Jo D'Hage, Katy Munson, Helga Groves, Mai Long, Geoff Lowe and others.

The mid 1990s was a great time to be the Australian ambassador in Vietnam. It was an exciting posting. We were witnessing the energetic and swift development of a very traditional and culturally strong society. One characterisation was a tiger on a motorbike. (Rapidly growing Asian economies were called tigers and the most rapidly expanding means of transport in Vietnam was the motorbike). The country was in a hurry to catch up, and the Australian Government and Australian companies were there early, building relationships and ready to help.

When I arrived in Vietnam, in 1994, the United States was convinced that the Vietnamese were deliberately not cooperating in locating the remains of American troops that had gone missing in action during the Vietnam War. The US administration refused to recognise Vietnam officially and maintained a boycott of trade and business relations. Thus, there was no US Embassy or US Consulate in the country, and there was only a very small American business presence. Vietnamese businesses might have preferred to work with American companies under Đổi Mới, but that was not possible. Australia was there and available. Australia worked hard to capitalise on this advantage, and the embassy was deeply involved. This was rewarding work.

All Vietnamese businesses were state owned and run. The new economic policy adopted by the communist government encouraged an opening up to the west, and Vietnam was keen to find foreign strategic partners. Some of the earliest overseas businesses to build collaborative commercial relationships in Vietnam were Australian, by forming joint ventures or creating other ways for organisations to work together. The Australian and Overseas Telecommunication Corporation, the forerunner of Australia's large telephone company Telstra, persuaded the Vietnamese Government that Vietnam needed modern telecommunications to facilitate trade development, and so it became an adviser to the Vietnamese state-owned Telecom. BHP Petroleum worked with PetroVietnam on a new oil and gas field – Đại Hùng, or Big Bear – in the South China Sea. ANZ was the first foreign bank to win licences to operate in the country, in Hanoi and Ho Chi Minh City. Phillips Fox was the first western law firm allowed to practise in Vietnam. Headed by Bill Magennis, it translated Vietnam's investment laws into English and trained Vietnamese lawyers. It helped a myriad of foreign investors into Vietnam. Two talented young business entrepreneurs, Susy Barry and Rachel Edilson, set up a small human resources enterprise which helped many Vietnamese and Australian companies. They worked with Swinburne University, the first Australian university to launch courses in Vietnam. It was a thrill to attend their first graduation ceremony in Hanoi, and fun, as the orchestra surprisingly struck up jaunty fairground music as the university procession left the hall.

Madame Tôn Nữ Thị Ninh came from an aristocratic family from the former Royal Court at Hue. She had spent the war years in Paris, at the Sorbonne, working for the North Vietnamese political cause. By the time I arrived in Hanoi she was the deputy head of the Vietnamese foreign ministry. She was elegant, highly intelligent and super smart. Her friend Madame Phạm Chi Lan was head of the Vietnam Chamber of Commerce and Industry and was the original architect of the Đổi Mới policy. Vietnam was in the process of corporatising many of the state-owned businesses, and Ninh invited me and the only other female foreign ambassador, Christine Desloges, from Canada, to join the two of them in forming an international women's business network, to help the many women heads of the state-owned enterprises with the challenges they faced in doing business with the west. Christine and I were of course delighted to help and in the process got to know Ninh and Chi Lan quite well. We called our group the Gang of Four. We got to know many women heads of Vietnamese business enterprises, in the north and in Ho Chi Minh City, and helped make useful connections for them. Two whom I got to know best were the chief executive officer of the Saigon Cosmetics Company, the manufacturers of the Miss Saigon perfume, and the head of a glass and ceramic decorative objects business. The embassy arranged for them to visit Australia in business delegations and make invaluable contacts.

In 1994, the Australian Department of Defence in Canberra agreed that it might be timely to negotiate the opening of a defence cooperation agreement between Australia and Vietnam. For the first time since the end of the Vietnam War, Australian navy ships, military attachés and staff college delegations could be in Vietnam. This was a significant step, since the Vietnamese were extremely sensitive on defence matters. Defence welcomed this assessment: they had been thinking along similar lines. So, on their behalf I carried out careful discussions with the foreign ministry, which consulted the Communist Party, and it was agreed that the first step would be a study visit from the Australian Joint Services Staff College in 1995.

There were emotional moments during this inaugural visit. Our host at the first official dinner at the National Defence Academy of Vietnam, in the Hanoi Citadel, revealed that he had fought in Phước Tuy province against the Australian unit in which his Australian counterpart, the leader of the Australian Staff College study group, Brigadier John Wilson, had served. As the evening was warming up, our host leant across the table and said to Wilson, 'You know we have met before?' It was an arresting moment. His military unit had observed Wilson's unit in action. He was full of praise for the Australian soldiers, who, he said, were honourable, with very high levels of professional competence. 'You Australians can hold a position for days', he said, adding that, unlike the Americans, Australian troops were fully professional and had not abused the local civilian population. This was an exhilarating and promising start.

After this initial contact, the Vietnamese authorities agreed to receive the first Australian defence adviser to join the embassy in Hanoi in 1999, enabling systematic contacts with the Vietnamese military leadership and exploration of ways to work together. The Vietnamese were cautious at first, but careful work slowly built trust and opened up information exchanges. The first Vietnamese officer to attend the Australian Command and Staff College course in Canberra did so in 1997. Vietnamese military staff attended maritime security exercises at Australia's Jervis Bay on the NSW coast. In 2014, HMAS *Larrakia* visited Ho Chi Minh port – the first Australian naval visit to Vietnam since the Vietnam War. Vice Admiral Tim Barrett, chief of the Australian Navy, was also present.[14] The visit was preceded by joint submarine rescue training and other defence staff exchanges. Australia also assisted Vietnamese peacekeepers in 2014 by providing English language training before they joined the United Nations peacekeeping group in South Sudan.[15] I felt quiet satisfaction at my roles in alerting Defence in Canberra that the time was ripe to pursue the defence relationship, conducting initial exploratory negotiations with the Vietnamese authorities in Hanoi and easing the first contact.

Similarly a new partnership for the Australian Federal Police was negotiated, some of whose officers became based in the embassy and worked with their Vietnamese counterparts on international law and order issues, including drugs, money laundering and people smuggling. The Vietnamese foreign ministry was initially opposed to the idea of having foreigners look more closely at Vietnamese police operations, which were, at the time, undergoing internal investigation for possible corruption. We carefully explored the mutual advantages of such an exchange, but we eventually learned that the difficulty was caused by the ministry's extreme sensitivity about foreign police in uniform roaming around Ho Chi Minh City. Once it was clarified that the Australian police would be in plain clothes and would be based in the Hanoi embassy, the way was cleared for the ultimate agreement. The Australian Federal Police representatives took up their positions after I left the embassy, and in due course they were allowed to operate out of the Australian Consulate-General in Ho Chi Minh City and soon established an admirable track record of international crime disruption. Among other results, this operation significantly reduced the flow of drugs into Australia from the Golden Triangle – the major drug producing area where the borders of Thailand, Laos and Myanmar meet.

The plans for the new embassy in Hanoi were originally for a two-storey office building, reflecting the mission's small size. It was clear that we were likely to need room for defence and Australian Federal Police staff, as well as for the Australian Centre for International Agricultural Research and a new education officer. As these positions, however, were not yet formally established when the plans were drawn, the respective departments in Canberra could not formally bid for space in the new building. We in Hanoi were able to persuade the architects to include an extra floor, which we originally designated formally as 'exercise space' and which eventually provided for the anticipated expansion of the embassy operations. Before coming to Hanoi, I had visited our embassy in Jakarta when it moved into its new chancery building and it was then already too small. In this environment, it seemed reasonable to take risks. I generally operated on the principle of 'do it first and seek permission afterwards', which mostly worked, although it was not in line with formal bureaucratic procedures.

In October 1994 Australia opened a consulate-general in Ho Chi Minh City in the south, where the Australian Embassy had been located during the Vietnam War. One of the most moving successes of the embassy in which I was involved was helping

Australian veterans to find the original Long Tân Cross and have it on permanent display in the Đồng Nai Museum at Biên Hòa in the south of Vietnam. Australian soldiers had erected a concrete cross with a metal plaque on the site of the battle in August 1966, but by the end of the war the cross had disappeared. The director of the museum discovered that a Christian community nearby had taken the cross to mark the grave of their pastor and was using the original plaque as a cooking plate. He recognised the historical importance of the cross, took it for safekeeping and hid it in his museum. After the war, he assisted Australian veterans in the construction of a replica of the cross and plaque and to erect it on the battle site. But he kept the existence of the original cross a secret, fearing that Australia would insist on taking it to the Australian War Memorial, in Canberra. Following a tip-off from Australian Army veterans, Russ Properjohn, the first secretary, and I visited the museum in 1994 and persuaded the director to produce the original cross and display it appropriately in the museum. I assured him that Australia recognised the cross belonged in Vietnam and that the government had no intention of asking for it. We provided the museum with funds to pay for the appropriate display of the original cross. The cross in the museum and the memorial in the middle of a rubber plantation remained sensitive issues with the local Vietnamese, many of whom had been members of the Army of the Republic of Vietnam, fighting with the support of the Americans against the northern communist Viet Cong.

In 1996, after a long negotiation, Vietnam agreed to a visit by the Australian deputy prime minister Tim Fischer, the minister for Veterans' Affairs Bruce Scott and a group of Vietnam veterans to mark the anniversary of the Battle of Long Tân and all who had died in the war. The Vietnamese authorities confined the ceremony to the old airstrip at the former Australian base at Núi Đất, not at the battle site at the Long Tân Cross memorial. Small groups could make private visits to the cross. Tim Fischer and I climbed up a hill at Núi Đất to the site of his tent when he was an army officer in the war. It was an extremely emotional moment as we squatted at what had been the entrance to the tent. Fighting back tears, Tim looked out at the unchanged view and talked about his time during the war. Little Pattie, the Australian singer, had been performing to entertain the troops at the Núi Đất base when the Battle of Long Tân was fought. She was also part of the group visiting with Tim Fischer. It was all very moving.

The recurring conflict between veterans wishing to visit and honour the site and Vietnamese reluctance seems to have been resolved with the gift of the original cross by Vietnam to the Australian War Memorial in 2013.

The Australian governor-general Bill Hayden visited Vietnam in April 1995 and, as is the usual protocol, as Ambassador I escorted him throughout the visit. He was formally hosted by President Lê Đức Anh, who was the commander of North Vietnamese forces in the south during the war. The president was welcoming but not at all receptive to the representations on current Vietnamese human rights abuses which Hayden raised with him towards the end of the formal meeting. The president responded angrily, accusing Australia itself of carrying out human rights abuses through its very participation in the war and the violation of Vietnamese sovereignty. This exchange created a mutually hostile atmosphere at the very end of the meeting, and after a tense silence both leaders accepted the suggestion that the topic might be further taken up at the dinner scheduled for that evening. Following the meeting, Vietnamese foreign ministry officials took up with me the president's anger, and they were indignant that Hayden had gone off script. They threatened to abort the rest of the visit. Hayden agreed privately that he might have given advance warning of the topic. We managed to smooth things over. The topic was not, of course, raised again at the dinner, and the visit concluded without further incident. Hayden had made his point, and the human rights question had been put on the official record at the highest level. The following day the governor-general, a Vietnamese vice minister and I turned the first spades of soil for the construction of the new Australian Embassy at Văn Phúc, a developing area of Hanoi (see picture insert figure 18).

Paul Keating visited Vietnam in 1994 – the first visit by an Australian prime minister. He established a special personal relationship with the Vietnamese prime minister, Võ Văn Kiệt, and agreed to his request for Australia to build a bridge over the Mekong River at Mỹ Thuận, under the Australian aid program. This important crossing was a bottleneck, impeding the easy transport of agricultural products from the rich delta of southern Vietnam to consumer markets and export ports in Ho Chi Minh City. Laden trucks were waiting days for places on the small ferries which crossed the river there. Perishable cargoes were affected. Many small eating places had set up to serve the needs of the waiting truck drivers, including hammocks at the many cafes, as well as prostitution. The bridge would open up the south and encourage new horticultural enterprises and provide alternative employment opportunities.

Planning for the bridge was well under way when, in 1995, an Australian parliamentary delegation visited Vietnam. It was headed by Labor senator Stephen Loosley, chair of the Joint Committee on Foreign Affairs, Defence and Trade. The deputy leader was the opposition's shadow foreign minister Alexander Downer. The agenda included human rights–related visits and discussions. In due course, we were able to open discussions which led to the development of human rights studies at the Ho Chi Minh National Academy of Politics, the Communist Party school. During this visit, Downer warned the embassy that if the conservative parties won the forthcoming Australian federal election, they would scrap the Mỹ Thuận Bridge project. Subsequently, upon taking office in 1996, the new Coalition government, led by Prime Minister John Howard, announced this intention. It argued that public opinion polls had indicated that the electorate did not support large infrastructure projects within the aid program. The Australian public wanted aid restricted to projects directly relieving poverty.

The embassy and the Australian business community in Vietnam saw this broken promise as a disaster. Reneging on a former prime minister's personal assurance to the Vietnamese prime minister would send a range of negative signals about Australia's reliability and affect the partnerships which Australian businesses were carefully establishing. The bridge was a highly visible keynote project.

An ambassador's job is to inform their government about developments which affect their country's interests and to advise on policies which would further those interests. I wrote a careful assessment of the situation and sent it back through DFAT to our new minister, Alexander Downer. I also reported faithfully on representations from the Vietnamese Government and on the concerns of the Australian business and aid community in the country at this move.

Initially, it was to no avail. I realised that reports from an ambassador urging a reversal of new policy were neither welcome nor a priority early in the life of the new government at home. We needed other methods of getting our message through. A prominent Australian plastic surgeon was leading the Operation Smile project in Vietnam, reconstructing the faces of children born with facial defects or those with serious injuries, including burns. He had close connections with the Downer family and agreed to raise the issue through his personal channels. The firm which had the design contract for the bridge also had family connections to the new government and agreed to weigh in. But the most important link was a very prominent Melbourne business family, a significant funder of the Liberal Party, which had several business projects in Vietnam that could be affected by the policy change. A senior family member who had close links with John Howard undertook to raise the matter with him personally, explain the consequences and urge reconsideration of the decision.

At this time, I received private reports from Canberra that Alexander Downer, the foreign minister, was saying, 'Will someone tell our socialist ambassador in Hanoi to tell her commie mates that there's been a putsch in Canberra? They'll understand', and, 'Whose fucking ambassador is she, anyway? Ours or Vietnam's?' This was worrying. I made an appointment to see the minister and flew back to Canberra. With my heart in my mouth, I told Mr Downer that I had heard what he had been saying about me. I could not continue to serve as Australian ambassador if I did not have the government's confidence. If I didn't have its support, I was prepared to resign. He referred to the many close friends I had in the Australian Labor Party. I did not deny these longstanding friendships and told him I had friends across the political spectrum and had served faithfully and well governments of all political persuasions since I joined the foreign service in 1970. After a tense silence, and a smile, he asked me to return to Hanoi and serve out the remainder of my term. I later heard that he also sought opinions of my performance from some of the senior business leaders I had helped in Vietnam.

The government did reverse its policy on the Mỹ Thuận Bridge and allowed the project to proceed. Mr Downer, his wife, Nicky, the deputy secretary of DFAT, John Dauth, and I flew by helicopter into the Mỹ Thuận site, on the banks of the Mekong, on 6 July 1997, to join the Vietnamese ministers in turning the first sods of the project.

Alexander Downer and I had a satisfactory professional relationship for the rest of my career. He later appointed me consul general in Hong Kong and then high commissioner in Fiji, and we worked collaboratively through the challenges of the Speight coup and the restitution of democratic government in Fiji.

The Mỹ Thuận Bridge was formally opened on 21 May 2000, without my presence, due to the Speight coup in Fiji, where I was by then posted. In 2011, I paid a private return visit to Vietnam and saw the completed bridge for the first time. Chantelle Woodford, consul at the Australian Consulate-General in Ho Chi Minh City, and Dr Bill Kean, formerly of the World Health Organization, came too. The Vietnamese Department of Transport gave us a full briefing on the significant benefits to the economy of the south provided by Australia's generosity, then took us to the bridge. We were joined by the chair of the bridge authority, an elegant woman wearing the traditional Vietnamese *áo dài* dress and carrying a parasol to shade us. We drove to the highest point of the bridge, then our escort invited us to walk down towards Cần Thơ, the major Mekong regional centre, with a police vehicle protecting us from the traffic. This was a very special moment. The bridge was a real success, and the benefits to Vietnam as well as Australia were considerable, in political, economic and social terms, and were well worth the risks I took personally and professionally.

At the Victoria Hotel in Cần Thơ the manager joined us in the lounge. He said he recognised me as the former ambassador and that he and others knew of my personal role in the bridge project. He wanted to thank me, on behalf of everyone who had benefited. He quoted the Vietnamese proverb 'When you eat the fruit of the tree, you remember the person who planted the seed'. I was quite emotional, recalling the anguish, fear of failure and possible negative consequences for the project I cared deeply for. It was now a time for a sense of relief and achievement against the odds. Bill Kean and I had a celebratory glass of champagne.

Western visitors continue to be amazed at how well they are treated in Vietnam. Part of the embassy's mission was to help Australian visitors understand that Vietnam is not a war; it is a country. For the United States, the Vietnam War was the longest it had fought – and lost. For Vietnam, it was the shortest war it had fought – it battled for longer against the Chinese and the French – and also won. More than half the population when I was there had been born since the end of the war. The war was etched deeply into the psyche of visiting Americans and Australians, but the Vietnamese were busy getting on with life.

In 1995, Democrat president Bill Clinton persuaded the US Congress to normalise relations with Vietnam, and the United States' first ambassador to Vietnam, Pete Peterson, arrived in 1997. He was an inspired and brilliant choice, and we welcomed his arrival in Hanoi. He had been an American airman and was shot down in the Vietnam War in 1966 and held in the infamous 'Hanoi Hilton' prison for six years. Upon repatriation to the United States, he entered politics, became a Democrat member of Congress and worked assiduously to normalise relations. He held no grudges. He was especially welcomed by the Australian trade commissioner, Miss Vi Lê. Vi was a stunning and smart Vietnamese Australian who had arrived in Hanoi with the initial ANZ bank team. In 1996, Austrade lured her from the bank and appointed her Australian trade commissioner. We got on well and made an effective professional team and a positive public statement about women in positions of authority. People noticed that the top four Australian Government officials in Vietnam were all women: the ambassador, the trade commissioner, the consul general in Ho Chi Minh City Lisa Filipetto and the Austrade representative Kerryn Mansell (see picture insert figure 22).

Vi Lê and Pete Peterson soon fell in love, and they married in Hanoi in May 1998. The American press had a ball: reporting to the effect of 'American ambassador, former prisoner of war in Hanoi, marries Vietnamese girl'. At their wedding, the Australian deputy head of mission, the wry Neil Mules, said that the headline should rather be 'Australian senior diplomat marries American ex-con'. They were married according to Vietnamese law, at a small private ceremony at the Hanoi People's Committee offices. I then officiated at the very large second marriage ceremony, attended by the international media, at one of the new hotels in Hanoi. They also had a religious ceremony in St Josephs Cathedral in Hanoi. The weather was extremely warm, and the tall, white candles in the church all melted and drooped. I whispered to Pete Peterson that I hoped this was not an omen!

In 1998, we celebrated the twenty-fifth anniversary of the establishment of the Australian Embassy in Vietnam. Former prime minister Gough Whitlam, who had made the decision to recognise Vietnam in 1973 travelled to Hanoi and participated in a seminar on the history of the two countries' relationship. He also gave one of his well-informed, instructive and entertaining speeches at the large, formal celebratory dinner at the Sofitel Metropole hotel. He placed the Australian presence in its historical perspective with great wit.

We held a large gala twenty-fifth anniversary celebration in the Hanoi Opera House, a splendid colonial showplace relic based on the Palais de Garnier in Paris. It had been seriously run down but by 1998 was newly renovated, and we held the first performance and reception there, for 650 guests. They included the Vietnamese deputy prime minister, Phạm Gia Khiêm, who had previously studied in Australia, and eight other ministers. The Australian parliamentary secretary for Foreign Affairs, Kathy Sullivan, opened the formal evening program with a special address. But the audience was only half listening. Its attention had been taken by a single, large rat, which had emerged from the back of the stage, wandered over and stopped immediately behind the unsuspecting parliamentary secretary, appeared to listen and then took its time to complete its parade before disappearing back into the wings, to a round of applause.

Following this, our guests were more conventionally entertained by a musical performance by the Australia Ensemble, on the impressive stage.

The reception after the concert took place in the splendid Mirror Room. A vertical banner was hung on either side of the grand staircase, with Vietnamese-language calligraphy on each. The Commonwealth Bank was a major sponsor of the event, and I asked its representative, Rob Pelley, to translate the words on the banners. Straight-faced, he responded, 'Your dong is safe in our hands'. (The dong is a unit of Vietnamese currency.) The ANZ bank's representative, not to be outdone, responded, 'We advertise with the slogan "A dong in the hand is worth a bird in the bush".' All very amusing. The event had been generously supported by the Australian business community and was rated a success and a demonstration to Vietnam of Australia's interest and competence across the spectrum.

While the prime minister and president of Vietnam were important leaders, real power lay in the hands of the Communist Party of Vietnam, and the most powerful person was the party secretary Đỗ Mười (1991 to 1997). He had met Paul Keating during the latter's visit to Vietnam and the two established a special rapport. In August 1995, Prime Minister Keating invited Đỗ Mười to visit Australia, and I accompanied him throughout his tour. He took a delegation of seventy-seven with him, including the top twenty-five business leaders in Vietnam – heads of all the state-owned enterprises, some of which were partnered by Australian businesses. This was the party leader's first visit to a non-Asian developed country (he had already visited Japan and Korea), and he was impressed by Australia's standard of living, economy and general happiness. The message went out on his return that Australia was the preferred business partner, and many opportunities opened up as a result.

The first stop for the Vietnamese leader and his party in Australia was Melbourne. The governor of the state of Victoria hosted us very comfortably in Government House. A rest day had been included in the program, but at dinner, Đỗ Mười said that he had been brought up on a farm in Vietnam and would dearly like to visit an Australian farm the following day. He did not need to rest. The details for the visitors' official program had been agreed weeks before, including the security aspects, but the Victorian state protocol department went into instant overdrive and overnight managed to arrange for us to visit a Gippsland dairy property the following day. The farmer and his wife were actually away from the property, in Melbourne on business, but his mother and their children agreed at short notice to host the visit. The children were highly entertained by the police who arrived early on powerful motorcycles to check security and gave them rides. The farmer's mother went into full Country Women's Association hospitality mode and called on neighbouring women to help with baking scones and making sandwiches, as well as laying the table with the best linen and china. We were royally welcomed when our official cavalcade went down the farm drive. The Vietnamese Communist Party leader and the farmer's mother had a long, personal conversation through our interpreter, in which both revealed that they had lost their respective partners. We observers wondered if a new special friendship was in the making.

During the tour around the dairy farm I made a dreadful clanger. A new calf was born while we watched, and I suggested to Đỗ Mười, through a member of his party, that he might allow the calf to be named after his daughter. Our interpreter, Phong Bùi, stepped in quickly. 'You can't do that, Sue! It is extremely insulting in Vietnamese culture for animals to be named after people'. I quickly apologised and explained our customs to the secretary. He responded jovially.

A few days later Đỗ Mười asked to make a visit to an Australian coalmine on the Sunday. This was also additional to the prepared program. An Australian company was working with the Vietnamese coalmine at Hạ Long Bay, an important tourism area on the Vietnamese coast, trying to modernise its operation. Vietnamese mines were grossly overstaffed, used inefficient technology, were polluting, and reforms were difficult. Processing methods were laborious and primitive. Đỗ Mười wanted to see an Australian mine and meet the workers for comparison. At very short notice, we arranged a visit to a mine that was in full production – totally operated by two men. Both were union members. We asked Đỗ Mười which one he wanted to meet. He was astounded.

At the end of the visit Keating hosted Đỗ Mười at the Mirage Country Club's golf course at Port Douglas, in Queensland. The prime minister personally drove the secretary around the course on a golf buggy, with the interpreter perched on the back. We in the official party were left hanging around the clubhouse, and we had no idea what was discussed by the two men. Fortunately, both appeared well pleased when they returned, and we took our visitor to the airport, from which a private plane flew him and his entourage home.

Vietnam's ambassador to Australia at that time was Nguyễn Thanh Châu, who had been one of the first students to travel to Australia from Vietnam under the Australian Colombo Plan international scholarship program. He had spent three years studying in Australia and knew the country and its culture well. It was very easy to work with him. Such relationships are invaluable in diplomacy and are a real help in avoiding and smoothing over difficulties. Diplomacy often involves making uncomfortable decisions, and the skill set of an ambassador includes pursuing the country's interests in difficult circumstances.

When the time came to leave Vietnam, I paid, as usual, courtesy farewell calls on all the ministers the embassy had dealt with. Each gave me an identical farewell gift: an embroidered tablecloth with matching napkins. Under the official government rules, I deemed all these as donations to the embassy and added them to the inventory at the residence. The education minister, however, gave me something different: a skimpy nightdress in peach-coloured silk, with matching negligee, and in my size! This, I decided, should be treated as personal. I could not see the Commonwealth having any use for it. The education minister also proposed to award me a medal, to recognise Australia's contributions to education in Vietnam. At that time, Australian ambassadors were barred from accepting foreign honours, so this presented a problem. Alexander Downer, however, was then visiting Vietnam and ruled that, as an exception, I should accept this honour. As the Vietnamese minister, with shaking hand, pinned the medal to my chest, I thought of the nightie!

Vietnam was an extremely busy post which tested and developed all the skills needed to be a good head of mission, and there were high levels of stress. As in my other posts, it was friendships and support from the staff in the embassy and in the Australian community which helped me through. I spent many weekends exploring temples and historical sites outside Hanoi and on each occasion invited friends to come along too. I took a good picnic lunch and bottle of wine with us, as well as mats to sit on, so we had excellent days out and I got to know friends better. Each was also getting to know Vietnam and was open in sharing experiences. I had an excellent support group of clever, kind and talented friends.

One friend accompanying me in the official head of mission vehicle towards the end of my posting commented to my driver, Mr Thi, that he must by now be expert in Vietnamese temples. He responded that the former ambassador Michael Potts had actually been passionate about Catholic churches and had visited them at weekends. And indeed, at the end of his posting, Michael had presented to the head of the Catholic Church in Vietnam a very handsome book of photographs of these historically significant buildings.

In my own experience, I found the value of reading as much as possible about the country of the posting, including folk tales, and learning at least a bit of the local language. I did an intensive Vietnamese-language course in Sydney before leaving. It was so easy to make inadvertent mistakes. By the end of my career I had a good knowledge of three languages as well as English, and a lesser knowledge of three more. Even if the main language of communication in the new country was English and there were professional interpreters, people appreciate it if you are interested in them and, at the very least, can pronounce their names properly. And you will learn more if people are talking in their own language.

For me it was very hard to learn Vietnamese. It was the first tonal language I had had to deal with, in which a single-syllable word might have six different meanings, depending on the tone. For example, in the market, buying grapefruit, getting one tone wrong communicated that you wanted to buy men's balls. The Vietnamese had lot of laughs at foreigners' expense. But I had sufficient Vietnamese to brief Alexander Downer that the names of three men he was about to meet, Húc, Phúc and Chúc, were not to be pronounced Huck, Fuck and Chuck.

I learned to be tolerant when foreigners make mistakes when speaking in English. Fred Hollows was an Australian eye surgeon who established a not-for-profit organisation supporting an international network of clinics dealing with cataracts and other eye disorders. I was the guest of honour at the opening of a new clinic and the interpreter tried so hard to get the introductions right. But he introduced me as 'Mrs Shoes-on Boy, Ambassadress Extraordinary and Plenty Potential of the Republic of Australia'. Almost all completely wrong! My friends had a T-shirt made for me with 'Ambassadress Extraordinary and Plenty Potential' printed across it.

Learning early on about different styles and cultures is important. In my first staff meeting in Vietnam I wondered why the Vietnamese staff were polite but unforthcoming. I later learned that they needed to take any new idea and discuss it among themselves and then with the ruling Communist Party and reach a consensus. At the time of the first meeting, they were not ready to give their views to the ambassador, but once they had gone through that internal process and had a position, they stuck to it and there was confidence that it had been carefully thought through. This was also the case in negotiations with the foreign ministry and other relevant ministries, such as the ministries of education and justice. Once they had provided their response, it could be relied on. This was not always the case in other countries where I was posted.

Differences in culture can also be dangerous. Early in my posting, Queensland Rail was seeking to build a business relation-ship with Vietnam Railways, to provide rolling stock and modern communication systems. The Queensland representative from Brisbane invited me to his introductory lunch with the Vietnam Railways representative in Hanoi. As always, the Vietnamese opened the discussion by asking the visitor about his family. 'I hope your mother is in good health?'

'Oh yes', replied the Australian. 'She's ninety-two now and still lives by herself. She's fantastic'.

The Vietnamese was shocked. What sort of a barbarian was this, who allowed his aged mother to live by herself? It is the duty of the sons to look after the parents. Is this man the sort of man you want to do business with? What standards does he live by?

I learned always to assure my interlocutors that my sister took good care of our mother while I was overseas.

When Tim Fischer visited Hanoi, knowing his enthusiasm for railways, we arranged for him to visit Hanoi's central station to farewell the evening train to Sapa, which often carried Australian tourists. This modern train had incorporated some Australian technology. Tim was invited into the driver's cabin and sounded the departure hoot. As soon as the train pulled out, however, there came a much more interesting hoot, several platforms away, from a very old, Czech-made, black puffing billy. Tim's eyes lit up, and he bounded down the platform and across the tracks to see this treasure, his accompanying party struggling to keep up. He was one very happy trainspotter!

Tim's visit to the station had opened with a very cordial meeting with the head of Vietnam Railways, with a mutually interesting conversation about trains conducted through interpreters. Towards the end, Tim said, 'I am convinced that railways will never disappear, because steel wheels on a metal track generate much less friction than rubber tyres on a road'. The response from the other side was, 'But our trains don't have rubber wheels'. Something had got lost in translation!

In staff management and leadership terms, during my career I learned the absolute value of appropriate diversity in teams. I developed what I called the 'Christopher Robin theory of management', borrowing names from A. A. Milne's Winnie the Pooh books. I learned the value of having an Eeyore in the team, however irritating. They are the doubting, unenthusiastic ones. 'Do you really think this is a good idea, Sue?' 'Do you think the minister and the department would want us to do this?' 'Do we have enough resources?' 'What do you want us to put aside so we will have time to take up this new idea?' The Kanga role is also important: the kind one, who looks after everyone and checks on their health and comfort. And Tigger, totally disruptive, jumps around all over the place but may introduce new ideas and keep everyone on their toes. Then there has to be a Pooh, the solid, reliable one, who gets things done and is a bit of a philosopher. And every team has a Piglet, the excitable one, who runs round all the time agreeing with everyone. 'Yes, Pooh'. 'No, Pooh'. 'Whatever you say, Pooh'. All are important. I had all these characters in the Hanoi Embassy team.

13

Hong Kong and Macau, 1998–99: fiddling about

**Not my favourite posting. Hong Kong after the handover
had few international challenges and I was bored,
found little interest in the huge expatriate community
but nonetheless rang up a few achievements.**

In May 1998, I moved from Vietnam to become Australian consul general in Hong Kong. Australia had a longstanding presence there, but the former British colony had been handed over to China the previous year. While there was a vibrant local government, education, arts, social and business scene, any policy decision which might be of interest to Australia was now made in Beijing. Of interest to Australia were cases in the High Court which concerned the status of Hong Kong in relation to China. Australian Judge Tony Mason served on the court and was generous in sharing relevant information, and I followed these cases closely. But otherwise, there was not much work of any real interest for me to do. Everyone else in the large consulate had serious and satisfying work: the immigration, Austrade, Australian Federal Police, defence, education and consular staff had plenty on their plates. However, unlike in Vietnam, there was little useful supporting political role the head of mission could play. Hong Kong had an identical international trade position with Australia. Business was done directly by businesses, with no need of government support. There were no trade policy issues.

Nonetheless, I kept myself occupied. The Asian financial crisis gripped much of East and South East Asia beginning in July 1997 and there were fears of worldwide economic difficulties. Hong Kong had a dominating economic and commercial position, with its concentration of international banks and financial institutions and was particularly affected. I took the opportunity to renegotiate the lease on the consulate's office space at Wan Chai, the commercial area. This was a good time to secure a more advantageous lease, when there were competing offers in buildings whose owners wanted Australia's prestigious presence. I reorganised the office staff and introduced new technology. I also took an interest in the Australian International School and helped it raise funds for new premises. There was an opportunity to bring the Reserve Bank of Australia and the Hong Kong central bank together, so that they jointly become strong enough to earn their way into the international group of central banks and financial institutions working to create a new international financial architecture, within which countries would survive the crisis.

I enjoyed very much also being accredited to Macau. It was then still under Portuguese administration and when I presented my credentials, I was able to speak in Portuguese to the Governor. He was impressed, as were the media when I spoke with them following the ceremony. Macau had a more leisurely approach to life than Hong Kong. There were the casinos of course and some splendid old buildings and cobbled streetscapes beautifully restored, and attractive shopping streets and antique shops and excellent restaurants. There was no official business between Macau and Australia, though there were Australian interests in the casinos.

China had let the Portuguese know that it wanted Macau's status to remain unchanged, after the handover of Hong Kong, and arrangements for a similar change in status were underway. The Governor and his entourage returned to Lisbon in 1999 and a new Portguese consul general took over.

When I paid my last visit to the Governor, in 1999, to say farewell before leaving for Fiji, he said they were sorry to see me go. I could speak their language, had taken an interest in the place and had developed relationships with the governor's staff. He said they felt they knew me. For the most part, foreign consuls arrived, presented credentials and then two years later came to say farewell. The governor told me that, among themselves, they said, 'who the hell was that?'. That wasn't the case with Australia.

The residence of the consul general in Hong Kong was beautifully located, perched on a cliff, overlooking Deep Water Bay, on the other side of Hong Kong Island from the office. The ground under the residence had become unstable and considerable work was underway to prevent the building sliding down the slope. I spent the first months staying in a hotel near the office in Wan Chai. Eventually, I moved into the house and set about refurnishing and entertaining in it. It was one of the last few large, prestigious, freestanding houses in Hong Kong, with its own garden, overlooking the bay. People loved invitations to visit it.

Hong Kong is seriously into good food and wine, and these were major imports from Australia. Excellent Australian chefs who were already working in Hong Kong came and showcased their talents at official dinners I hosted. In 1988 the large Australian wine company Penfolds launched a new wine campaign led by Jackie Chan as its wine ambassador. The message was 'moderate drinking with friends'. Jackie was well known as a daring stunt actor in countless films, and he lived near me. He was brought up in Canberra, where his father was chef at the prime minister's residence. He was a good choice. Penfolds provided several bottles of its famous Grange Hermitage, as well as other suitable wines, and paid for the catering for the dinner hosted in the residence. The company invited the leading wine buyers in Hong Kong. The food and wine were superb, the guests stayed on late into the evening, and, much to my disappointment, there was no Grange Hermitage left over for the residence's wine cellar at the end of the night.

At one official dinner in Hong Kong I found myself seated next to a 92-year-old Hong Kong Chinese film mogul who was boasting about his new girlfriend. I told him about a friend who said she liked affairs with older men: they were always so grateful. He retorted that he liked affairs with older women: they thought it might be their last time, so they gave it all they'd got!

On the way home from a dinner held in an excellent Chinese restaurant, I told my driver Chan Kan, who was a bit of a philosopher, about each of the amazingly creative dishes which had been served to us. He grunted. 'You go to restaurant and eat dinner which cost hundreds of dollars. I go eat bowl of noodles which cost four dollars. We both go home, go to bed, wake up next morning, go to toilet. Same thing!'

Once, commenting on the size of the three-storey official residence, he said, 'You lucky you have good staff to clean so many rooms. Chinese say, "Rich man have many rooms, but still sleep in only one bed"'. Chan Kan's hobby was keeping caged songbirds. Like many people in Hong Kong, he took his pet birds to the park at weekends and evenings so they could sing and socialise with other birds, similarly caged and hung in the trees. He was devastated when the bird flu hit Hong Kong and all his birds had to be put down. He still treasured their cages, and I was very touched when, saying farewell at the airport on my departure at the end of the posting, he gruffly gave me a small brown paper bag in which was a pair of small, exquisite, Chinese porcelain water bowls from one of the cages.

For the 1988 Australian general elections, Hong Kong had the second-largest polling station in the world, after the Australian High Commission in London. The Australian community in Hong Kong was very large: there were twenty-three different Australian community organisations. All wanted my presence at their breakfasts, lunches, dinners and social and professional events. But all that was required of me was to enhance the prestige of the event: be there, be dressed well, with matching shoes and handbags and good jewellery, and be congenial. Intellectual input was rarely required. There were no policy questions. My heart was not in this job. Coming from the hectic and full-on life in

Vietnam, where I could make a difference, I did not feel that there was any really meaningful and useful work for Australia which used my talents. So I asked the secretary Ashton Calvert to move me, if there was a suitable job elsewhere.

In mid 1999 the phonecall came. Trouble was brewing in Fiji, where they feared a possible coup. The current Australian head of mission, Greg Urwin, had just been promoted and had to move back to a policy job in Canberra. I was a sensible, competent officer with a safe pair of hands, and the Secretary thought I was just the right fit for Suva and its expected crisis.

My friends in Hong Kong wondered what I had done wrong. They saw Hong Kong as the centre of the universe – rich and sophisticated. Fiji was seen as a holiday destination. Surely I was not prepared to move there? But I was delighted to accept. Fiji was in the centre of Australia's area of interest in the South Pacific, and there was real work, which mattered. I moved with alacrity. Before going, I had a long telephone conversation with Greg Urwin, who was an experienced Pacific hand, to pick up as much information as I could. I mentioned to him the practice I had built of inviting star Australian chefs to the residence to prepare top-class and innovative meals for official dinners, and I asked him what arrangements he had in Suva. 'Don't worry about that', he replied. 'Pacific islanders just like simple food, and plenty of it'.

14

Fiji, 1999–2003: the Speight coup

**Plenty to keep me busy. The Chaudhry government
overthrown by George Speight and parliament is occupied.
Australia's role in finding the path back to democracy.
Threats to my life and living with bodyguards.**

On the morning of 19 May 2000, soldiers from the Fijian army
led by a little-known businessman George Speight stormed Fiji's
Parliament, took hostage Prime Minister Mahendra Chaudhry and
all sixty-four sitting members and occupied the parliament building.
Laurie Marquet, the clerk of Western Australia's Legislative Council,
was working in the parliament on a Commonwealth exchange. He
escaped and telephoned the Australian High Commission: we
were the first to hear about it.

News soon spread, and an unruly procession in support of the
coup rampaged through the streets of Suva, looting businesses
on the way. Crowds filled the parliamentary grounds, providing
a human shield for the hostage takers. The crowd included
ultranationalist chiefs, retired army personnel and villagers
coming in from the hills. Shots were fired, one just missing the
Australian trade commissioner Peter Murphy as he was standing
in the driveway of his home, just beyond the parliamentary
boundary fence. He arrived back in the office physically shaking,
while I was on the phone with the Australian foreign minister,
Alexander Downer. I gestured towards the fridge in my office, and
Murphy happily grabbed the bottle of vodka.

The 1999 elections under a new constitution had been won by the Fiji Labour Party, led by the Indo-Fijian Mahendra Chaudhry. The new constitution recognised the multiracial, multicultural nature of Fiji. The most numerous groups, almost finely balanced, were the indigenous Fijians and the Indo Fijian Community. The Indo Fijians had been imported as indentured labourers from India during the British colonial rule, principally to work in the sugar cane industry. But there were also independent entrepreneurial settlers from the Indian state of Gujerat. To add to the racial mix were Chinese, European settlers, Solomon Islanders and many of mixed race. The new constitution sought to give each of these groups appropriate recognition. Once elected, Chaudhry led a multiracial government, but many indigenous Fijians were unhappy to see a non-indigenous leader. Among the discontented were some of the chiefs, whose traditional power was in any case eroding as Fiji became a more educated and urbanised society. Rumours of a possible coup had been around for some time, but there seemed to be no leader for those wanting change by force. That altered with the surprise emergence of George Speight – a mixed-race, fast-talking, impeccably dressed young man who had been thwarted in business and sacked by Prime Minister Chaudhry.

The crisis lasted for fifty-six days – a busy and varied time for the Australian High Commission and one of most stressful but most rewarding periods of my 34-year career in the Australian foreign service. I recalled Gough Whitlam's questions: What's going on? What does it mean for Australia? And what should we do about it? Answering those questions kept the Australian High Commission in Suva very occupied

There were serious issues for Australia, which had a long-standing and major presence in Fiji. Australia was concerned about stability in the region, trade and investment, and the many people-to-people links between the two countries. The seventy staff at the high commission looked after immigration, defence, trade and investment, an aid program and security issues for the whole of the South Pacific, as well as economic, political and development issues. What happened in Fiji was important to Australia.

The Fijian armed forces were led by Commander Ratu Josaia Voreqe (Frank) Bainimarama, a traditional chief who had been commander of the Fiji Navy. ('Ratu' is the generic Fijian title for 'chief'.) Some army leaders were unhappy with his elevation from the 'junior service', and the parliamentary coup was carried out by a group of disaffected officers and men. In the days following the coup, Bainimarama himself faced a mutiny in the barracks and was fired upon by his own soldiers, a highly traumatic event. The commander, like several of Fiji's military officers, had previously received professional training in Australia.

The Australian High Commission compound, in the suburb of Tamavua, was located within 4 kilometres of the army barracks. During the mutiny, rounds of ammunition rained on the roof and landed in the front garden, narrowly missing staff members who were outside listening to the exchanges of gunfire and watching as army flares lit up the night sky. Staff with family members in houses near the barracks were worried and wanted to get home. We were concerned to learn later that such ammunition maintains sufficient velocity to maim people within a relatively short range. Two individual civilians in the neighbourhood were hurt: one when ammunition entered through his bathroom window while he was showering, and the other in her garden, while she was hanging out washing. I was more than worried.

Bainimarama was absent from Fiji on 19 May, when the parliamentary coup took place, but he flew back the next day and took control of the situation. He imposed a curfew, restored law and order in the city and started the long process of negotiations with George Speight and his backers. Retaking the parliament by force was not an option. The hundreds of people gathered there provided a human shield and soon settled in for the long haul. Speight managed the media skilfully. He was clean-shaven, including his head, and dressed always in the traditional Fijian *sulu* – a smartly tailored man-skirt – and an impeccably laundered white shirt. He spoke engagingly and convincingly. He was well educated and had been chief executive officer of the Fiji Hardwood Corporation. Fiji had gone to international tender for the management of its substantial and valuable mature mahogany forests and plantations. Prime Minister Chaudhry alleged that one of the tendering companies was bribing Speight and summarily removed him. Speight had good motivation to join and become the figurehead for the coup plotters, though this backstory emerged only later.

I was also away from Fiji on 19 May, on a plane to Sydney, when the coup happened, and the deputy head of mission, Margaret Twomey, was acting high commissioner. I had been invited to the formal opening of the Mỹ Thuận Bridge in Vietnam, connected to my time as ambassador there. I'd worried long and hard about whether I should go, leaving Fiji at that juncture. The police chief had assured me only the previous day that nothing was about to happen. Qantas staff met me off the plane at midday in Sydney, told me the news and put me promptly on the next flight back. I used the waiting time to phone Margaret in Suva, get her brief on the situation and discuss what the high commission was doing in response. I then telephoned Greg Urwin, my predecessor in Fiji but by that time the head of the Pacific Division at DFAT in Canberra. Urwin was married to a Samoan and was an experienced Pacific hand. He knew Fiji well and had family connections in the region. He had plenty of useful comments and advice. An important call was to our very experienced consul in Suva, Brian Pullen, about looking after the several thousand Australians living, working or holidaying in Fiji.

Ensuring the Australian community was safe was a priority. There were some 4,000 Australians living permanently in Fiji, and tens of thousands visited as tourists each year. The evacuation plans and formal networks of key Australians around the country were checked. The high commission worked with DFAT in Canberra on appropriate travel advisories.

The high commission team needed to find out what was happening and brief the foreign minister, Alexander Downer, and the prime minister, John Howard. The prime minister had considerable personal sympathy for Mahendra Chaudhry, a fellow Commonwealth leader, and was very concerned for him.

Other tasks were to tease out what had led to the coup, how the hostages could be protected and eventually freed, and which participants in the complex matrix – chiefs, political leaders, the military and civil society institutions, including the churches – could combine to bring the crisis to an end. How could Australia best be helpful? How could Australian interests be protected and promoted?

Only a few days earlier, on 18 April, I had been at a traditional eightieth-birthday celebration for Fijian president Ratu Sir Kamisese Mara on his distant home Lau island of Lakemba. He also held the traditional position of Tui Nayau, the paramount chief of the Lau Group of Islands. This was possibly the last ever of the impressive and elaborate traditional days of feasting, dancing, singing, praying and celebration for a paramount chief in the Pacific, and I had been deeply honoured to be one of the five ambassadors invited. This was a family, not a state, event. Ratu Mara was not only president of Fiji but a major player in the development of a modern Pacific. As a birthday gift, Australia had given him a truck to be used to carry young men and women from around the island of Lakemba to attend the agricultural college he had founded. I had formally presented the vehicle to him at Government House in Suva the day before the coup. He started the engine and drove away from the imposing colonial-style building, between the lawns and palm trees, and was very pleased. Looking on in admiration were his military guards, smartly dressed in the Fijian armed forces uniform of tailored, red jackets bearing their many medals and jagged-edged, white, formal *sulu* skirts.

I next saw Ratu Mara two days later, on 20 April, early on the morning after the coup, and confirmed Australia's support for him in finding a constitutional way through the crisis. The administrative attaché brought a satellite phone along, and Foreign Minister Alexander Downer was able to speak to the president directly from Phnom Penh, in Cambodia, where he was on an official visit. I reminded Ratu Mara of the strength and range of the Australian presence and interests in Fiji – Australian companies were among the most prominent, and its aid program one of the largest in the country. Australian interests also controlled most of Fiji's industry sectors. He drew on this information in his address to the nation on Fijian television that evening. As I left Government House, the Fijian chief justice, Sir Timoci Tuivaga, arrived to offer his advice. I had attended his wedding only a few weeks before and golfed with him frequently.

Joe Brown, official secretary to the president, came to see me in my office at the high commission the following day, to talk through possible scenarios and to warn me that the president and his family might be removed from Suva. During our discussions I asked Joe about his own personal security. He showed me the army revolver he had under his jacket. As he left at the end of the meeting, my personal assistant, Wendy Welsh, returned his mobile phone. (We banned mobile phones within the secure areas of the office.)

I said, 'Wendy, you took his mobile phone. Did you also know he was carrying a gun?'

'Oh yes', she replied. 'But I knew what our policy was on phones. I didn't know what our policy was on guns!' She was the wife of one of our defence cooperation staff, and it took her some time to live down this event. Margaret Twomey wickedly entitled her cable on Joe Brown's call 'Is that a gun in your pocket, or...?'

As Joe Brown had foreshadowed, on 29 May, the president and his family were taken aboard one of Fiji's naval patrol boats, which then cruised around the island of Beqa. These patrol boats had some years earlier been donated by Australia to several Pacific island states, to help them secure their own exclusive economic zones. The following day, the ship was boarded by Commander Bainimarama; the police chief, Isikia Savua; the head of the Fijian Great Council of Chiefs and former prime minister, Sitiveni Rabuka; and the president's son-in-law Ratu Epeli Ganilau. The delegation formally presented Ratu Mara with the traditional whale's tooth, the gift most laden with traditional cultural and spiritual significance, and requested him to abrogate the constitution. He refused, resigned and ceded power to an interim military government led by Bainimarama. The delegation returned to shore, and the ship then sailed to Lakemba with the president and his family. In a later radio interview Ratu Mara said that, in the circumstances, he had no choice but to stand down. He never returned to power and had an impressive state funeral in Suva when he died on 19 April 2004. He was then returned to Lakemba by patrol boat, with all ceremony, to be buried on his home island.

I met early with Frank Bainimarama, accompanied by Margaret Twomey, and assured him of Australia's support for his interim military government, provided that he moved as quickly as possible to resolve the crisis and return Fiji to constitutional democratic government. Bainimarama noted Australia's deep interest in Fiji and agreed to keep us informed of his plans as the situation developed. I knew him and his wife well enough to express my concerns about his personal situation as well as the huge formal responsibility he now carried, and I offered him personal as well as official support. Informally, I told him that in my experience, men in power were extremely attractive to women, and men in uniform even more so. I suggested he be very careful about his moral behaviour in his new role. He protested, 'Sue, you are talking to me like my *talatala*' – his priest. We did not include this last exchange in the official record of the meeting.

In the meantime, Speight and his gang held thirty-five members of parliament hostage within Parliament House for fifty-six days. The parliamentarians, young and elderly, men and women, were kept in the parliamentary chamber, where they slept, and were escorted by soldiers to and from the bathrooms. Chaudhry was beaten up, but other members were apparently not physically mistreated. They were fed. The head of Fiji Red Cross, John Scott, was allowed daily access. He took in letters, clean clothing and food from the families of the hostages. Australia respected the neutrality of the Red Cross but quietly funded this operation. Scott was under a lot of emotional pressure. He was an especially close friend of Margaret Twomey, who knew his family well, and we were very worried about the pressures on him.

At the same time, the crowd within the Parliament House grounds became permanent campers. Over the next days *lovos*, earth and rock pit ovens, were dug so food could be cooked. Washing was dried on bushes. Prostitutes moved in and set up shop. Military-style training exercises took place. A visiting group of New Zealand cadets created a stir when, in uniform, they went down to see what was going on. Speight thought an armed Australian military rescue mission was about to take place and rounded up all the parliamentarians and held them at gunpoint. News of this promptly reached the high commission, and a junior staff member called Speight on his mobile phone, assuring him nothing of the sort was going on. He relaxed, and the parliamentarians were relieved to be able to move freely back into the parliamentary chamber.

As the days went by Speight released some of the hostages one by one. Soon after their release they each came to the high commission to report what was going on. They also joined the daily lunchtime vigils of prayer for the hostages being held in the Anglican cathedral, which I attended. Some of the released hostages took advantage of Australia's offer of post-traumatic stress counselling and treatment in Australia. The oldest parliamentarian sobbed in my office as he related how he had managed to keep a simple daily journal until Speight had found it and ripped it to pieces. I found myself choking back tears of sympathy for this old man and all the others being held for so long.

Over the fifty-six days of the hostages' confinement the high commission staff members met with all the players who were vying for influence and trying to find a way through the crisis. Most people wanted to talk to us and gauge Australia's reaction as possible scenarios unrolled. Every morning I woke wondering who we would need to influence that day.

Speight set aside Fiji's constitution and tried to form a revolutionary government of his own. We learned that one prominent woman known to the high commission staff had been invited to serve in this government, and I phoned her to talk through the implications and possible consequences if she accepted. She decided to decline Speight's invitation. Much later, when it was all over and the crisis had been resolved, she came to see me, bringing a gift. She said she was so grateful for our conversation. She had been deep in prayer: 'Blessed Mary, Mother of Jesus, help me in this hour of need, send me a sign. At that point, Sue, you telephoned! I was so grateful!'

Relatives of some of the locally engaged embassy staff were involved on different sides of the conflict, but they came to work each day and continued to do their jobs well. For them, the office was a haven of safety and normality in an increasingly unsafe and uncertain time. Their loyalty was highly appreciated.

At one point I consulted all the senior Australia-based staff and concluded that the situation had become so serious, with lawlessness and general disruption, that all the families and nonessential staff should be evacuated and either housed in hotels at the other end of the island or sent back to Australia. Essential Australian staff were concentrated into the four houses on the high commission compound, including the official residence, and I made sure that they were eating properly and getting rest. So that we could keep our communication system open, the defence adviser, Commander Keith Egland, and his deputy set up camp beds in their offices, as well as stocking up on supplies of tinned baked beans and sardines. All the other foreign embassies left Suva; Australia was the only one which stayed put throughout, though fully fuelled and supplied vehicles were parked at the back gate, ready to leave if necessary. The New Zealand high commissioner phoned to let us know that he and his staff had pulled out and were on the road to the tourism and business hub of Nadi at the western end of the island, 190 kilometres from the capital Suva, which is located on the south eastern coast of the main island of Viti Levu. With Australia's the only diplomatic mission remaining, DFAT Deputy Secretary John Dauth questioned me closely by phone about whether we should also leave. The high commission was located a little way out of town and quite far from Parliament House, and we did not expect further problems from the barracks. We did not feel ourselves to be a direct target and Suva was a town well served by mobile phones. I was confident we would find out in good time if the situation was about to change. But I have to admit to feeling some nervousness on going to bed the night we decided to remain in Suva, the responsibility weighing heavily.

Our defence adviser Keith Eglen did not agree with my decision to evacuate staff and appealed to the Department of Defence in Canberra to overrule me. He was told promptly that I was the commanding officer and he should respect my decisions. I explained to him that while seasoned military personnel might feel comfortable with, and perhaps even excited by, the challenges of the dangers we were facing, I was concerned about civilian staff, their wives and children, and vulnerable members of the Australian community.

During my career I developed a range of different leadership styles. My default style was to be consultative. It's important not to appear weak or indecisive. In the end, the decision is yours, but it must be respected by the team members, and they deserve to have their ideas and points of view heard. I learned in my first industrial democracy training course that any fool can make decisions; it is making decisions stick which takes skill. People are very good at undermining actions with which they disagree. In industrial democracy workers are involved in making decisions and sharing responsibility and authority in the workplace.

Margaret Twomey and members of the political and economic section of the high commission kept up a flow of high-quality reporting by cable to Canberra, shared between DFAT and the Department of Defence, as well as with the intelligence agencies and ministers' offices.

Not long after we had evacuated some of the staff, DFAT in Canberra passed on information from a usually reliable source that I had become a target and my life was threatened. Until then I had kept it all together, busily worrying about everyone else and focussing on all the different tasks to be done and stakeholders to be looked after. This information really knocked me. The stress had been unrelenting, and I realised that I was no longer capable of staying in charge. I shared this with Margaret Twomey and Brian Pullen, and they agreed I should hand over the leadership of the embassy for the weekend and join the staff who had been temporarily moved to the beachside Pearl Resort, an hour's drive outside Suva. My driver, Tagi, who was formerly an army driver and had worked for the prime minister, drove me there. The domestic staff closed up the residence and went home.

The Australian staff who had been evacuated to the Pearl with their families were welcoming and cosseting. There were a few glasses of good Australian wine, and then two of the little girls asked whether they could give me a massage. That seemed like a lovely idea in the circumstances, and I lay out on the sofa and succumbed. After a little while I heard them whispering.

'You ask her'.

'No, you ask her'.

I came out of my massage trance. 'Ask me what?'

Tearfully, one of the girls blurted out, 'Dad told us that you said we couldn't have a dog. Is this true?'

I explained that as all our houses were on the compound and there were no garden fences, it really wasn't practical for people to have dogs. They would have to wait until they had a house with its own garden, when they returned to Australia.

'That means we'll never have a dog,' they sobbed, 'because we don't have a house in Australia!' This was clearly a much more important issue and helped regain my equilibrium.

The coup kept the Australian diplomatic representation in Fiji busy for many months and plunged me, as the high commissioner, into difficult challenges. Following the threats against my life, an

Australian Federal Police team travelled from Australia to provide close protective security for me. I had never had bodyguards before, so at our initial meeting at the residence I checked what the procedures were. Did they have to sleep at the residence? Did I have to provide meals for them? How did it all work? It turned out that they stayed at a hotel downtown, looked after their own food and came to the high commission to look after me on a roster. They checked out places I was going, escorted me there and kept watch. On days when I did not need to leave the compound, they exercised and planned. I felt rather obliged to leave the compound and go and do something every day, so they would feel useful. The team stayed for several weeks, to provide protection for as long as we deemed necessary. They were highly trained and dedicated. They were prepared to die to protect me but, as they preferred not to, they spent some time training me in useful protective security measures. They checked my route, whether it was to the office or on private house calls, to official receptions or to the hairdresser. (The hairdresser thought they were gorgeous! 'Uru, madam, uru!') At weekends, they were out on the golf course with me, discreetly making sure I was safe. The golf course was a good place to maintain contact with Fijian leaders and members of the Australian and other international communities, to exchange information about what was going on. I developed a high regard for the professionalism of the Australian Federal Police group, who stayed until the situation calmed down sufficiently. Once the hostages were released and an interim government was formed, the Australian government withdrew me from Fiji, as a mark of disapproval at the non-constitutional turn of events and the irregular state of its politics, and I spent a short while in Canberra. But the security group remained to look after the acting high commissioner, Margaret.

That Australia's was the only foreign mission to stay and work hard to help Fiji through this crisis was widely noted and served us well. The complex situation was eventually resolved through the involvement of the Great Council of Chiefs, individual chiefs and the Fijian military, as well as business leaders and the churches. The Australian mission team followed and sought to understand the situation as it evolved.

On 13 July 2000, the hostages were released from parliament as part of a negotiated deal, the Muanikau Accord. George Speight and his cohort were arrested and imprisoned on a small island off Suva. They were charged and went to trial. Australia assisted in the appointment of Queenslander Peter Ridgway as the deputy public prosecutor. The high commission staff continued to have full access and influence as the immediate crisis was resolved and Fiji moved back to parliamentary democracy. Foreign minister, Alexander Downer, visited Fiji as a member of a Commonwealth special delegation established to help the country through the crisis. The Pacific Islands Forum was the regional organisation with membership by all island states, Australia and New Zealand. It was headquartered in Suva in specially built premises which housed a meeting hall and secretariat offices. The President of Samoa, Tuiaepa Aiono Sailele Malielegaoi, invited Forum Foreign Ministers to hold a special Pacific Islands Forum meeting in Samoa to find a regional consensus on helping Fiji return to normality after the release of the hostages. I flew from Canberra with Downer and the experienced deputy head of AusAID, Annmaree O'Keeffe, and a small DFAT delegation for the special meeting. Kaliopate Tavola, interim foreign minister of Fiji was there and impressed the Forum foreign ministers as being reliable, sensible and pragmatic.

With international encouragement, Frank Bainimarama ceded political leadership on 4 July 2001 to an interim civilian government headed by Laisenia Qarase, a prominent Fijian business leader. The international community encouraged Qarase to hold elections for a new, democratically elected government and to reconvene parliament. I had several private meetings with the interim foreign minister, Tavola, and Qarase, urging them to move quickly to elections and defusing their various objections and demands. Parliament House was trashed through the Speight occupation, so there was nowhere for a new government to meet. Would Australia fund the refurbishment? We would assist an international appeal for this. Drawing up new electoral rolls covering all the islands of Fiji was a huge task which would have to be completed before any elections could be held. This precluded an early election. Assistance was provided by the Australian Electoral Commission, and Fiji's request for help from the United Nations was supported. I headed off all efforts at procrastination. History has shown that governments which come to power unconstitutionally become comfortable in their situation, and the longer they remain in power, the more they resist any moves to restore constitutionality. So the sooner a new constitution could be agreed and elections held, the better.

I had got to know foreign minister, Tavola, and liked him a lot. He had previously headed Fiji Sugar Marketing. He lived quite near my house, and during the period when we were avoiding official contact with the illegal government, I often took a bottle of Australian red wine around to his house, ostensibly to talk to his wife, Helen, who was a New Zealander and came to the aquarobics classes held in the high commission swimming pool, as well as being a member of the same book club as me. Tavola and I could talk frankly.

The elections took place in August 2001, just fifteen months after the coup. I and other officers from the high commission visited several polling stations informally, both in the city and in further flung mountain areas. One polling station we reached in the mountains had just closed – all nineteen registered on the electoral roll had already cast their votes. The polling officers invited us to join them for a curry lunch. An international election observer mission which had travelled through Fiji's many islands declared the election had been free and fair. Australian prime minister John Howard and his wife visited to congratulate the government on having returned Fiji to a democratic parliamentary country. This was a major achievement.

However, problems remained. Some fundamental hurts had not healed, and tensions between the indigenous Fijians and

Indo-Fijians remained. The traditional chiefs were struggling to retain their authority, and the discord within the armed forces was not resolved. Relations between Prime Minister Qarase and Bainimarama, the commander of Fiji's armed forces, were deteriorating, and this worried Australia and Fiji's other friends and allies. All were mindful of the situation which had recently arisen in Papua New Guinea, where the armed forces had defied the convention that they were there to serve under the democratically elected government, broke out of their barracks and seized power.

A group of high commissioners and ambassadors in Suva met to discuss the worrying situation in Fiji, and I was asked to represent the group in a discussion with Qarase. He told me he had offered Bainimarama two prestigious overseas postings in an effort to remove him from the scene. Bainimarama had refused to go: he told me that he was not interested in cocktail parties and being nice to people; he liked messing around in boats and playing rugby. I urged Qarase to call Bainimarama in for a meeting. It was important that he and the armed forces commander understood each other and worked together for the good of the country. Qarase, however, continued to sit on his high horse and argued that it was for Bainimarama to take the initiative to meet him – his door was always open. When in turn I spoke to Bainimarama about the situation he said it was up to Qarase to invite him.

Qarase and his government were developing increasingly nationalist policies, which were unacceptable to Bainimarama and those who supported a fair deal for all ethnic groups. The British high commissioner Charlie Mochan had a close relationship with a former head of the armed forces, Paul Manueli, whom Bainimarama respected and regarded as a valued mentor. The Brit had long conversations with Manueli, urging him to use his influence on Bainimarama. Manueli said he was also worried about the situation and was trying hard, but Bainimarama could not be moved.

My time in Fiji came to an end before there was any sign of a rapprochement. The government became increasingly nationalistic in the eyes of some, who saw Qarase as governing in the interests of the indigenous population rather than in those of the country as a whole, including the significant Indo-Fijian portion – almost 50 per cent – of the population. Frank Bainimarama took this view and claimed that the constitution gave him the responsibility of looking after the security and interests of the whole country; Bainimarama himself led Fiji's third coup, in 2006.

Many international commentators blithely assumed that Fiji's politics were about the struggle between indigenous Fijians and the Indo-Fijian community, but they are much more complicated. Bainimarama led the country through new elections under yet another constitution. At the time of writing, Fijians seemed resigned to the new situation and prepared to live with its imperfections in the interests of a peaceful life and some order and predictability. This is quite understandable for the inhabitants of an island nation. There is nowhere to go, so you have to compromise and find a way to get on. But old hurts are not forgotten or truly forgiven.

There have been respected Chinese families in Fiji for generations, but during the time I was in Fiji new Chinese settlers had been conspicuously arriving in the country, many illegally. China increased its diplomatic presence and aid program, including building a new Olympic swimming complex and upgrading the Kings Road, which runs along the northern coast of Fiji's main island, connecting the capital, Suva, with the tourism and business hub of Nadi. The influence of China has grown as Bainimarama seeks to broaden Fiji's international connections, beyond its traditional links with Australia and New Zealand. The Australian High Commission is still busy. For Australia the Pacific remains an area firmly within the policy focus but maintaining and developing the relationship is getting more complicated. It is an excellent place to have a posting.

15

The not-so-peaceful Pacific, 1999–2003

High commissioner in Fiji, Nauru and Tuvalu. Managing the Pacific Solution.

While in Australia in 1999 preparing for the new Fiji posting, I met staff at the Queensland Museum of Contemporary Art, which was the only Australian institution seriously collecting and exhibiting works from the Pacific. During my career I found the arts to be useful in gaining understanding of each new culture and building links between Australia and the country where I was posted. The most common art forms in the Pacific islands are performance art and artefacts connected with important dance and other rituals. Domestic arts are also strong, such as woven mats, pottery and the intricate patterns of fibre ropes used in timber buildings.

I also visited Artbank to choose artworks for the high commission in Suva. Artbank was an Australian Government organisation which purchased works by contemporary Australian artists and then rented them out to government departments, private businesses and overseas embassies as part of Australia's soft diplomacy – pursuing Australia's interests by indirect means. Artbank's head Antonia Syme had previously helped me choose paintings, prints and sculptures for the embassy in Hanoi and for the consulate in Hong Kong when I was posted there.

Ray Crooke was the best-known Australian artist working in the Pacific. He had spent considerable time painting in Fiji and still made working visits each year, staying on Toberua Island, near Suva. Artbank provided one of his splendid, large island scenes, which dominated the dining room in the residence and was much admired. Ray deeply appreciated the beauty of Pacific people and was in turn highly respected both in Fiji and in Australia. His work was included in a public exhibition of Australian contemporary art held at the high commission in 2002. This brought together works by various Australian artists which were usually hung in the offices, residence and public spaces of the high commission, and additional works by Ray which were held by private collectors in Fiji were borrowed.

Ray opened the exhibition, along with Antonia, the Artbank director. Antonia gave a couple of public lectures on art in general and on the works in our exhibition specifically. There were a number of serious contemporary artists in Fiji expressing their ideas through carvings and paintings. These included students at the University of the South Pacific in Suva who came from other Pacific islands, like Solomon Islands, with strong artistic traditions. I admired many of these and bought works for my own personal collection. Many of the artists were impressed and inspired by our exhibition. Indeed, one man who painted for the tourist trade was encouraged by it to successfully direct his skills to the production of serious works. He had assumed such works would not be of interest to the public.

The arts all came together on Lakemba for Ratu Mara's eightieth birthday on his home island, which I have described in an earlier chapter. This was a huge celebration. The islanders had prepared for months. Before dawn, each island family had prepared the *lovos*, or pit ovens, and had started cooking pigs, chickens, fish and vegetables for the feast. At sunrise hymns were sung outside Ratu Mara's house, and the celebrations continued with a day of feasting and dances performed by large groups of island men and women, splendidly dressed and painted. Some dancers wore leg bindings bearing masses of shells, sounding like the crashing tide on the beach. The shelters for the paramount chief and other guests were arranged to enclose a large circular *rara*, a flat, grassy area, where the dances and rituals took place. Timber cages held live pigs, which were important ritual gifts. Taro roots, the vegetables which are a staple of the island diet and also an important offering, were piled in mounds as high as small huts. Ratu Mara and the guests sat in open-sided huts decorated with traditionally patterned *masi*, tapa cloth made from the beaten bark of the mulberry tree. We all sat on specially designed and woven mats. Bright, colourful flower decorations were everywhere. Visitors were all lodged in local houses with families, who sat with their guests and cared for them during the feast.

Ratu Lui, one of Ratu Mara's sons, made a ritual tour of the assembly, wearing, on behalf of his father, specially decorated *masi* clothing prepared for the paramount chief, with an extremely long train held up by thirty island women. These women were also specially costumed in matching dresses, with flowers around their neck and in their hair. It had taken months to make this celebratory costume.

The Maori queen flew in from New Zealand and wore her ceremonial feather cloak. She was accompanied by a party of celebrators, who all made an energetic contribution to the dancing. The New Zealand high commissioner to Fiji, Tia Barrett, also Maori, arrived with them and danced as energetically as anyone else.

I was invited in 2002 to visit the Polynesian island of Rotuma, the farthest flung of Fiji's territories. We travelled in a specially chartered plane and there was room to take other members of the embassy staff. Rotumans are ethnically distinctive, being Polynesian as compared with the mainly Melanesian indigenous inhabitants of the major islands of Fiji. We witnessed how Rotuma's history was captured in dance and song. A welcome ceremony began soon after we arrived; it reflected a centuries-old tradition of wet and tired visitors arriving on the island in canoes following a long sea journey. We were welcomed with gifts of food and dry clothing to meet our initial needs, and pigs and yams as food for the first few days. The following day an organised phalanx of men and women dancers, progressing row by row, welcomed us to their island with a special song and dance composed to record and commemorate my visit. 'The sun is shining; it's a beautiful day, singing and dancing along the way, to welcome High Commissioner Susan Boyd'. They had practised for weeks and were led by John Fatiaki, who was Rotuman. John, his wife and children spent a whole school term on their home island each year, so the children would not lose their culture. For the rest of the year they lived in Suva, where he was the doctor for several high commission staff.

The Rotumans hold a special place in Fijian society. They are well educated, hardworking, creative and relatively wealthy. The island settlements have good infrastructure – water, roads, waste disposal, schools and a hospital. The community is tight and mutually supportive. The children ran around freely after school, kicking footballs or going fishing in small boats on the reef. There was no hotel: visitors like us were hosted generously by local families. The Fatiakis had spent some time studying in Australia, and this was reflected in the architecture of their well-designed bungalow, which they had built, incorporating traditional elements, and in which I stayed. They were extremely hospitable. The four other members of the high commission staff who had accompanied me on this visit were similarly hosted by other families.

The Australian Aboriginal Bangarra dance company was a great hit when it visited Fiji later in the year. The stunning athletic and sensuous skill of the Aboriginal dancers and the stories they communicated resonated perfectly with the Pacific islander audience. But it is not the Pacific way to watch in respectful silence. The audience came and went; children were nursed or packed off to play; conversations were carried on. The whole community participated as they did in the special ceremonies in Lakemba and Rotuma.

As well as being high commissioner in Fiji, at the same time I was also accredited to Nauru, and also accredited to Tuvalu, a country consisting of a group of nine small islands in the southern Pacific Ocean with a total population of 10,000. Visiting involved a flight of a couple of hours from Fiji in a frighteningly small plane. Tuvalu is easy to miss in the vast Pacific Ocean. The islands are only a few metres above sea level. The main island atoll with the capital, Funafuti, lies on the rim of an extinct volcano, and there are spectacular coral reefs within its lagoon. Funafuti is largely occupied by its airstrip, which doubles as a sportsground. It also has a hotel, a restaurant, a hospital, a school, permanent shelters where parliament sits and a formal meeting place of thatched timber with open sides – a *maneapa*. The sole restaurant was opened by a Chinese traveller who found himself stuck in Tuvalu because of visa problems. There is also a single permanent diplomatic mission, that of Taiwan. Australia does not recognise Taiwan diplomatically, so formal relations are not possible. But despite this, I always found time for a useful chat with its representative in Funafuti. All other countries had nonresident diplomatic representatives to Tuvalu who are based in Fiji. The Tuvaluan population is largely Polynesian, with a strong culture whose emphasis is on traditional ways and an easy island lifestyle. Protestant churches are influential. Tuvalu also has vigorous and energetic ritual story dances involving large numbers of men and women in special grass skirts and skilfully woven garlands. Large numbers are involved, including the prime minister. These are performed on special occasions, such as a visit by a high commissioner.

The Tuvalu Maritime Training Institute is located on Funafuti atoll and produces about one hundred cadets each year, to prepare them with the basic skills necessary to be seafarers on international cargo ships. When so employed, these seamen are an important source of funds sent home to their Tuvaluan families.

Between 1985 and 1997 Australia constructed twenty-two Pacific Forum class patrol boats, which were donated to Pacific island states. Tuvalu received one of these which is operated by

Tuvalus's police force, supported by two Australian navy staff. They are posted to Tuvalu for long periods and occupy well-built simple houses on Funafuti. They always welcomed the regular visits to Tuvalu by the high commissioner and Australian staff from Suva, who brought fresh meat and fruit with them. The naval staff usually hosted a barbecue in their garden, to which I could invite local guests, including the prime minister, to reciprocate the generous hospitality the government extended to me on my visits. The navy fellows also took us in their small boat to snorkel on the best coral reefs I have ever experienced. As I snorkelled, the Beatles' Octopus's Garden song was in my head. The reefs were a refuge and escape from the madness of the human world.

In 2000 I travelled with the Australian naval crew on the patrol boat to visit Tuvalu's largest island of Vaitupu, which had just over 1,000 inhabitants. The whole island is surrounded by an unbroken protective rock and coral reef; it has no harbour. The Australian patrol boat had to anchor beyond the reef, and the ship's lifeboat was used to surf in to the beach. But I could not manage the rope ladder down to the smaller boat, when it was in the water and heaving with the waves. So the crew winched up the lifeboat, put me in it and then winched it back down into the sea. A dignified way for the high commissioner to arrive on an official visit. A seriously sick islander was taken back to the Funafuti hospital when we left, and we shared the lifeboat as it was winched back onboard for the journey home.

Unlike the coral atoll of Funafuti, Vaitupu island is volcanic, has the best soil and largest agricultural area of Tuvalu and houses a boarding secondary school. Shortly before we visited, in March, a fire at the school had trapped the girl students inside their locked dormitory, and, tragically, several had died. We paid tribute at their graves and joined the islanders in their mourning. We made a donation to the school in memory of those who had died and presented books for the school library.

The attorney-general of Tuvalu had visited Vaitupu the previous year to identify possible projects for the special United

Nations fund set up to ameliorate the effects of sea level rise – a serious concern for Tuvaluans. We were told that an old man had stood up to reassure the attorney-general that there was no need to worry. 'God told Noah that there would never be a second flood'. The attorney-general took the local church minister along on later visits. Tuvalu has been very effective in making the international community aware of its environmental concerns.

Tuvalu's prime minister Ionatana Ionatana CVO, OBE, died later that year, in December 2000. I had respected him and spent long periods with him on my visits, and I was pleased to be invited to go to the funeral with all the other heads of diplomatic missions dually accredited from Suva. The visitors all stayed at the single Funafuti hotel and were shuttled the 300 metres to the church in the government's single car, one by one, in order of precedence. Each head of mission had been asked to have their national car pennants with them, and each one in turn was attached to the little flagstaff at the front of the vehicle for the short trip to the church.

Tuvalu's protocol officer had briefed everyone on their role in the funeral. In order of precedence, visitors were seated on a dais in front of the altar, with the prime minister's coffin lying on the floor in front of them. The protocol officer told us that we should each, in turn, approach the coffin, bow and return to our seats. Ratu Epeli Nailatikau, the Fijian representative, arrived by special plane just before the funeral and missed the protocol briefing. I was sitting next to him. He was the one to lead and at the appropriate time I tapped him on the knee and whispered what we were supposed to do. Ratu Epeli was an imposing figure. He approached the coffin, bowed and then proceeded to circle it, bowing and touching it at each corner. On the way around, he kissed the late prime minister's wife, who was seated at the head of the coffin. She was visibly surprised. Well, we all then felt obliged to follow suit, so the service took considerably longer than planned. I'm not sure the widow was entirely comfortable with all the kissing.

After the church service, the coffin was moved to the *maneapa* for more cultural ceremonies and speeches. We then walked with the coffin to the burial site – a pit carved out of the coral rock of Funafuti – into which the coffin was placed and then covered with a heavy cement slab, put in position by six muscular Tuvaluan men. Wreaths were laid on top; they had been brought from Suva and mostly consisted of plastic flowers, which were easy to transport and would last.

In the evening all the mourners were invited back to the *maneapa*; we sat on mats around the edge and ate a dinner of fish, meat, rice and crunchy sea vegetables followed by fruit, all placed on individual banana leaf trays on a mat before each guest. The master of ceremonies then announced that it was the Tuvaluan tradition that this coming together was the end of the funeral proceedings, and anybody who wished to say anything about the departed prime minister should do so. We quietly gasped when he said he would allow twenty-five speeches. It was to be a long evening. The diplomatic corps agreed among themselves that the New Zealand high commissioner, Tia Barrett, should speak for everyone. He gave a rousing Maori speech of tribute in both English and the Maori language, with singing and elegant hand movements. Maori, being close to the Tuvaluan language, was understood by most of those present.

Tia was a veteran of such events and had carefully chosen a place to sit on the mats where he could lean on a strong supporting wooden pole. I had followed suit and sat next to him, sharing the pole as back support. His speech was about number six. Speech number twelve was given by the Tuvaluan high commissioner to Suva, Enele Sopoaga. He stood and, having paid tribute to the late prime minister, said he wanted to tell all his fellow Tuvaluans about the diplomatic corps that had all come especially from Suva and to welcome everyone to his country. He said that he had overheard people in the church discussing who we were and supposing that the two women among us were wives of male ambassadors. Enele assured his people that we were all individually formal representatives of our own various countries, including the women, who were not married to anyone but were respectively the high commissioners of Nauru and Australia.

The speeches then continued, and there was a lull at about number eighteen. The others urged me to speak. So I stood and, after paying tribute to the late Ionatana Ionatana, said that, as I had been leaning against the same pole as the New Zealand high commissioner, people could be excused for thinking that I might be married to him. I wanted to emphasise that I was the Australian high commissioner. I wouldn't mind being married to Tia, but he already had two wives (which was sort of true – he was in the process of a divorce). I was single, because I found that men were like parking meters, either occupied or defective. This went down very well and caused some amusement. Funafuti had just two roads, few cars and certainly no parking meters. I was told later that for the next few days the men of Tuvalu had gone around asking each other, 'Are you a parking meter?'

A posting in the Pacific means lots of public speaking – like at the launching of a new aid program, at a meeting of women, at significant ceremonies or anywhere as the chief guest. The important thing to know is that people really want to hear a speech. It is not a case of stand up, speak up, shut up. Oral traditions are strong. Many have often come a long way, and they expect to be entertained. A storytelling style is the Pacific way. So a short speech will generally not do.

Serious events in the Pacific also involve presenting gifts – woven mats, carvings and, for extra special events in Fiji, a whale's tooth and maybe a pig. In the Pacific, gifts are meant to circulate, and there are many occasions, including funerals, at which mats in particular could be passed on. Whales' teeth, however, could not so easily be regifted by us in Fiji. They had particularly high cultural significance and there were few occasions where it was appropriate for the high commission to present them, and by the end of my posting in 2003 the high commission had accumulated a fair number. The teeth had considerable market as well as cultural value. The newly arrived Australian accountant at the high commission thought they should be sold and the proceeds placed in our official funds. But the Fijian local staff assured her that that would have been seriously contrary to Fijian cultural expectations. So before my return to Australia, I presented most of them to the Fiji foreign ministry, which needed them for formal welcoming ceremonies for very senior official visitors. This gift was turned by the foreign ministry into a special, formal act and was marked by the drinking of kava, to recognise its cultural significance.

Kava, a mildly depressant drug, is derived from the root of the *Piper mesthysticum*, a plant common in the South Pacific. It is commonly drunk socially or at culturally formal occasions. Through my three years in Fiji, I drank a lot of kava served in coconut shell cups, and developed a taste for the drink and an appreciation of the formal ceremonies where it was ritually prepared and served. At such ceremonies, I was accompanied and assisted by the *mata ni vanua* ('eyes of the country'), the high commissioner's traditional protocol spokesman, a position occupied by our driver, Tagi, a very dignified and respectful former soldier. He could speak the special, formal, ancient Fijian language and understood the appropriate rituals for the ceremonies.

The work of the high commission in Suva was not all dancing and celebration. In the wake of the coup came the formation of several temporary governments with which Australia had to deal and which we tried to influence. As part of Australia's expression of disapproval at the formation of extra-constitutional governments, and wishing to influence appropriate developments, the Australian government had instituted a series of 'smart sanctions'. These included a ban on visas for any Fijian who had been actively involved in the coup or had served in the first unconstitutional governments. This hit Fiji hard, since the ban was applied to sports teams as well as individual travellers. It made Australia very unpopular. The smart sanctions also affected the aid program. Australia was careful not to suspend those parts of the program which worked at the community level, in health, education, community development and human rights. However, it discontinued those which had government level impact, such as the judicial support program. These moves were very unpopular in Fiji, particularly the travel bans. As the situation improved, the high commission had the opportunity to negotiate the appropriate restitution of the aid program.

Just as the high commission was working its way through the aftermath of the coup and Fiji had achieved a new constitution and a constitutionally elected government, a new professional and personal challenge for me arose. In August 2001, the Australian coalition government, led by John Howard, refused to allow the Norwegian freighter MV *Tampa* to transport to Australia 438 refugees it had rescued from a stranded Indonesian fishing vessel in international waters. This triggered a divisive political controversy in the run-up to the 2001 federal elections in Australia. Numbers of people seeking asylum and claiming to be refugees had been arriving in Australia by boats via Indonesia or countries further away. Australia was not a country of first asylum as defined in the 1951 United Nations Convention Relating to the Status of Refugees. Those heading for Australia had already found refuge somewhere else. The government argued that Australia was a generous recipient of numbers of refugees and asylum seekers who had been assessed as such by the office of the United Nations High Commissioner for Refugees. Many others were currently resident in other countries following their refugee applications, awaiting resettlement. Australia was not prepared to deal with those who deliberately set off to Australia from other, safe countries, their travel facilitated by people smugglers.

As a measure to thwart and dissuade the people smugglers who were organising the boats, the government refused to allow the *Tampa* refugees to land in Australia. The government quickly introduced a new Border Protection Bill and stipulated that the refugee claims should be assessed offshore. They should be prevented from setting foot on mainland Australia, where they would have access to the Australian legal system. The government argued that others should also be discouraged from setting off for Australia. 'Stop the boats' became the policy slogan. The *Tampa* passengers were temporarily housed on Christmas Island, an Australian territory, which was hurriedly excised for legal purposes connected with the handling of such asylum seekers.

As high commissioner I was instructed to ask Fiji and the other Pacific islands to which I was accredited to partner with Australia and establish processing centres in their countries for the *Tampa* passengers and other refugees and asylum seekers trying to arrive in Australia by boat. The 'Pacific solution', as this came to be called, caused staff in the high commission, and me personally, great distress. I did not agree with the policy and was extremely reluctant to put the request to the poorer governments of Fiji, Tuvalu and Nauru. I thought deeply about what to do. The role of an ambassador is to give the government policy advice. Once the government has made a policy, however, your duty is to carry it out. In the Pacific we had several aid programs encouraging good governance in the island states of Solomon Islands, Vanuatu and Fiji. The Pacific solution was a policy made by a constitutionally elected government, with, if the media and opinion polls were correct, the support of a significant proportion of the Australian population. But it was a policy I personally disagreed with strongly.

Australia is a wealthy and generous country, and I was deeply opposed to the demonisation of human beings seeking refuge from unbearable conditions in their home countries and to the refusal to allow them to seek refuge with us. I also knew that the vast majority of undocumented immigrants, refugee and asylum seekers arrived in Australia by air and were dealt with locally; the number arriving by boat was much smaller. The Pacific solution targeted those who did not have the capacity to arrive by air. Australia is a country successfully created by migrants, including refugees. Indeed, the postwar boom in settlement in the 1950s and 1960s was made up largely of southern Europeans and eastern Europeans displaced by World War II, many of whom had been assisted in Europe by people smugglers.

I also found the Pacific solution internationally embarrassing. Australia is a successful multicultural nation, strong and wealthy because of the contribution of such a diverse community. I saw Howard's policy as an opportunistic and racist move to play on and encourage fears in the electorate shortly before an election which the opinion polls were predicting would be a defeat of the incumbent conservatives and a clear win for the Australian Labor Party, led by Kim Beazley. The Pacific solution was a strong domestic political move.

I was deeply unhappy and ashamed of my government's move, but what were my options? The government's directions to me were unambiguous and lawful. I could have refused to carry them out and resigned. That would have made no impact on the policy, which would still have been carried out by others. After deep thought and discussions with my team in the embassy, I decided that the best way forward lay in using my skills and experience to ensure that the Pacific solution was applied with the least possible damage to Australia's interests.

I spoke to the prime ministers of Fiji and Tuvalu. Fiji was just getting over its own coup-related political divisions, including between Indo Fijians and the indigenous population, and the presence of a new group of refugees would not be welcomed. However, Fiji valued its relations with Australia and could not say no outright. Prime Minister Qarase responded cleverly, saying that this was a serious matter and needed to be referred to Fiji's parliament, which in due course referred the matter to a parliamentary committee, which took its time in considering the request. An immediate response was not forthcoming.

The prime minister of Tuvalu, Saufatu Sopoanga, was shocked and immediately refused. Tuvalu is a tiny nation of 10,000 people spread over a group of small coral atolls, with little agricultural land and no capacity to implement the request. In addition, as has been discussed earlier, it is extremely low-lying and has well-founded fears of sea level rise induced by climate change. It was already experiencing historically high tides. In addition, the people of Tuvalu felt hurt by Australia's ongoing rejection of Tuvalu's request to specifically guarantee refuge for Tuvaluans affected by rising seas in future. By contrast, New Zealand had generously provided Tuvaluans with an easy migration option. Tuvalu and other Pacific island states blamed the industrialised west, including Australia, for causing the climate change which could impact them so severely.

Nauru was the third island state to be approached. A Pacific Islands Forum Leaders meeting was imminent. It was actually Fiji's turn to host, but Fiji's internationally unacceptable interim military government made the location impossible, and Nauru stepped into the breach and offered to host the forum instead, from 16 August. Due to the upcoming Australian general elections, Prime Minister John Howard chose not to go to Nauru for the meeting but remained in Australia and sent Peter Reith in his stead. Reith asked Nauru's president, René Harris, to host Australia's refugee assessment centre. Harris accepted with alacrity. Australia had found the place for its Pacific solution.

For Nauru, a triple-mortgaged, bankrupt, small island state with 10,000 inhabitants, the Australian proposal was a heaven-sent gift. Nauru's wealth had previously resided in its phosphate deposits, which at one stage made it the wealthiest country in the world, per capita. But no longer. The phosphate had been practically mined out. Nauru's offshore investments (including property and West End stage shows) had all turned sour, and its income from licences for pelagic fishing was minimal. Its offshore banking licences had been exploited by international cartels to launder money from international crime, including drugs, and international pressure had caused it to close these banks. The water desalinator had broken down, and Nauru could not pay for its repair, so drinking water was at a premium. Public servants had not been paid for six months. International fuel companies were refusing to supply Nauru until earlier debts were paid. There was little to buy in the single store on the island, since Australian and New Zealand suppliers were also waiting for outstanding invoices to be paid. Nauru, when wealthy, had decided not to build sophisticated medical facilities on the island but rather to pay for Nauruan citizens to be treated in Australian hospitals. Nauru has an extremely high incidence of diabetes, and considerable sums were owed to hospitals in Queensland. In return for the refugee processing facilities, Australia agreed to cover all of these debts and to repair the desalinator. Australia also agreed to create a new annual aid program for Nauru.

Soon after the offshore processing facility was set up and refugee and asylum seekers had been moved there from Christmas Island, I visited Nauru with the foreign minister Alexander Downer, to sign an agreement with René Harris and inspect the facility. We flew in from Canberra in the government's small Royal Australian Air Force VIP jet, arriving late afternoon. Nauru's single hotel, the Menen, was already full, housing the immigration officials working in the refugee centre. Some had agreed to double up in their hotel rooms to accommodate our party.

The program the following day began with a briefing from immigration staff over a working breakfast of coffee and croissants. We later learned that the flour for the croissants had been borrowed from the refugees' kitchen, since the hotel had no supplies. During the morning we visited the camp, which was well set up but heartbreaking, and where we were presented with several petitions from women and men desperately seeking protection and a new life.

The agreements with the Nauruan Government were signed before lunch in the Chinese restaurant next to the airport, and token gifts were exchanged. I felt deeply uncomfortable about all this human misery and Australia's role but went through the motions of the program arranged for us. I had no stomach for the Chinese food in the restaurant, when the refugees located not too far away were suffering and desperate.

After lunch the foreign minister's party thankfully reboarded the jet, relieved to leave Nauru and all the problems. We buckled in, took off our shoes and began to relax for the flight onwards to Fiji. However, soon after take-off, the plane flew into a flock of large frigatebirds, a couple of which were sucked into the plane's engines, forcing us to turn back to Nauru. Some wit suggested that 'Frig it' might have been what the pilot uttered. Our plane was beyond local repair, and a second aircraft was despatched from Canberra overnight to bring in a mechanical crew and pick us up. So we had an unplanned second night at the Menen Hotel. The immigration officials who had moved back into their own hotel rooms once we had departed now had to move out again. All our towels were in the laundry, and there were no fresh ones, so Downer and I were given towelling bathrobes instead, and the rest of the party had to use their own dirty shirts to dry themselves after their showers.

The hotel was only able to rustle up tinned pilchards on toast for our dinner, so I was eagerly looking forward to a good breakfast on the new Royal Australian Air Force plane which arrived during the night. Catering on the VIP flights was always exceptional. But alas! They had not had time to load supplies before flying from Canberra, and all they had onboard were small packets of biscuits. We were flying to Fiji, where the day's program began with a lunch given by the Fiji Australia Business Council. I was famished by the time we arrived and made short work of the great Fijian lunch on offer!

In the meantime, Fiji had still not responded to the Australian request to host a processing facility. However, besides Nauru, Papua New Guinea had agreed to one, on Manus Island. I judged that the need for a Fijian facility might now be less pressing and put it to our minister that the urgency had passed and that we would gain more by withdrawing our request to Fiji. Minister Downer agreed. Prime Minister Qarase and Foreign Minister Tavola of Fiji were immensely relieved.

16

Afterlife and how I got there, 2003–20

Retiring from DFAT in 2003. Resettling in Perth;
finding employment and making a new 'retirement'
life. Gold Corporation Board; Senate of the University
of Western Australia and St Catherine's College.
Working with Aboriginal Traditional Land Owners
in the East Kimberly and the Pilbara; resident lecturer
on MV *Orion*; re-energising the Australian Institute
of International Affairs; executive business coach.

My posting in Fiji finished in 2003. Ashton Calvert, the DFAT secretary, told me that there was just one more post coming up which I would fit: Rome. The government, however, was looking for a couple of suitable places to make political appointments, and Rome was very attractive for any politician the prime minister wanted to shift or reward. There was no guarantee that Rome would hold. On the other hand, if I were to retire, at the age of fifty-nine, there was an attractive redundancy package available, with a re-training component, in addition to my superannuation. And they wanted me to remain in Fiji for an additional year.

It was the right time to retire. I was not looking forward to going back to Canberra after ten years of relative autonomy, to be another cog in the DFAT machinery of government, with even closer involvement with ministers. Nor did I really savour the idea of a posting in yet another country, with another culture and language to learn and more staffing and administrative challenges. My father had died, my mother was alone and getting older, and I wanted to have quality time with her as she aged and not just parachute in at the end of her life. I was not nervous about retiring.

I had been quietly thinking for some years about what I would do after my time with DFAT ended. I knew that I wanted to leave young enough to still have some working life left in me, not just to go on with DFAT until I had no alternative but to wind up in retirement mode. I did not fancy a retreat to a life of golf or endless walks at the beach or constant travelling just for the sake of it. Travelling with DFAT spoils you for pure tourism. It is so much more interesting to be an insider, a professional player in a new country, with something serious to contribute. Looking at new things, I want to *know* about them. What makes these people tick? Why is this country like this? What is likely to happen? Why? I do enjoy relaxing at the beach with a book or in a beautiful mountain spot, but not for too long! There was also that old ingrained duty: to continue to be of service.

With these thoughts rumbling about in my subconscious, I had started preparing for this next phase some years earlier.

The first questions were where I would live and how my finances were. I had a house as well as an investment property in Canberra, the former of which had been my base during my thirty-four years in the foreign service. I had good friends and former colleagues there. But employment opportunities for retired ambassadors were scarce, limited to joining a university or another government agency. And, comfortable as Canberra is, I felt, after my experience in Sydney, that I wanted to live in a larger, more varied city. Several colleagues had decided to retire to Sydney and Melbourne, but in the end there was no choice for me: I wanted to go home, to Perth. In anticipation I sold my Canberra properties and bought the perfect house in Claremont, Western Australia, two years before I actually retired.

I'd had a financial adviser for some years, and it looked as if I would be financially secure. My pension from DFAT after thirty-four years of superannuation contributions would be adequate to live on, and it was indexed. It would be useful to find some remunerated employment, but I could afford to give time pro bono to organisations and projects which interested me, where I could use my skills and make a useful contribution. People warned me that as soon as I was available I would receive many approaches for my services and I should wait a while before accepting anything. This was sound advice.

I had consciously collected business cards and details of people who might be useful contacts when the time came to find something else to do. I had kept box files on women in business, and, as I wrote earlier, I had welcomed the invitation, when I was in Sydney, to join Chief Executive Women, a network formed by some of those few pioneer women business leaders, who found networking with men useful only so far. There were things that they were experiencing in working in a man's world that needed a woman with similar experiences to share and to offer advice. I was the first senior woman leader from the government sector invited to join the organisation in Sydney, and I found exchanges and friendships with those other women leaders encouraging and supportive. When faced with my dilemma about the Pacific solution, it was to these women I had turned. With chapters eventually opening in all the Australian states, the once-small group developed into a formidable body of prominent women business leaders in Australia who worked tirelessly and intelligently to promote the advancement of women in senior management roles and on boards.

When I retired and first got home to Western Australia I found there was no senior businesswomen's organisation in Perth, so, building on our experience and membership of Chief Executive Women in Sydney, Tracey Horton, Dean of the University of Western Australia's Business School, Professor Leonie Still, former Director of the Centre for Women and Business at the University of Western Australia and I founded a Perth chapter of Chief Executive Women and worked to identify and recruit appropriate women locally. When I was writing this, the chapter had some forty members and was growing: a sign of the changing times in Western Australia.

In Sydney, I had welcomed wholeheartedly the opportunity to work with and learn more about Australian business, with half an eye on whether I could do this after DFAT. The Chamber of Manufactures of New South Wales invited me to join a business delegation visiting Singapore and Indonesia, and I grabbed this opportunity to be on the road with small-business insiders and learn from them. The DFAT business liaison program I built up in Sydney was also useful experience. And earlier in my career, the department's leadership had bemoaned its lack of power and leverage in the government budgetary processes, especially before the merger between the departments of Foreign Affairs and of Trade. In the business community there was a powerful domestic constituency supporting the foreign service and its diplomatic and aid activities. I had continued my interest in Australian business when I became ambassador in Vietnam and then consul general in Hong Kong, and I had continued to learn, to build my network and to prove myself a useful interlocutor.

So I had started to think about some involvement in business after I retired. Non-executive directorship of commercial or not-for-profit enterprises seemed a good place to start. After retiring, I joined the Australian Institute of Company Directors and undertook their new company directors' training course. This gave me useful knowledge as well as the business language and terminology I needed for meaningful discussions, as well as networking opportunities. I started looking at the boards of companies I was dealing with and seeing which ones really needed women directors. At my last diplomatic post, Fiji, a vacancy came up on the board of a not-for-profit organisation in the human rights and development area, and I signalled that I could be interested once I was retired. And so, a couple of years later, I was invited to join the board of the Pacific regional human rights organisation, the Regional Rights Resource Team, based in Fiji. This was a non-remunerated board, but it funded regular travel back to the Pacific, including to countries I had not before visited. It built on and extended my previous experience in international development cooperation.

My mother and closest family were in Perth, as were my oldest friends and strong university, business and social networks which had sustained me over the years. My sister Lynda had remained in Perth, and had a son, Ben, by her first marriage. Family was important to me, and my going home gave us the opportunity to be more in each other's lives. They had visited me in several of my posts, and Lynda and her husband Brian had held their wedding at my official residence in Suva. They had then lived and worked in Fiji for a short period. Lynda had been the ongoing support for our parents, staying in Perth and helping more as they grew older, while I had come and gone freely over the years. She was an expert in sales and marketing and had held several good jobs, but for her, family always came first. I was glad to be able to shoulder more of the family responsibility and to appreciate even more my sister's loving, selfless character.

While retired ambassadors were two a penny in Melbourne, Canberra and Sydney, they were scarce in Perth. Mike Horobin, a headhunter I consulted about finding non-executive business directorships, told me that while I would undoubtedly be an excellent director, he would have difficulty actually placing me, as my curriculum vitae was so different from others on offer. The business scene in Perth was heavily male; there were very few female directors, and it was hard to persuade the chairs of boards to take on women: they were more comfortable with people who were like themselves. If they did take on a woman director, she had to have legal, accounting or mining qualifications.

But with Perth being a town where it was who you knew that mattered, Horobin was confident that my own network would deliver opportunities. And so it turned out. I had always known the importance of developing and nurturing networks. Somebody you helped years before and have forgotten will sudden reappear years down the track and be helpful to you. So it was in Perth.

Fiona Harris, a woman business leader I had helped during my time in Sydney and then forgotten about, re-entered my life and helped me land my first board position. She welcomed me warmly, introduced me to a women's networking organisation and then invited me to a private box at the Hopman Cup Tennis, where I met a minister in the state government who was looking for new directors for government-owned businesses for which he had authority. He offered me a position on the Gold Corporation Board. I was launched!

When first stepping back from a position of some responsibility in which your identity is integral to your occupation, it is common to feel a bit lost when you first retire. My identity as an Australian ambassador was strong, and it was strange to just become 'Sue Boyd'. Who was I? The cachet of my previous position carried over to a degree, but I now had to prove myself in a new role. I also had to restructure my life. No secretary, no driver, no supporting office or domestic staff, no-one to help with computer issues. I had to learn to fend for myself and find suitable help where necessary. I soon developed a stable of technical staff to call upon – a computer man, electrician, plumber, handyman, gardener and cleaner. I was lucky being single: it was only me who had to adjust. Some colleagues had spouses who found the transition from ambassador's wife to daily life in Australia challenging. If I'd had a partner, their transition would have been important too.

At the beginning, I felt a bit naked going to business networking events with nothing on my name tag except my name. It is easier to engage with others when wearing a business clue as well. I was going through a classic process of 'identity bridging' – shifting from one identity to another. My first post-DFAT appointment, was international adviser to the United Nations Development Fund for Women. I proudly displayed the fund's abbreviated title, UNIFEM, on my name tag. People thought I was with a tampon manufacturer.

It became easier when I joined the board of Gold Corporation, which runs the Perth Mint and also an international precious metals refinery. A historic company, it was established originally as a branch of the London Royal Mint to manage and process the large amounts of gold produced during the Western Australian gold rush in the 1880 and 1890s. Its sole shareholder is the Western Australian state government, and it is extremely profitable. This made it easier to start conversations. It was not, however, a comfortable board to serve on. I was a nominee of the Labor state government, and the chair resented my being parachuted in without any consultation with him. He patronised me constantly at board meetings, referring to me throughout the three years I served as 'the new board member' and taking up board time with 'educating' me in simplistic terms about aspects of the business he assumed I would not understand. Coming from the public sector, I was concerned about equity issues and, for example, expressed my opposition to the company's practice of allowing employees to use frequent flyer points for personal travel. This was not allowed in the public service, which prohibits private reward from expenditure of public monies. These concerns were rejected out of hand. But the treasury undersecretary was also a member of the board and supported me. The board was so dysfunctional that in the end an external firm was commissioned to conduct a board review, at the conclusion of which the government reassessed the required skill set of the board, and several members, including me, took the opportunity to move on.

My previous overseas experience in community development proved invaluable when, in 2004, I joined representatives of the Gidja and Miriuwung peoples on the governing boards of the two Argyle diamond mine trusts established under the first Indigenous land use agreement in Australia, between the Aboriginal traditional owners of the land and Rio Tinto, operators of the mine. The board members agreed to name the two trusts the Gelganyem Trust and the Kilkayi Trust. Gelganyem was the Miriuwung name for the Argyle mining area. Kilkayi was the Gidja name for the same place. The Gelganyem logo, by Miriuwung artist Jodie Hall, is shown in artwork insert figure 10. The Kilkayi logo was created by the Gidja elder and artist Madigan Thomas. These trusts were the vehicles for mutual cooperation between Rio and the traditional owners in developing the mine and sharing the profits with the on-country communities. I felt very honoured to be the first independent female director. It was a privileged position, to join ten Aboriginal people and a male independent director, Ian Williams, on the governing boards and to be accepted by clever, wise and dedicated Aboriginal community leaders as we found ways to make the trusts work for the benefit of all. Gelganyem invested carefully for the longer term, beyond the life of the mine, and funded a wide range of projects, including provision for renal health education and care, school holiday programs, indigenous plant propagation and fish-farming businesses, literacy and maintenance projects, vehicles, equipment for houses and schools, tourism development and education of young men and women in traditional knowledge, law and practices. There were school scholarships and programs to help students to remain in schools, as well as literacy projects for mothers and young children at home.

My fellow directors patiently welcomed, educated and tolerated their two independent, non-Aboriginal directors. We were both appointed after being vetted by the Aboriginal elders on country. Ian Williams had worked with traditional owners for much of his senior mining life in northern Australia before retirement from Rio Tinto and had an excellent reputation. He was the perfect fit. The two independent directors had to have between them significant community development or financial and business experience. My community development experience was derived largely from knowledge of Australian and other aid programs gained while posted with DFAT and a short period of volunteering with Oxfam in Amazonian Brazil in 1979. Ian knew all about finance and business and had worked closely with traditional owners of the land where the mines that he had headed in Queensland were located.

The other ten board members were chosen by the traditional owner families who drew as their representatives younger

Aboriginal people who had experience in both the traditional and the non-aboriginal world. Ted Hall was the first Gelganyem chair. His experience was in community broadcasting and tourism. The first deputy chair was Maria Morgan. She and her husband and children ran a successful on-country tourism business, providing touring, camping and learning. Another director, Paddy McGinty, went on to establishing his own waste-management company, providing services to the Argyle mine.

The trusts were backed by a council of elders which provided wise guidance and support to the boards. These elders carried the traditional knowledge, had battled and negotiated long and hard for the rights of their people and were the signatories of the agreement with Rio Tinto. It was a privilege to spend time with these new friends and colleagues, to meet and travel with them through their stunning and spiritual country, accepted as an insider. It was a unique opportunity to learn and respect Aboriginal ways and rich culture. Ian and I were both blessed in welcome to country ceremonies, with smoke and water, at the creek at Second Gorge, Mandangala, as the spirits were asked to recognise and protect us on country. I learned about kinship taboos, which regulate where people may physically be in relation to their relatives. I learned not to try to arrange people in a photograph. Each knew where they could and could not stand. Several of the elders received national recognition through the Order of Australia and travelled to Perth to have their order bestowed by the state governor.

I was asked to draw on my new experience by reviewing another trust, the Gumala Foundation, which provided benefits from the Rio Mine at Mount Tom Price to traditional owners spread over the Pilbara region of north western Australia. Again, this was stunningly beautiful country. Gumala was one of the earliest agreements between a mining company and traditional owners and was fundamentally flawed in its design and provisions. There were deep governance problems which facilitated corruption, and benefits were not flowing to the Gumala members, some of whom lived on newly created homeland settlements on country but were mostly scattered through the modern coastal communities of the region. Mining companies had learned from this experience, and newer agreements, like the Argyle agreement, worked much better.

In reviewing Gumala, I worked with South Australian Bob Burton of Parakeelya, an organisation with considerable experience with Aboriginal people and mining companies. Bob and I found that the most fruitful way to conduct consultations was to take a box of fruit and sandwiches, make a camp in the middle of a community, light a campfire, boil a billy and make tea. Residents would come over to see what was going on, and before long we would have a productive community meeting going. In the towns, we sent out notices of meetings, but this did not work very well: addresses were out of date, the post was unreliable and people had other things to do. Aboriginal people are busy! Best practice was to make a little campfire in a park and spread the word through human chains.

Our report made strong recommendations which would have improved the administration of Gumala, strengthened its governance and ensured a better distribution of benefits. The management of Gumala buried the report, which was critical of them, but we ensured that many others with influence saw it. It took two more reviews by eminent Australians with wide knowledge of Aboriginal affairs, including my old friend Fred Chaney AO, (founder of WA's Aboriginal Legal Service, former Minister for Aboriginal Affairs, Deputy President of the Native Title Tribunal and Chair of Reconciliation Australia), before the chief executive officer could be replaced and the processes improved so that the intended beneficiaries could be properly served.

My involvement in the South Pacific continued after I left Fiji and retired from DFAT. Sarina Bratton, a friend from my Sydney Chief Executive Women days, broke away from a mainstream large cruise ship company and established her own small, luxury, adventure cruise company, leasing her own ship, the MV *Orion*, which carried only 100 passengers. In 2003 Sarina asked me to join the *Orion*'s crew as resident guest lecturer as she cruised through the Pacific on her maiden voyage. What a lovely job! We took over the ship at Papeete, in French Polynesia, and as a training voyage sailed with a small number of passengers to Sydney, where we received an exciting, full formal welcome in the harbour, with water cannons and hooting ships. I went on several subsequent Pacific cruises with the *Orion*, stopping in Fiji, Vanuatu, Solomon Islands, Noumea, Papua New Guinea and New Zealand, lecturing on Pacific politics, culture and history, and telling my own personal stories of the Speight coup in Fiji.

On one *Orion* cruise, in 2005, we visited the remains of Rabaul in Papua New Guinea, which had tragically been destroyed in a volcanic eruption in 1994. The DFAT trainees in 1970 had been fortunate in being able to visit the stunningly beautiful and historic town before it disappeared. From the cruise ship MV *Orion* the passengers were able to walk over the lava ashes around what had been the golf course and to visit the remains of the Japanese war installations, half buried in lava. I felt very sad. The volcano was still erupting and shedding fine black ash, and the captain deployed crews to clean the ship continuously while we were in port.

On these Pacific cruises I sometimes held informal workshops in the bar in the evening, showing passengers the culture and practice of kava drinking, buying kava in markets along the way. In Fiji once we had to share a welcoming kava ceremony with another visiting cruise ship, and my group felt very superior in knowing the right way to behave.

In 2004, I joined the board of the Regional Rights Resource Team, known throughout the Pacific by its initials, Triple R. T. This had been founded as a small, indigenous not-for-profit organisation in Fiji by the super-impressive, globally recognised Fijian human rights lawyer Dr Imrana Jalal. The Regional Rights Resource Team was an organisation which was growing fast. It had developed from its Fijian base to work in several Pacific island states. It tackled human rights issues at several levels in society, educating and encouraging human rights norms and working with Pacific island governments and courts to frame and enforce appropriate legislation for human rights protection for citizens.

The organisation had readily attracted funding from international aid agencies working in the Pacific. Here was a local organisation performing important service to a global standard, with indigenous staff working with their own island communities and governments. The organisation supported a woman suffering domestic violence as she went to complain to the local police. It educated the police to know that this was a criminal offence and not something to be taken lightly or a 'normal part of family relations'. It encouraged the magistrates to administer the law, taking into account human rights concerns. And it worked with lawmakers and parliaments to ensure appropriate laws and practices were in place. It fought perceptions that human rights were a foreign flower planted by westerners in the Pacific islands, with no basis in traditional law or culture. It also worked closely with and encouraged women's organisations throughout the Pacific. During my ten years on the board, I saw the organisation grow and develop and become a mainstream part of aid programs funded by major donors, including Australia and New Zealand, through the Pacific Community, the regional development association of the Pacific island states.

The organisation's chief executive officer Sandra Bernklau was an experienced community development leader. She was married to the Fijian architect Masimeke Latianara, who was renowned for his work, with Habitat for Humanity, in developing economical cyclone-proof housing for the Pacific islands. I learned a lot from them, and I think I contributed in encouraging a strategic perspective in the board and senior staff, especially by keeping the organisation going in difficult times, such as during coups, and by assisting with government relations and fundraising.

In 2004 my old university asked me to join its senate, as a nominee of the state government. I was chair of the External Environment Committee and of the Centenary Committee, steering the university's 2013 celebrations held not only in Perth but also in major regional centres throughout the state. School-children in Mount Magnet, 574 kilometres from Perth, gazed in awe at the heavens through an array of telescopes and had fun with scientific experiments involving water and fire. Teachers there said our project had opened the eyes of the schoolchildren to the prospect of a life outside the small and remote town. The medical school demonstrated rural medical capacity and demands in the goldfields region around Kalgoorlie. The chief justice of Australia, the Honourable Robert French, an alumnus and later chancellor of the university, delivered a centenary lecture to the legal com-munity in Bunbury. In Geraldton, the School of Design worked with local planners and community members to design ways to activate the old centre of the city and the port precinct. I loved the opportunity to see Western Australia close up, to drive the long distances and be part of the university team running the projects.

The celebrations included a photography competition involving images incorporating the figure 100. Mt Magnet is an important rest and refuel centre for the long and heavy road trains serving the mining and agricultural industries in the north. These are powerful trucks pulling four or five heavy trailers. They are very common features of West Australian long distance roads. I approached the driver of one of these road trains at the Mt Magnet rest stop, and asked to photograph him and his rig posed with our large wooden '100' figure display.

'Okay', he said reluctantly, 'as long as you don't get my feet in the photo'.

Why?

'The boss would fire me. I'm supposed to wear safety boots instead of these thongs!'

The highlight of the centenary celebrations was the captivating and clever animated projection onto Winthrop Hall of aspects of the university's first 100 years. On the same evening there were a number of entertainment and arts events throughout the campus. An estimated 20,000 people were expected to come. In fact, 35,000 turned up! There were no unpleasant incidents, everyone was patient and cooperative, and somehow it all worked, because everyone wanted it to work. I commented to Vice-Chancellor Paul Johnson the next day, 'If we'd told you 35,000 people would turn up, you'd never have let us do it!' The risk management approach would have kicked in. Very luckily, the celebration turned out well, with the sole injury being a sprained ankle for a young man who tried to climb in over a fence.

The key to the success of the whole centenary program was the patient work done in the years before, helping all parts of the university to accept ownership, invest their energies and creativity and see that all would benefit from the occasion.

From 2004 I worked as an executive business coach with Foresight's Global Coaching, helping some of the most senior business leaders in the state develop their leadership capacity. When Denise Fleming, who owns the company – offering 'coaching for business leaders by business leaders' – initially asked me to join as a coach, I was reluctant. I did not see myself as a business leader. Denise dismissed this concern: 'You led organisations with large numbers of employees. You operated in a variety of different environments, some very difficult. You administered very large budgets. You managed a variety of stakeholders, including government and commercial. You were instrumental in policy formulation and development. What do you mean you have no business background?' And indeed, I have found my experience entirely relevant. Foresight's coaches work across several sectors, helping leaders to develop new skills, including strategic thinking, and to navigate their way through perplexing and constantly changing business scenarios. The work is confidential, and Foresight's coaches work in more than half of the ASX top 100 companies, do not advertise and have considerable repeat business.

I have coached in mining, petroleum and gas companies, public utilities, education, law firms, accountancy and consulting companies, each client having different needs. On the whole, I have found that the people we coach see it as positive that their company chooses to invest in them, and they like the fact that I come from a different background. Being a former ambassador has some cachet, and I can share exotic stories and examples. My gender is irrelevant. There has been only one potential client who refused to accept a female coach. On the other hand, there was one client to whom we proposed a male coach. He went to our website, reviewed all the coaches and decided he wanted me – I was different, and he was likely to learn more from me.

The senate and St Catherine's College of the University of Western Australia have been my most engaging and enjoyable post-retirement engagements. They call on all my skills and, most importantly, keep me in touch with younger, talented people. And the university is at the cutting edge of research, new knowledge and better practices.

I have also greatly enjoyed work as president of the Australian Institute of International Affairs in Western Australia (AIIA) expanding its reach and number of members and building a good executive team. The AIIA created its Young Professionals Network, which helped attract younger members to the venerable institution, and they introduced modern ways to manage. The AIIA is the only fully volunteer organisation in Australia to encourage interest in and study of international affairs. The Western Australian branch was established in Perth in 1946. By 2003, it had dwindled to a small group of older enthusiasts – an organisation which recorded its financial information on its cheque book stubs and communicated by snail mail. At the time of writing it had a solid membership and excellent program.

Perth is one of the most isolated cities in the world. The nearest Australian capital city is Adelaide, 2,551 kilometres away. Singapore, nearly 4,000 kilometres away, is nearer than Sydney. Perth is an excellent and easy place to live. But it's important to travel, to keep learning, to see what is happening elsewhere. Retirement has given me time for this: I have travelled to Fiji, Solomon Islands, Vanuatu, Berlin, Vietnam, Portugal, Ireland, the United Kingdom, France, Italy and the United States, as well as seeing much more of Australia. And there is more to come.

The end: for the time being

The Pacific regional response to trouble in Solomon Islands; a suitable ending to my career; Prime Minister Qarase's dinner of appreciation.

In 2003, as my posting in Fiji was coming to an end, Prime Minister Laisenia Qarase and his wife Leba invited me to be their guest on his home island, Vanua Balavu, in the Lau Group, and I flew there with our newly arrived second secretary, Adrian Morrison. The prime minister of Solomon Islands, Alan Kamakeza, had just asked the Australian Government to intervene in the civil war wracking his country and to help restore law and order. Just before my departure, DFAT briefed me that they would be sending instructions to seek Qarase's views on this, both in his role as prime minister of Fiji and as the chair of both the Pacific Islands Forum and the EU-ACP Partnership, the affiliation of the European Union and Pacific, Caribbean and African states. DFAT wanted to know whether Qarase would support a positive Australian response to Solomon Islands, whether Fiji would commit forces to a proposed regional intervention, whether he judged that other Pacific states would join and, finally, whether he had any general advice to offer. The confirmation came via the only telephone on the island, located in the prime minister's house. He was courteous enough to move to the veranda, out of earshot, as I received the call.

I put these questions to Qarase later, as we sat on a fallen coconut tree on a pristine beach, sipping coconut water from a coconut shell and eating fish prepared freshly, especially for us, while we waited for the small fishing boat which was to take us on a tour of the island. Qarase responded immediately and decisively. He supported the initiative, pledged Fijian troops and police and stressed the importance of engaging civil society, especially the churches, in the rebuilding of Solomon Islands society. I had to wait until later in the afternoon, when we returned from the boat tour, to telephone Canberra and report back.

Consequently, the Regional Assistance Mission to Solomon Islands was set in train. My final official duty in Fiji was to lead the Australian delegation at the Pacific Islands Forum Regional Security Committee meeting in Nadi at which Solomon Islands formally asked for regional help, which was pledged by the representatives of the island states present. It was the first such collaborative mission launched by the forum to address a security challenge in a Pacific member state. Previously, the approach always taken by the forum had been that member states did not become involved in each other's internal problems.

This was a satisfying way to end my posting to Fiji and my foreign service life. When I left Fiji I was farewelling both a country and a career spanning thirty-four years, including four postings as head of mission in the Asia-Pacific region. At the small farewell dinner he gave for me in Suva, Prime Minister Qarase thanked the Australian Government for our role in restoring normality to Fiji. He said that he had found our policy discussions extremely helpful. Often, he said, his policies and courses of action had been influenced by what I'd had to say. Given the active and sometimes tough role that Australia had played, I felt encouraged that we remained in good standing in the Pacific, making a contribution while ensuring that our own interests were advanced. I felt I had faithfully responded to Gough Whitlam's questions.

Notes

1   'The ranker general', Lt Col (Rtd) Derek Boyd, *Army Quarterly and Defence Journal*, vol. 106, no. 4, October 1976, pp. 440–50.

2   Susan I. Ginbey, 'A case study on Phyllis Dagmar Rolfe Norris: presented as part of the requirements for the third year sociology option course at Mount Lawley Teachers College, 13 September 1972, in family archive. Susan Ginbey was related to Phyllis Norris through the marriage of Gerald Alexander Laurence Boyd to Bethwyn Ginbey.

3   A.A Milne, *Winnie-the-Pooh*, Methuen and Co Ltd, London, Reprinted 1972, p. 45.

4   Vladimir Peniakoff, *Popski's Private Army*, Reprint Society, London, 1953.

5   A. R. Taysom, 'Women should not be trade commissioners', minute to the director, Trade Commissioner Service Directorate, Trade Commissioner Service, Australian Department of Trade, 13 March 1963, National Archives of Australia, Canberra, A3120, 106/1/6, pp. 24–5.

6   Jacqueline Boysen, Das "Weisse Haus" in *Ost-Berlin: die Ständige vertretung der Bundersrepublik der DDR*, Links Verlag, 2010, p. 265.

7   Anna Funder, *Stasiland: Stories from Behind the Berlin Wall*, Text Publishing, Melbourne, 2002.

8   Cynthia Guttman, *In Our Own Hands: The Story of Saptagram, A Women's Self-Reliance and Education Movement in Bangladesh*, Basic Education Division, UNESCO, Paris, 1994.

9   Jim Collins, *Good to Great*, Random House, UK, 2001.

10 Margaret Byrne, 'Workplace meetings and the silencing of women', PhD thesis, UWS. See also additional valuable material on meeting skills at <https://ugmconsulting.com>.

11 Sheryl Sandberg, Lean In, see bibliography.

12 Pat Duggan, email to author, 28 May 2018.

13 David Irvine, speech at author's DFAT farewell party, 2003.

14 Gary McHugh, 'Chief of navy pays visit to Vietnam', *Navy Daily*, 30 September 2014, viewed 6 January 2020, <https://news.navy.gov.au/en/Sep2014/Fleet/1454/Chief-of-Navy-pays-visit-to-Vietnam.htm#.XhLCkS9L1TY>.

15 'Defence cooperation program', Australian Embassy, Vietnam, viewed 7 January 2020, <https://vietnam.embassy.gov.au/hnoi/Defence_section.html>.

Bibliography

'25th anniversary celebrations in the Hanoi Opera House', *DFAT News*, vol. 5, no. 10, 23 March 1998.

AsiaLine, *Special Focus on Australia-Vietnam: 25 Years of Diplomatic Relations*, Australian Department of Foreign Affairs and Trade, Canberra, March 1968.

Blood, Thomas, *Madame Secretary: A Biography of Madeleine Albright*, St Martins Press, New York, 1997.

Bolton, Geoffrey, *Paul Hasluck: A Life*, UWA Publishing, Crawley, 2014.

Boyd, Sue, 'Diplomacy and crisis management', in Moreen Dee and Felicity Volk (eds), *Women with a Mission: Personal Perspectives*, Australian Department of Foreign Affairs and Trade, Canberra, 2007.

Broinowski, Richard, *Driven: A Diplomat's Autobiography*, ABC Books, 2009.

Byrne, Margaret, 'Workplace meetings and the silencing of women', PhD thesis, UWS.

Carr, Bob, *Diary of a Foreign Minister*, NewSouth Publishing, Sydney, 2014.

Chey, Jocelyn, *Lodestar China: Navigating the China Relationship, 1956–1996*, Australians in Asia, no. 21, Centre for the Study of Australia-Asia Relations, Griffith University, Brisbane, 1998.

Collins, Jim, *Good to Great*, Random House, 2001.

Debenham, Howard, *Waiting 'Round the Bend*, Echo Books, 2013.

Durack Clancy, Perpetua, *Elizabeth Durack: Art and Life; Selected Writings*, Connor Court Publishing, 2016.

Edwards, Peter, *Arthur Tange: Last of the Mandarins*, Allen & Unwin, Sydney, 2006.

Evans, Gareth, *Incorrigible Optimist: A Political Memoir*, Melbourne University Press, Melbourne, 2017.

Fewster, Alan, *Trusty and Well Beloved: A Life of Keith Officer, Australia's First Diplomat*, Miegunyah Press, Melbourne, 2009.

Fewster, Alan, *Keith Waller: Three Duties and Tallyrand's Dictum*, Australian Scholarly Publishing, 2018.

Flood, Philip, *Dancing with Warriors: A Diplomatic Memoir*, Arcadia, 2011.

Funder, Anna, *Stasiland: Stories from Behind the Berlin Wall*, Granta Books, 2003.

Gate, Richard, *From Coup to Coup: Diplomatic Experiences in Five Asian Countries*, Australians in Asia, no. 16, Centre for the Study of Australia-Asia Relations, Griffith University, Brisbane, 1996.

Gattung, Theresa, *Bird on a Wire: The Inside Story from a Straight Talking CEO*, Random House, 2010.

Gyngell, Allan, *Fear of Abandonment: Australia in the World since 1942*, La Trobe University and Black Inc., Melbourne, 2017.

Harry, Ralph, *The North Was Always Near*, Australians in Asia, no. 13, Centre for the Study of Australia-Asia Relations, Griffith University, Brisbane, 1994.

Hearder, Jeremy, *Jim Plim: Ambassador Extraordinary*, Connor Court Publishing, 2015.

Irvine, David, 'Farewell speech for Sue Boyd', German Embassy, August 2003.

McKew, Maxine, *Tales from the Political Trenches*, Melbourne University Press, Melbourne, 2012.

Miller, Rachel, *Wife and Baggage to Follow*, Alstead Press, 2007.

Morris, Malcolm, 'Letters to my grandchildren', unpublished, 1945–90.

Peniakoff, Vladimir, *Popski's Private Army*, Reprint Society, London, 1950.

Priestly, Raymond Edward, *Breaking the Hindenberg Line*, T. Fisher Unwin, London, 1919.

Quoc Te, 'Vietnam–Australia, 1973–1998: cooperation and development', *World Affairs Weekly*, special supplement, Hanoi, February 1998.

Rimington, Stella, *Open Secret: The Autobiography of the Former DG of MI5*, Arrow Books, 2002.

Robertson, Robbie, *The General's Goose: Fiji's Tale of Contemporary Misadventure*, ANU Press, Canberra, 2017.

Rowland, John, *Two Transitions: Indo-China 1952–1955, Malaysia 1969–1972*, Australians in Asia, no. 8, Centre for the Study of Australia-Asia Relations, Griffith University, Brisbane, 1992.

Sandberg, Sheryl, *Lean In: Women, Work and the Will to Lead*, WH Allen, 2013.

Torney-Parlicki, Prue, *Somewhere in Asia: War, Journalism and Australia's Neighbours, 1941–1975*, University of New South Wales Press, Sydney, 2000.

Smith, Fred, *The Dust of Uruzghan*, Allen & Unwin, Sydney, 2016.

Stuart, Francis, *Towards Coming-of-Age: A Foreign Service Odyssey*, Australians in Asia, no. 2, Centre for the Study of Australia-Asia Relations, Griffith University, Brisbane, 1989.

Taysom, A. R., 'Women should not be trade commissioners', minute to the director, Trade Commissioner Service Directorate, Trade

Commissioner Service, Australian Department of Trade,
13 March 1963, National Archives of Australia, Canberra, A3120,
106/1/6, pp. 24–5.

Waller, Keith, *A Diplomatic Life: Some Memories*, Australians in Asia,
no. 6, Centre for the Study of Australia-Asia Relations, Griffith
University, Brisbane, 1990.

Woolcott, Richard, *The Hot Seat*, HarperCollins, 2003.

Kim Akerman, unpublished email to Sue Boyd in response to query about
mining of an Aboriginal sacred site near Leonora, 9 June 2010. Cites
official correspondence.

Acknowledgements

Krystal Hartig, my volunteer research officer, the international relations graduate who bullied me into actually sitting down and writing the book, after I had talked about it for years. Dr Maureen Smith, literary fiend and experienced editor, who patiently battled through my first draft, and made many useful suggestions. Her partner, Kevin Smith, and my friend Bill Kean, who both came up with the book title simultaneously. Everyone who knows me thinks it was apposite. The now late Sheila Drummond, literary agent, who suggested important changes which would help the book appeal to a wider audience.

Nicholas Hasluck AM, widely published author, who encouraged me, gave me some legal hints and educated me on the ins and outs of publishing. Emeritus Professor Dennis Haskell AM, poet and English language guru, for encouragement and advice. The Hon. Kim Beazley AC, very long-time friend and Governor of Western Australia, former politician and Ambassador in Washington, who encouraged me at every step and offered to write the introduction. I am grateful for his special insights. Dr Alexandra Ludewig, Professor of German, who read the Berlin chapter with insight and encouragement.

Emeritus Professor Peter Boyce AO for his gentle advice on writing an autobiography: 'You will be modest, won't you?' It is hard to exclude yourself from an autobiography, but I hope he is not too disappointed. David Irvine AO and Robin Irvine, long-standing and supportive friends, through University and our years in the foreign service. With them I have a generous and caring home-away-from home in Canberra as well as endless discussions on contemporary politics. Richard Rowe PSM, who checked the manuscript for any glaring foreign service errors. Vietnamese teacher Nguyễn Văn Ninh who provided the Vietnamese language diacritics and initially introduced me to the perfect chair for writing and reading, a vital step in actually getting me down to work.

For all the students of international affairs I have lectured to and discussed the endlessly fascinating topic, who have asked so many questions about the profession and life in the foreign service, and particularly being a pioneering woman. 'What does the Department of Foreign Affairs and Trade actually do, and how do I get into it? How else can I work internationally?' Your questions were the trigger for this book. I hope it is helpful.

For the members of the Australian Institute of International Affairs, who carry on the work of encouraging interest in and research on international affairs. I am particularly grateful to members and leaders of the West Australian branch, who have been so supportive of me.

I am extremely grateful to the holders of the copyright on the artworks from my collection, who have generously given permission to use these images, which are so central to the story. Eva Fernandez has done a superb job in photographing them professionally. Nancye Miles Tweedie has volunteered at the AIIA in taking professional photographs of the speakers and participants in the events, and patiently produced the current photograph of me which appears in this book. The idea of using my old diplomatic passports for the cover design came from Professor Ted Snell and I thank Alissa Dinallo for the striking design.

I must thank Terri-ann White, Director of UWAP, who encouraged and advised me over the years and eventually agreed to be the publisher; Kate Pickard, the careful shepherdess at UWAP; and Penny Mansley, whose punctilious and challenging editing made this a much better book.

My superb colleagues in the Department of Foreign Affairs and Trade and the staff, both Australia-based and local staff, in the many Australian diplomatic missions around the world, who cooperated professionally and shared their friendship, families and insights, in good times as well as in times of danger and stress. I appreciate in particular 'The Dhaka Mafia' for their deep and enduring friendship. And there have been so many superb colleagues, from so many nations, who have made invaluable contributions to my life.

Sadly, my parents have both died, and I dedicate this book to their memory. Most importantly I acknowledge with gratitude my sister and brother, Lynda-Jane and Gerald, who agreed that I should write about the family, and whose love and support have been unconditional. They are fully responsible for the next generations of the family. I have merely been the eccentric aunt.

About the author

Sue Boyd's whole life has been international. Born in India into a Raj British and British Army family which moved around the world – to the United Kingdom, Ireland, Germany, Egypt, Cyprus – she embraced change and was educated in thirteen schools in five different countries, learning several languages. Upon leaving school in England in 1964, she volunteered for a year, teaching in Africa. She and her family migrated to Western Australia in 1966. At the University of Western Australia she completed a bachelor of arts degree in English and politics and a postgraduate diploma in education while working part-time as a journalist at the Perth *Daily News*. She was energetic in student political life and was the first woman elected president of the Guild of Undergraduates. The University of Western Australia gave her an honorary doctorate. In 1970, she joined the Department of External Affairs in Canberra and played a pioneering and ongoing role in improving the status of women. In her 34-year career in the Australian foreign service she was head of Australian diplomatic missions in Bangladesh, Vietnam, Hong Kong and Fiji and worked in other roles in Portugal, East Germany, the United Nations in New York and DFAT offices in Canberra and Sydney. She retired from the foreign service in 2003 and settled in Perth, Western Australia. She has worked with the Argyle diamond mine and the Miriuwung and Gidja communities in the East Kimberley. She has been on commercial, not-for-profit and educational boards, she mentors other women and students, she has lectured at the University of Western Australia and Murdoch University, she rejuvenated the Australian Institute of International Affairs in WA, and she works as a senior executive business coach. Sue was awarded a Member of the Order of Australia (AM) in 2022 for her service to international relations, tertiary education and women's affairs.

www.ingramcontent.com/pod-product-compliance
Lightning Source LLC
Chambersburg PA
CBHW031425270326
41930CB00007B/573

9 781760 801496